DANCE NOTATION

Dance Notation

The process of recording movement
on paper

Ann Hutchinson Guest

DANCE HORIZONS – NEW YORK

DEDICATION

This book is lovingly dedicated to
my husband Ivor, whose devotion to
accuracy and thoroughness in research
I have tried to emulate, and to the
memory of Cyril Swinson who first
suggested that I write it.

This edition first published in 1984, by arrangement with Dance Books Ltd., London, by Dance Horizons, 1801 East 26th Street, Brooklyn, N.Y.11229.

ISBN 0–87127–141–9

Design and production in association with Book Production Consultants, 47 Norfolk Street, Cambridge

Typeset by Set Fair Limited.
Printed in Great Britain by The Thetford Press Limited, Thetford, Norfolk.

Contents

Acknowledgements

I cannot begin here to give full credit to all those who have helped in the preparation of this book. I am indebted, first, to Cyril Swinson, who many years ago suggested that I write this book. I must also acknowledge the encouragement of Anthony Mulgan, of Oxford University Press, who inspired me to pull the material together. For information on the Benesh system, I must thank Monica Parker, Faith Worth, Julia McGuinness and Adrian Grater. Noa Eshkol graciously expressed confidence in my knowledge of her system when declining my request that she check the statements made concerning that system. Muriel Topaz provided important facts concerning speed of professional notating and copyright matters and Ray Cook many ideas on the role of the dance director. Michelle Nadal graciously provided me with additional information on the Conté system while Doris Sutton checked the Sutton pages and contributed additional material. For information on the Stepanov system I owe much to the research of Roland John Wiley. For specific use of the system by Sergeyev much interesting material was contributed by Dame Ninette de Valois and Bridget Kelly Espinosa. Tracking down a good copy of the Cervera manuscript entailed the aid of Lolita de Pedroso and also Maria Carles who kindly wrote letters in Spanish for me and translated the answers. Elizabeth Souritz sent most helpful letters on the subject of Russian dance notation systems. My Italian research on the Chiesa system was in the capable hands of Lisa Finzi and of Manuela Riga, who painstakingly translated the material describing his sytem. Many libraries cooperated in my research for information, and though these are listed elsewhere I must give special thanks to Sibylle Dahms of the Derra de Moroda Dance Archives, to Genevieve Oswald of the Dance Collection of the New York Public Library, to Jeanne Newlin of the Harvard Theatre Collection and to Knud Jürgensen of the Royal Library, Copenhagen. My thanks to Robin Howard and Richard Ralph of the London School of Contemporary Dance for giving me access to their copy of the catalogue of the New York Public Library Dance Collection. The British Copyright Council checked my facts on copyright law, as did Robert Fawcus of the Centre for Clinical Communication Studies of the City University in London with reference to phonetics. Much valuable information on miscellaneous systems of notation was provided by Mary Skeaping, Mary Jane Warner, Sigurd Leeder, Raymond Lister, William C. Reynolds, Roland Buelens and Jean-Philippe Van Aelbrouck, many of whom also donated materials to my collection. Very welcome were the promptly supplied information on Doris Humphrey's system from Nona Schurman, and a needed illustration sent by Gretchen Schumacher.

I am indebted to those people who had already collected information on systems of notation – to Helen Priest Rogers whose 1938 thesis first made me aware of other systems, to Nancy Brock whose articles further stimulated me, to Ann Czompo, who was unable to complete her detailed information on each system of notation, to June Layson and Joan White, whose theses provided valuable organization of the information they had been able to collect. All my requests for information on computer use of notation were met with generous contributions of material and information from Stephen Smoliar, Norman Badler, Thomas W. Calvert, William Robertson, D. Herbison Evans, Dave Sealey, Jaysia Reichardt and John Lansdown. I only hope that by the time this book comes out the reports on their work will not be too hopelessly out of date.

Over the years during which my interest in other systems of notation grew, I was fortunate in having much help and cooperation. Albrecht Knust years ago made available copies of certain of his materials. Many of the inventors of notation systems whom I met personally were most friendly and cooperative. In particular I remember with pleasure my discussions with Margaret Morris. Others such as Walter Miszlitz whom I have not met have also written most helpfully.

In concluding, I must not forget my colleagues at The Language of Dance Centre who have contributed so much to making this book a reality. My thanks go to Patty Howell Phillips for taking over my teaching responsibilities so that I would be free to work on this book. To Renee Caplan who has typed the book more than once, to Sandy Mitchell for the many accumulated hours of standing at the photocopying machine on my behalf, and to Nancy Harlock who has undertaken with great patience and perseverence the task of compiling the index and, together with Gillian Lenton, many other organizational matters connected with the book. Among those who kindly undertook to read the book and whose specific comments have been most helpful were Peter Brinson, Selma Jeanne Cohen, Mary Clarke and Irene Glaister, and, of course, Ivor Guest. To Juli Nunlist must go my particular thanks for eliminating my misplaced modifiers and my dangling participles, as well as clarifying my punctuation. If the book reads smoothly I must hand the blame to her. In all matters historical – text as well as illustrations – my husband Ivor has been an unfailing help, quite apart from, as a writer, understanding another writer's needs.

Foreword

Dance is science – the science of movement – combined with art. The art of dance is what we as creative human beings, as artists, bring to the science of movement. But a science can only be developed, described, discussed, disseminated through being recorded – in words, figures, and/or symbols – in brief, through notation. Movement notation is a creative tool, the means of communication in the language of dance. Hence its basic inclusion in 'The Language of Dance' method of teaching. As Rudolf Benesh said: 'Reading is the gateway to knowledge; writing is the tool of thought.' The advent of a practical, functional dance notation system has been called 'a Gutenberg revolution in the dance'.

Of the eighty-five or so systems, major and minor, which have evolved through the centuries, each has certain weaknesses and certain strengths. Each system has a point of view on how to look at and analyse movement and a technique for transferring it to paper. Quite apart from the choice of signs and the degree of theory underlying a notation system, there is the question of how it works in actual practice. This can only be known from practical experience, and evaluation of a system must result from comparison with other systems.

Though dance notation in one form or another has been around for five centuries, it is only now beginning to come into its own as a tool in everyday use. In that sense it is in its infancy. The development of any branch of learning depends on the suitability and efficiency of its notation. Just as learning to read opens the door to wondrous worlds to be discovered between the covers of books, so dance (movement) notation opens the windows to a deeper understanding and experience of dance. Much has to be gained by moving dance out of the restrictions of the 'oral-visual' tradition into a literate one. Choreography has been called 'the throwaway art' because so many ballets were allowed to be forgotten, no attempt being made to make even verbal notes or draw floor plans. Nadia Chilkovsky once wrote: 'If you value your choreography – write it down!'.

As I write these words, it is very probable that somewhere an ardent enthusiast is busy inventing yet another system with which to record movement. Perhaps I should say 're-inventing' for it is most likely that the ideas chosen will be similar to ones already put forward in the near or distant past. Full development of a notation system is a lifetime's work which should not be undertaken alone; other minds and knowledge need to be brought to bear on it. The first requisite is a deep understanding of the phenomenon of movement, the second a comprehensive knowledge of what others have already done. This book is only a first introduction to how movement may be viewed and the variety of systems that have emerged. If it serves to reveal what a rich and detailed subject dance notation can be, and at the same time provides some perspective, then it has served its purpose.

Introduction

Dance notation – what is it?

Dance Notation! What is it? Why is it needed? How does it work? Who uses it? Are there many different systems? Can other movements besides dance be written down? How did it all begin?

At the mention of dance notation these and many other questions arise, particularly now that dance notation has become less of an esoteric subject. The purpose of this book is to examine the background of dance notation in general and explain the process of recording movement on paper without specifically investigating in depth any one or other of the many systems which have evolved over the centuries.

Though dance has been the field which has felt the greatest need of a system of notation, we need, in fact, to look at the wider field of *movement notation*, the recording of any kind of movement, be it gymnastics, sports, therapeutic exercises, anthropological studies, or the actions of men and objects in outer space.

On hearing that dance notation is nothing new, more questions arise. When was the first system evolved? Who have been the inventors? Which is the longest 'surviving' system to date? How far has each system evolved? How widely has any one system been used? Are there libraries of notated works? Is there a career in becoming a specialist in dance notation?

Purpose of this book

It is intended that this book will answer these questions and many others. The non-practitioner with a general interest in dance, the person who is merely curious about 'secret codes', and those intrigued by the ideas and inventions which have been devised to provide a written movement 'language', will each, I hope, find this book interesting and informative. Several non-dancers have, over the years, mastered dance notation to a high degree. These have admittedly usually been musicians, though one mathematician with two left feet, who felt too embarrassed to appear in a dance class in tights, decided he could learn about dance through notation. This indeed he did – his hobby took the form of writing down the various sequences he observed during evening ballet classes.

For the dance student it is hoped this book will give an insight into an important tool which is rapidly becoming part of the dance scene and about which every dancer should know. For the reader already learning or using a system of movement notation, much in this book may already be familiar. However, the survey of the past and of the present may give a broader perspective on the subject as a whole.

But first a definition.

Definition of Dance Notation

Dance notation is the translation of four-dimensional movements (time being the fourth dimension) into signs written on two-dimensional paper. (Note: a fifth 'dimension' – dynamics – should also be considered as an integral part, though usually it is not.)

> Dance notation is (or should be) to dance what music notation is to music and the written word to drama.

Though our main concern in this book is with the recording of dance, inevitably, as we shall see, it is movement notation in its broadest sense which must be considered and discussed, for dance of the peoples of the earth encompasses the total range of movement, much of it naturalistic, much highly stylized, much with complex rhythmic patterns, much with intricate group formations and much with highly imaginative and delicate use of instruments or objects. Life is movement, and civilised man has come to respect and value movement in many areas of specialized study.

Our main emphasis will be on western dance culture and the European heritage, though movement notation has long since spread to many other regions of the world and fields of movement study.

In this book much space has been devoted to consideration of how movement is viewed before any actual writing takes place. This is because it is too easy to think of writing movement as comparable to jotting down a grocery list. Movement is far from simple. This is its great joy and richness in relation to dance, its great range in relation to the many forms of sport and gymnastics. It is through movement that the artist paints, sculpts, the musician plays, the sailor handles a boat and the gardener tends his plants. Movement is life, and reflects life's complexities. No study of movement is simple if one is to delve beyond the superficial. There is no possibility in any system of movement notation for a complex action to be represented faithfully on paper by a few simple strokes. But we can select parts of actions to represent the known whole and thus simplify when such simplification is appropriate.

One further note: to simplify the text, reference to a dancer, choreographer, notator or inventor of a system of notation has taken the form of 'he', 'him', 'his', which in no way reflects any male/female bias or neglect of the role women have played, but merely avoids the irritation of constant reference to 'he/she', 'him/her', 'his/hers' throughout the book.

ONE

Why is Dance Notation needed?

Except for a few innocents who still believe that dancers make up the steps as they go along, improvising their way through full-length ballets, most non-dancers, while understanding that dancers rehearse, are unaware that rehearsal does not automatically include notation. Because the dance heritage has been handed down through visual demonstration, from person to person, one generation to the next, one may ask: 'Since dance seems to have managed perfectly well without notation, why is it needed?' Many in the dance field also ask this question. Why, when such glorious dancers as Margot Fonteyn, Rudolf Nureyev, Fred Astaire, and Gene Kelly, have achieved such brilliant careers without notation, should any future generation need it?

Preservation of choreographic works

The first area in which a real need is felt is in the preservation of ballets, of choreographic works. Like the message in the party game which, whispered from one person to the next down the line, emerges grossly distorted, so the classical ballet heritage, in being passed down person to person, has undergone change. Of the many 'authentic' versions of the Lilac Fairy's dance from the Prologue of *Sleeping Beauty*, who can say which is nearest to the original? In the first production of *Sleeping Beauty* the Lilac Fairy was a mime role; the variation was interpolated later. Ballerinas in previous times often interpolated their favourite steps since there was no one on hand to insist that they keep to the 'script'. In rehearsals roles are taught rapidly, and usually no time is available for careful, detailed explanation of the movements and the ideas behind them. It is considered sufficient that the outline be grasped. Inevitably the material gradually loses definition and takes on an altered form.

Many a wonderful ballet has been completely lost because ten years have been allowed to slip by before it was revived; by then it was too late because no one remembered enough to 'pull' it together. Other ballets have been 'saved' by retired dancers being called in to demonstrate what they can remember. The music is played and, bit by bit, phrases come back, and something is pieced together. Often the results are inadequate because not enough is remembered. Even if the choreographer himself is on hand, he may lack inspiration to re-create a work from another period of his artistic output, and would rather start on a totally new work in which he can

1

experience the excitement of creation. To appreciate what notation means in the preservation of dance, one has only to contemplate the theatre without the written word. What of Shakespeare's plays would we have inherited – if anything? Our musical heritage too would be almost non-existent if no music notation had been developed and – equally important – had achieved wide acceptance and use.

New ballets and revivals

Notation has a practical role to play in the creation of ballets.* At present the creation of a new dance work is carried out in a manner inconceivable in the field of music or drama. Imagine the dramatist meeting with the cast and telling each person the lines to say, changing his mind as the rehearsal proceeds and better ideas come to mind. Imagine, too, the actors memorizing entirely what has been told them, because they also do not have the 'tool' of written language to help them. Equally grotesque is the thought of musicians operating without music notation, the composer humming each part to the members of the orchestra, checking to hear if they have the right notes, questioning whether they are indeed playing what he had hummed the day before, and so on. To complete the analogy, imagine the other members of the orchestra sitting around, waiting for his decision while he is trying out ideas.

Under such conditions the revival of a play or musical composition would follow lines similar to what now happens for the most part in dance. Differences of opinion as to what exactly were the steps, who passed in front of whom, on which count the dancer kneeled and so on result in great loss of time and energy. There can be no argument as to whether it is C or C# in music, as to whether O'Neill wrote 'different' or 'indifferent', because the structure of the work has been recorded on paper. Dance will have enormous advantages to gain when dance notation is also universally known and used. With ever rising costs and union restrictions, company directors can no longer afford to waste time in the rehearsal studio. Where now a whole rehearsal is called to replace one dancer, through notation that dancer can come prepared, knowing the steps and his stage location in relation to the other dancers. In the future it is probable that a generation of choreographers will arise who can record their creations, in part if not in whole, before meeting with the dancers.

Comprehension of movement

The cultural and educational benefits to be derived from use of notation begin with teaching small children the joy of understanding the movement they are experiencing, and range through to advanced comparative study of

---

*Note use of the term 'ballet' for the 'danse d'école', the classical form of the art, and 'a ballet' or 'ballets' for choreographic works which may be in styles other than classical ballet.

cultural and choreographic styles at university level.

Recording movement involves more than a straight statement of facts on paper. Many people suppose movement notation to be equivalent to recording numbers in that, whether verbal or written, the information is the same, only the form is different. Converting movement into signs on paper can be directly related to language. Language, through choice of appropriate words, expresses thoughts and ideas as well as facts, and movement can be just as elusive as thought. The ability to organize thoughts, to express what one wishes to say, indeed to know *how* to say it is a direct result of education in the use of words. One is taught to look beyond the first word that comes to mind, to be aware of the subtle differences between words with similar meanings, to be choosey about which one selects. In the 'language of dance' a similar situation applies. Two notators often describe the same movement differently. What they 'see' in the movement and how they choose to describe it is a direct result of their movement education. The notator who is well versed in the language of movement, familiar with the whole range of movement possibilities, and aware of the subtle differences in movement can most faithfully translate movement into written form.

Dissemination of knowledge

Human communication is based on signs, which may be verbal or written, and on visual signals, i.e. particular body movements. Over the centuries knowledge of the various disciplines of mathematics, science, music, phonetics, etc. has been transmitted through the establishment of semiotics, the language of signs. Now semiotics also encompasses movement through the existence of movement notation. Just as verbal communication is based on linguistics and the meaning is apparent or clouded according to correct or inappropriate usage, so in movement the logical use of a grammar comparable to linguistics makes communication easy. Coherent movement has its own logic, a 'kinetic logic', which involves its own 'parts of speech', its own organization of 'nouns', 'verbs', 'adverbs', etc. into 'words', 'phrases', 'sentences' and 'paragraphs'.

To serve organized movement, a system of notation must have its own semiology, and its own semantics. The better its semiotic and linguistic organization, the more easily information will be imparted through the sign sentences.

In the traditional handing down of dance from person to person, the knowledge has been transferred visually through physical demonstration accompanied usually by verbal explanation. Translating movement into symbols on paper allows the information, the knowledge, thus captured to be used by people around the world. Great teachers can only benefit those able personally to study with them. Their words of wisdom may reach only a small audience. But much of the specific knowledge which great teachers impart can be captured in notated form and hence enrich other teachers and students elsewhere. No one should learn to dance from a book, but if one has taken a course in a particular subject, having that material available also in notated form for future reference is a tremendous advantage. It is a benefit enjoyed in other fields of study – why not in movement?

Availability of the written form increases an audience's enjoyment and appreciation of plays and music, before or after attending a performance. So it can be with dance. Through notated scores dancers and dance scholars can become acquainted with choreographic works and derive greater enjoyment and benefit from seeing performances of them. Dance will have a literature, and all the benefits which literature and literacy bring. Since this literacy is still in the distant future for most dancers and teachers, it is hard for them to envisage what it will mean. But once they can read and write as a matter of course, they will bless notation.

Lessons to be learned from music notation

Before investigating past history and present use of dance notation, a look at the development of music notation, and a look at language, may help in understanding why movement notation has taken so long to emerge. In relation to the slow establishment of dance notation it is comforting to realize the centuries of evolution which went into standardizing western music notation, the notes, staff, keys, etc. as we know them today.

A thousand years ago music scores used neumes. These signs, developed to serve plainsong, did not give precise pitch or rhythm but served as a memory aid to indicate to the singer which of the songs he already knew were to be sung. Exact pitch resulted from introduction of the staff, first of four lines, later of five. Present day notation was codified as recently as the seventeenth and eighteenth centuries. From its early evolution in the monasteries music inherited a cultural respectability and the attention of the educated classes. It continued to be part of the cultural development, with no disastrous break in the heritage.

The greatest flowering of dance notation occurred in the eighteenth century when it was used by and for the educated classes. But following the French Revolution, notation fell into decline partly through the fact that development of dance became centered in the theatre rather than in the Court. Professional dancers came from the 'lower classes'. The stigma which the educated classes attached to dance, particularly in the Victorian and Edwardian eras, discouraged the emergence of literately inclined dancers and hence impeded the development and use of a notation which would function in the same way as music notation. Dancers were not expected or encouraged to have brains, their brains were in their feet. Only now are dance and education encouraged to intertwine. The future holds promise for a literate art of dance, but, alas, there is no unbroken tradition to give it the initial advantages which music notation enjoyed. Despite its imperfections, music notation has played a crucial part in advancing the art of western music. It has preserved a rich musical heritage and has made it possible for a composer in one country to have his works played by orchestras around the world. Contemporary composers are, however, dissatisfied with the standard music notation. It is more cumbersome than need be. Its inflexibility has hampered avant-garde composing by restricting the range of inventiveness. No provision is made for quarter-tones. Intricate rhythms can be notated only clumsily, if at all. The passage of time often needs to be marked in seconds rather than the standard beats and metres. Several avant-garde composers indicate duration by length (*see* Fig 1.1); a device first introduced by the American Joseph Schillinger who used graph paper in teaching rhythms.

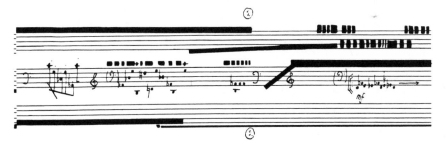

The original is printed in green, red, blue and black.

Fig. 1.1 *The Garden of Royan-gi* by Louis Andriesson, 1967. (A. H. Guest Collection)

Over the years many new ideas for systems of music notation have been put forward, though none so far has met with significant success. There has been an increasing trend in avant-garde music of incorporating extraordinary sounds, such as plucking or hitting different parts of instruments, for which no indications exist. Each composer must make up his own signs. In addition many composers are now giving freedom for improvisation within a general framework. As a result of these new trends, composers have resorted to fantastic devices to convey their ideas (or an impression of their ideas). (*See* Figs. 1.2 and 1.3).

Notation
The sign x—— is used for the right-hand stroke in pizzicato-glissandi and pizzicato-gruppetti.

Horizontal square notes denote a heavy bow pressure resulting in a controlled creak.

Arrows through stems denote varying rates of tremolando: forward arrows mean accelerate etc. . . .

Cross shaped note-heads (always open strings) are for playing behind the bridge.

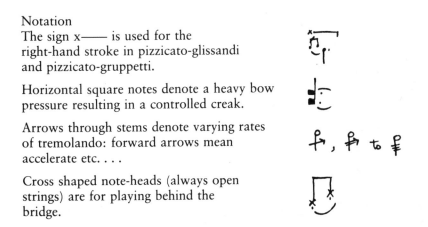

Fig. 1.2 Nicholas Bannan *String Quartet.* (Courtesy Nicholas Bannan)

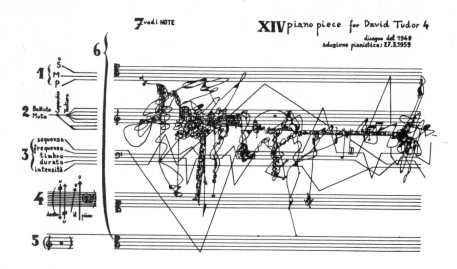

Fig. 1.3 Sylvano Bussotti, 1959. (A. H. Guest Collection)

How much such notations convey decipherable messages is debatable, but undoubtedly in using standard music notation so that orchestras can play his works, the composer may be forced to modify, simplify and, indeed, alter what he really wants to say. Is the notation, in the long run, the 'master' or the 'servant'?

Dance notation faces an identical problem. If the system used is too primitive, the movement description may distort instead of represent accurately. Even with a flexible notation tool there is a tendency to choose an easy way of writing, thus modifying the movement. The limitation may not be that of the system, but of an insufficiently skilled, lazy, or overtired notator.

The greatest chore a composer faces is the hours spent in writing down his musical composition. But this chore has to be undertaken for no orchestra can play a work by hearing it on tape. Similarly, a dance score requires many hours of work, and the chance of 'typographical' errors abounds in both.

Comparison with language

A look at the evolution of written language may also help in understanding the stages dance notation has gone through. The standardized English spelling, despite its frequent illogicality, appears to be here to stay. If one is concerned that a symbol on paper should represent a single sound, and no other, then phonetics should be used. Use of phonetics entails learning a larger alphabet, but has the advantage of consistency in symbol/sound relationship. Phonetics can therefore be applied to any language. Except for certain intonations, rise and fall, etc., the reader could speak lines correctly in a foreign language of which he knows nothing. On the other hand, in using phonetics, the simple word 'dance' could be written several ways, depending on local pronunciation, which ranges from the English 'dahns' to 'danns' and even 'dayens' in the U.S.A.* For universal communication there should be one standard form applicable to all.

The most highly developed system of movement notation works on the basis of phonetics. If a familiar action is performed in a slightly different manner, it is so written. This means that personal mannerisms may be captured in the notation by a conscientious notator, as indeed happened during the recording of Kurt Jooss' masterpiece *The Green Table* in 1938. Notating movements demonstrated by the performers, without Jooss at hand, made it impossible to distinguish what was essentially part of the choreography and what were personal variations. In traditional forms of dance, such as classical ballet, the standard performance of the vocabulary of steps is so well established that this standard version can be notated regardless of personal variations by individual performers. Because the ballet vocabulary is so well known, an abbreviation for each step can be evolved, comparable to speed-writing. But if a subtle change in style, a particular modification, is needed, the writer must resort to 'longhand' to capture the specific details.

In developing a dance notation system it is important that the written 'language' be rich and full in order to meet the needs of all movement disciplines. Some verbal languages are extremely limited, revealing the limited life experiences or needs of the people using them. The English language is rich in the choice of words to express subtle variations in thought. A comprehensive system of movement notation which can serve universal needs must be the product of many people experienced in a variety of movement backgrounds.

---

*dahns (S.E. England); dans (N.E. England); dæns (Midland); dæ:ns (West Country); dēans (Brooklyn, U.S.A.).

7

TWO

Why not use existing devices to record dance?

Can dance not be recorded, captured for posterity, by some of the means already on hand? Modern technology has advanced considerably since the days when eighteenth century dance masters struggled to record the dances they had just composed. Are present day notators just mad enthusiasts who are in love with little symbols on paper and oblivious to other seemingly obvious answers to the need?

Why not film?

A frequent question in relation to dance notation is: 'Why is it needed? Isn't film the answer?' Dance is a visual art; surely film, and video in particular, which records movement with immediate playback, can take care of the needs in recording dance. Dancers have always learned from watching others; they need only to watch the film. Why bother to learn any system of notation?

To put film and video into perspective, turn again to a comparison with music. Recorded music, tape and discs, has not obviated the need for printed music, either in the teaching process or in professional activities. Why not? Two obvious reasons: first, even if the work involves only one or two instruments, the student or professional performer prefers to read his part from the printed page, to get instructions about what he is to play from the clearly stated symbols on the sheet. This is certainly preferable to listening to a few bars on a tape or record, imitating it, going back to listen again, memorizing the next bit, and so on. The undertaking is compounded if there are many instruments in the piece; identification of the parts for individual instruments may then be difficult, if not impossible.

Few dancers prefer film if they have access to notation. During the years I worked with the New York City Ballet, on occasion the dancers came to check sections from the score. Some of these dancers had previous experience in learning their parts from film. Todd Bolender, for one, on being shown his sequences in the third movement of *Symphonie Concertante*, enthused over the ease of notation in contrast to working from film which he had experienced on several occasions and definitely disliked.

If such a learning procedure is hard for a professional, it is even more so for the student. Learning music with and through music notation has become an established way of life for every serious music student. The wealth of printed music literature provides further incentive to gain fluency in reading as well as in performing. High costs of rehearsal time in the profession mean musicians must be able to sight-read, or be able to take the parts home to practise.

The second reason that records and tapes are not used in rehearsing a work is that these do not represent the work itself but a *performance* of that work. This rendition of the composer's original idea bears the recognizable stamp of the conductor as well as the personal style of the leading soloist. Each performer and conductor wants to be able to go back to the work itself recorded in the notation and to bring the music to life in an individual, personal way. Learning a piece of music solely from listening occurs only when the player is unable to read music.

Having taken this look at recorded music, let us see to what extent the same situation exists in dance. As yet most dancers cannot read dance and so they turn to film and video out of necessity. What is the preference of those who can read? A quick glance at film is helpful, but for the actual learning process notation is to be preferred.

From the practical standpoint it is not as easy to learn a dance sequence from film or video tape as it would seem. Even if we overlook the fact that many dance films are recorded in unfavourable circumstances – poorly lit, part of the stage off camera – we still have to deal with distortion resulting from camera angle, movement hidden by other dancers or by props or costumes, and, quite frequently, poor or blatantly incorrect performance on the part of the dancers. What is on the film may not be what the choreographer intended. Since a choreographer seldom has a perfect cast with which to work the film can be a much watered down or distorted version of the planned choreographic sequences. To leave a record of what he *does* want the choreographer must record it in notation, with the hope that one day a cast will be on hand capable of his choreographic demands.

Of interest in the comparison between use of film and notation is the result of an experiment which took place a few years ago at George Washington University, in Washington, D.C. In his research project 'A Comparative Study of Video Tape and Labanotation as Learning Tools for Modern Dance',[1] C. Brook Andrews states:

> While studying Labanotation . . . I was also using video tape as a learning tool. . . . My first impression was amazement at the ease and speed of video learning. . . . The instant visual reinforcement seemed a strong selling point for video tape as a better learning tool than notation. Further investigation, however, revealed drawbacks to video tape learning, the greatest of which seemed to be the viewer's inability to see specifically what happened on the screen. Audience response to seeing a movement performance on video tape closely paralleled reaction to a television show. The viewer received an impression from the screen rather than extracting specific or detailed information. I noticed that dancers studying films of movement were unable to discern exact or specific movement from the total movement performance. Initially they were impressed with an overall aura surrounding the dancer. Later they criticized the performance as a total unit but seldom commented on specific movement parts. Their learning seemed hampered by a distortion

of depth, a tendency for images to appear overly large, a slowing down of the speed of movement and a reduction of movement dynamics. The possible interference of the above variables caused me to reconsider the reliability of learning movement from video tape.

These findings of Andrews are supported by others with similar experience. Merce Cunningham commented similarly on the distortions of video, but revelled in them as a spur to creativity. This is very different, of course, from trying to recreate faithfully a specific choreographic work and style.

Andrews' controlled experiment was a pilot project, a forerunner, he hoped, of other such tests. In it ten dance students learned two modern dance movement phrases through watching video, ten others learned the same phrases from Labanotation. The results were videoed for the judges to view, marks being given specifically for accuracy and for quality of movement. Andrews reports the results:

Two major indications are clear from studying the data of this research: 1) Labanotation subjects tended to receive higher scores than video tape subjects. Labanotation subjects in both experiments were able to perform better and obtain higher ratings. . . . [They] seemed more involved in what they were learning. Use of the notation system seems to necessitate a greater amount of concentration on the material than use of video tape. This dissimilarity is probably due to the negative characteristics inherent in video tape learning. The viewer appears to understand but the amount of concentration and the retention of knowledge do not seem so intense as with Labanotation. 2) Advanced dancers tended to receive higher scores than nonadvanced dancers. The intangible elements of dance performance ability have affected the research to a greater degree than expected.

Andrews points out the need for further research in which performance level, ability in reading Labanotation and other factors are equally ranked. Further evidence has been provided in the Chief Examiners' Report on the first examinations of the London University 'O' Level Dance syllabus for which the technical study was worked either from video or from the notated score:

'The range of interpretive skills that were expected appeared to be better from those who had worked from the notation than from those who had relied on the video tape. Teachers are advised to teach from the score whenever possible, using video merely as a check. It was reassuring that the best candidates had fully understood the style and produced performances that were rhythmically alive and full of character.'[2]

Another revealing experiment involving information obtained from film occurred when Valerie Preston-Dunlop compared two tennis strokes, one by a professional, the other by a student, to determine where the difference lay in the resulting proficiency. By painstakingly notating the actions observed on the film and placing the two notations side by side, it was possible to make a detailed comparison which revealed where the significant difference lay. This proved to be the action of the left arm, the 'passive' arm. Where the student did nothing with this arm, the expert used it to counterbalance the right, sweeping it backward in the follow-through. Such detail-by-detail movement correlation is not possible between two films. With the information on paper it is possible to locate and evaluate minor differences in movement patterns.

There are several other practical aspects in which notation has the advantage over film or video tape. Copies of the score can be handed out and referred to in the train, at home, on the beach. No special equipment is needed. Notation allows for random reference, the score can be opened at any point, whereas film has to be run through to find the appropriate place. It is comparable to having a pianist at a rehearsal who can start playing at any point instead of working with a tape on which the correct place has to be found. There is also the question of speed in learning. With notation the dancer can learn at his own pace, spending more time on certain phrases, if needed. Slowing down film and video causes further distortion and often the very detail wanted is not visible.

For soloists and principals another consideration is artistic integrity. A leading concert pianist or violinist may listen to recordings of other performers out of interest, but would prefer not to learn his part by listening to the rendition of another. Many dance soloists do not want to look at the film of a dance which they are to learn since they do not want to be influenced by the mannerisms and personal style of a previous performer. Actors are grateful to be able to start completely fresh, finding their own interpretations from the written words.

Until dancers grow up with notation and are thus fluent in reading, film and video in conjunction with notation will continue to play a helpful part in the learning process. Film gives an overall impression of a work, notation the specific details. They are not mutually exclusive.

Why not stick figure drawings?

Everyone can draw a little pin man, and with practice can make pin men convey a great deal of information. It has been said that a picture is worth a thousand words, but art lecturers reveal how long it takes to develop observation, to train the eye to *see*, and the mind to interpret all that a great painting contains. But our concern here is not with complex drawings but with simple stick figures. What do they tell us? Usually the general placement of the limbs, torso and head. Care in drawing is essential if wrong impressions are to be avoided. Is that short neck a mistake, or are the shoulders to be raised? Is one hip out of line? Should the figure be off balance, or was the writer careless?

Fig. 2.1

It does not take long before one faces the problem of showing the missing third dimension. Drawing perspective requires skill. The simplest solution is to turn the figure drawing and then devise some indication to state that the figure has not actually turned. At some point one must resort to signs to convey the message the figure cannot convey. Many movements are not pictorial in nature; they do not have a destination as their goal. Take for example a wiggle or a shiver, or a hand vibration. How does the hand vibrate? Back and forth? Up and down? Side to side? Or with very fast small rotations? The spatial displacement is too small to be drawn, other devices have to be used and that means resorting to symbols. The addition of such indications means evolving a systematic and logical sign use.

A stick figure captures a pose at a particular moment. Indication of timing for positions is simple when limbs, torso, head, etc. all move in unison. But so often arms, head and torso do not synchronize with the legs. Any subtle interrelation in the timing of movement of different parts of the body becomes difficult to indicate. The movement must be broken into segments and special indications used to show the duration for each individual part.

Not all movement to be recorded is in a finished form. General statements of movement and indication of basic movement ideas, as may be needed in the early stages of dance composition, are impossible with stick figures. No matter how simple, the stick figure is always specific. For example, to state merely the fact that the knees are bent, the writer drawing a stick figure has to give some spatial placement for the knees, i.e. some use of leg rotation – turned out, parallel, or somewhere in between. This leg rotation may be of no importance but in a figure drawing it cannot be left out.

Equally the instruction 'bend the arm' can be performed in a number of ways, but for a stick figure indication a particular placement and degree of bend must be chosen, and thus open choice is eliminated, and a desired freedom in interpretation impossible. Despite such limitations in flexibility, however, stick figures obviously offer a speedy memory aid of positions which are easily drawn and are familiar to the reader.

Why not word descriptions?

Since in many magazine articles and books, keep fit exercises and other movement instructions employ word descriptions, why not use these in an organized form as a system of notation? Words are common currency; why invent a whole set of symbols? To understand the inadequacy of words one has to experience both the actual writing process and the reading back of unfamiliar material. Those who have dealt with words – dance teachers writing notes for themselves, authorities preparing dance syllabuses for publication – know the frustrations met in turning movement into words and observing the range of interpretation and leeway for misundestanding when those words are turned back into movement. And speaking of 'turning back', the following examples taken from the 1972 C.O.R.D. (Committee on Research in Dance) special publication *Institute of Court Dances* illustrate the kind of problems met just in use of the word 'back'.[3]

'Step back to 5th position.' (Is this a step backward followed by a closing, or a closing which occurs after the leg had been extended forward?)

'Take the leg back.' (Probably a gesture in the backward direction.)
'In the back placement.' (Does this mean 'behind' the other foot, as in 5th
  position, or that the limb is extended backward?)

These examples were from a stylized dance form; let us now take a simple,
everyday word instruction. If the command 'Hands up!' is given, as in the
cartoon here, (Fig. 2.2), do you raise your arms toward the ceiling or
'overhead', i.e. past your ears?

Fig. 2.2 Labanotation Textbook. (Courtesy Dance Notation Bureau)

Will the words 'Hop, skip and a jump' mean the same thing to each person?
What is 'a jump'? Will everyone spring into the air from both feet and land
on both feet in performing 'a jump'? The problem is met in the historical
dance field in trying to reconstruct word descriptions in fifteenth century
manuals. Take the instruction: 'Three steps forward, left, right, left.' That
seems simple enough, but if performed in a circle holding hands where is
forward? As this appears such a simple example but reveals a basic problem
faced in recording movement, let us inspect it to find out why there could be
more than one interpretation.

Fig. 2.3

In the diagram in Fig. 2.3 a circle of people, represented by pins, are facing
in. (The point of the pin shows where the person is facing.) The performers
know that the circle should progress clockwise (note the arrow) so how then
are they to take three steps forward? If they walked into the direction they
are facing they would all end up bunched together in the centre of the circle.
If 'forward' means the direction that the circle should progress, then their

steps should go in that direction. Most students of these old dances have agreed that the direction of the circling *is* meant by 'forward'. But how is it to be performed? One interpreter felt that the dancers should remain facing the centre of the circle and so should take sideward steps to the left. Note the use of arrows in Fig. 2.4.

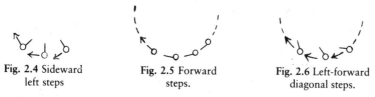

Fig. 2.4 Sideward   **Fig. 2.5** Forward   **Fig. 2.6** Left-forward
left steps   steps.   diagonal steps.

Another historical dance specialist decided that 'forward' should also mean forward from the body, so that each dancer should turn to the left, face the line of progression and take forward steps, as illustrated in Fig. 2.5. Yet another researcher decided that the logical interpretation should split the difference between figs. 2.4 and 2.5. The dancers should turn slightly to the left, and take diagonal steps as in Fig. 2.6, the step direction from the body being between forward and side, i.e. left-forward diagonal. When hands are held this version is comfortable and is often met also in folk dances.

Any serious system of movement notation avoids words because they are also a deterrent in international communication. Then there is the practical consideration that a symbol is briefer and can be read more swiftly than words. For example, 'right shoulder' takes thirteen letters. Even abbreviated to 'R shd' it takes up more room than: (Labanotation) or: A'6 (Benesh notation).

One of the advantages of a notation system is organization, the placement of information where it is easily located. There is no universal standardization as to where specific pieces of information will be placed in word descriptions. Usually the feet, supports, steps are described first. Finding information about the head may require skimming through many lines of type. Some publications establish columns in which verbal information is placed, a great help, but even here there is much variation between individual writers. Dance terminology is not universal. Even in classical ballet, in which steps and positions are clearly defined, the existence of different nomenclatures causes confusion.

Though words are not the tool with which to record a movement, they are a vital means of communication in learning to understand and master movement. Words should therefore be selected according to their scientific accuracy on the one hand and their expressiveness in evoking imagery on the other. As Zelia Raye so often said: 'Dance is science plus magic.' The body moves according to the laws of physics but dances in response to visions, images and concepts which depart from the practical to a striving for the unattainable.

To be considered is whether a notation system should only state the practical facts of a movement, or should also include the idea behind it, the concept, the motivation.

THREE

How is movement described?

How would you describe a handshake? Or grasping an object? Through a drawing, realistic or simplified? In words? Would you describe the shape of the action, how the fingers close in, the feeling, timing, intensity? Let us take grasping an object. Quite apart from your personal preference, the choice of description and the degree of detail would obviously depend on whether it is needed for:

dramatic purposes (training of an actor)
functional purposes (training of a worker in industry)
therapeutic purposes (rehabilitation of the injured)
psychological purposes (observing abnormal movement patterns for treatment)
stylized, artistic purposes (as in dance)
artistic educational purposes (as in acquiring skill in handling a musical instrument)

Each of the above purposes usually requires a different type of description and level of detail in recording how such a seemingly simple action as grasping an object is performed, or should be performed. In selecting how a movement should be described the notator inevitably faces the need to understand what is taking place. He must have a rich understanding of movement and be able to analyse it.

The question also arises as to whether the notation is descriptive or prescriptive, that is, should it represent the movement as it is being performed or as it should be performed, the goal to be reached.

Training the eye

In the various fields mentioned above, specialists are trained to observe movement in a particular way. They look at different aspects of a particular action. To make an analogy, in describing a person you have just met, would you speak first of his personality as it came across to you (warm, hearty, easy-going), or of his looks (red hair, large nose, hazel eyes), or of his clothes (short overcoat, collar turned up, baggy trousers), or perhaps of how he spoke, how he moved, what he said, how he related to you and to other people? Depending on who you are, and how and why you have met him, the content and emphasis of the description might vary considerably.

For each field of movement study the eye needs to be trained. We do not all see movement in the same way. Consider the visual art of painting. As every painter knows, the eye needs to gain experience in seeing the minor as well as the major features of a painting. To be observed are the overall design, the specific forms and shapes which emerge, the spatial relationships between the forms, the dynamic rhythm of intersecting, merging and diverging lines, and, of course, the added dimension of colour, a whole study in itself. All these and much more contribute to training sensitivity in eye and mind. In recording movement the writer may see only the main, outline features of a series of actions. What he records depends on his movement education, the type and depth of his training. In the case of an unfamiliar movement pattern, two notators will probably vary in how they choose to write it down. I say 'unfamiliar patterns' since, as mentioned before, a standardized 'spelling' will already have been worked out for familiar movement patterns such as appear in ballet. But let us leave until later this question of standard forms of movement and the pros and cons of falling back onto stereotype description rather than treating each action as a unique occurrence.

Development of a movement description

In approaching possible movement descriptions let us take first an example from everyday life, then later look at the same sequence performed as stylized dance movement. We need to consider the possible levels of description, from the most general, overall statement of what happens to the more detailed.

General outline
The bare essentials in describing a sequence might be: 'Man is seated. Sees visitor, waves, rises, walks, shakes hands.' Such a description might be used to record an action in a play or an episode in a psychotherapy session. The scope for interpretation is obviously wide, and may intentionally be so.

Stage instructions
When in a play a particular setting for a series of actions has been established, a memory aid description will serve for future reference: 'Seated in armchair, lost in thought. See nephew enter. Wave left hand, then rise. Pause before taking two steps toward nephew. Grasp his right hand, add left hand, shake twice, then let go quickly.' Such description serves as a reminder to anyone in the production of the specific actions (stage 'business') set by the director. Already a clear structural pattern is emerging, with suggestions of mood and interpretation.

Imagined dialogue accompanying actions
What goes through the performer's mind as he performs the series of actions is not part of the movement description, but will colour the actions since how the movements are performed will stem directly from the inner feelings and attitudes. In some cases it is desirable to include subjective thoughts.

Though words are not audibly spoken in dance performance, appropriate dialogue is often imagined and silently 'talked through' as each movement unfolds, thereby giving substance and 'colour' to the gesture. Such dialogue may be taught alongside the steps and gestures in a ballet to illuminate the character being portrayed, the situation and relationship to other participants. For example, in recording the traditional 1870 version of the ballet *Coppélia*, which had been preserved at the Paris Opéra, the 'dialogue' in all the dramatic scenes was as much part of the heritage as the movements themselves, and so the traditional words were written alongside the notation.

For the movement sequence being explored here, the following might be the thought, but unspoken dialogue:

> Uncle: seated in chair (thinks: How am I going to solve this problem? The solution escapes me, I need more time . . .).
> Jack: entering (thinks: There's the old fool, well, I must be nice to him). 'Hello, dear Uncle, hello!'
> Uncle: slightly startled (thinks: Blast! There goes my peace and quiet, that stupid young fool has arrived). 'Oh, hello there, Jack.'
> Jack: (thinks: Not a very warm welcome, but I'll chivvy him up). 'Lucky I found you here! Just the person I want to see.'
> Uncle: (thinks: Yes, I can imagine, probably wants money – as usual!). 'How are things?'

And so it might go. In each performance the unspoken words might vary somewhat, or from season to season they may intentionally remain the same.

Background information not included

The kind of information which cannot be conveyed through movement and which, obviously, must be told in words could be the following: 'While puzzling out a real estate deal, I was interrupted by my ne'er-do-well nephew, Jack, the one who borrowed that large sum of money from me and squandered it gambling. For his mother's sake, I must hide my dislike of him.'

Involved interrelationships (an unsympathic mother-in-law, a jealous cousin, etc.), past happenings, thoughts of future plans, etc. all affect present attitudes and behaviour, and hence movement patterns. Whereas the way the body is held and nuances in expressive use of gestures can be recorded in movement notation, the causes, such as those stated above, cannot. If needed, these must be explained in an accompanying text, as indeed they are in the programme notes of complex ballet plots.

Description of physical performance of the sequence

The following description concentrates on the physical changes. (Note: anatomical descriptions such as would be used in medical circles are not being covered here since these are very specialized and thus outside the scope of this book.)

'Seated, weight over to right side, right elbow resting on arm of chair, head resting on right hand, eyes closed. Head jerks upright, eyes open. Left

17

arm is raised with a wave of the hand. Lean forward to rise on both feet using support of right hand on chair arm to get up. Straighten up with difficulty. Take two steps forward, left, then right, toes turned slightly in. Right hand weakly grasps person's hand. Left hand joins in to provide more pressure. Two handshakes then quickly release, slowly lowering arms down to sides.'

This description could still relate to straight acting. As dance the movements will become stylized through subtle changes in timing, dynamics and variation in space and body patterns.

Stylized Movement – Dance
In taking the movement sequence already established and putting it into a stylized dance form for the stage, the following is one possible setting. Verbal descriptions given here purposely avoid unfamiliar technical terms.

Start: Uncle sits with legs crossed, right foot resting on left knee. Right elbow rests on arm of chair, head inclined to right, cheek rests on tips of index and middle fingers of right hand. Left hand grasps right biceps. Eyes are closed.

Counts 1–6. No movement.

Ct 7: Head jerks suddenly to upright position, eyes open, focused strongly forward on nephew, right hand opens wide, lower arm opening slightly out to the side.

Ct 8, 9: Hold.

Ct 10: Left lower arm is raised, palm facing toward nephew, at same time head and eyes drop slightly.

Ct 11, 12: Hold.

Ct 13–16: Right leg unfolds, extending toward nephew, making an arc as it lowers to the floor where it is placed in a deliberate manner next to the left foot. As the foot touches the floor, both hands grasp the arms of the chair with a stressed, emphatic movement.

Ct 17–20: Torso leans forward, rounded. Pushing up from chair with the right hand, rising starts swiftly then becomes slower and more deliberate.

Ct 21, 22: Now upright, looks at nephew, stands still for two beats.

Ct 23, 24: Slides the left foot forward, toe first, then takes weight on it with knee slightly bent. Straightens as the step is completed. Finishes the movement abruptly.

Ct 25, 26: Repeat the same with the right foot.

Ct 27–29: Right arm moves forward starting at the elbow, then lower arm and hand in succession. Left arm moves backward, fingers separated, rounded and tensed (his antagonism is revealed in this hand).

Ct 30: Right hand sharply grasps nephew's hand. Pause.

Ct 31: Left hand makes an upward arc on its way to grasping outside of nephew's hand. The final grasping motion has the quality of impact.

Ct 32: Hold.

Ct 33: The right hand mechanically shakes nephew's hand, the upward preparation coming before the beat, the downward action falling on the beat of 33.

Ct 34: Repeat 33 (second shaking of hand).

Ct 35: Sudden tense releasing of grasp with a sideward opening of both hands away from nephew's hand. Pause.

Ct 36–38: Energy draining away, a slow drawing in of the arms in a bent position close to the body, elbows back, weight moving unobtrusively backward to left foot. Tension reappears in a slight contraction of the torso. Eyes remain fixed on nephew's face. Fingers end touching outside of thigh, the last three fingers bent, while thumb and index finger are extended (almost a 'pistol shooting' hand position).

This same basic sequence could have a variety of settings, the chief variation being in timing and use of energy; many small physical differences might also alter the style. Choice of these would depend on the era being depicted (Victorian, the Gay Twenties), on the social status (noble lord, gangster, solid burgher) or national cultural style (Spanish, Japanese, East Indian). In highly stylized contemporary dance the hand grasping and shaking could even be indicated without any actual grasping at all.

Choice of description

How is such a movement sequence – or any other – to be recorded on paper? What type of description and what level of complexity are to be chosen? A simple notation system provides a single simple type of description; a highly developed system presents choices. The decision then must rest on the purpose for which the notating is being done. To make this decision the notator must understand fully the content of the movement and also the needs of those who will read and study the resulting notation. The problem of choice can be likened to a comparison between shopping in a village store, where the range is limited and the choice easy, and shopping in a bazaar with dozens of stalls and a dazzling range of choice. A particular need will be more accurately met if greater choice exists, but the notator must be trained to make appropriate selection.

For notating dance outsiders often stress simplicity. Is a complex, highly developed system of notation really necessary? Why choose more than one way to say 'the same thing'? A particular type of movement description may be applicable to certain situations or actions but be unsuited to others. To cite a simple, familiar example: It is considered correct to brush the teeth from the gums (the base) to the extremities. When I assured my dentist I knew the correct way, I stated: 'From the top down.' He pointed out that this is correct for the upper jaw, but not for the lower. For the lower jaw the instructions should be the reverse: 'From the bottom up.' The full set of instructions in those terms become rather lengthy, and we are not even taking into account the circus performer who might be brushing his teeth while standing on his head – where then are 'up' and 'down'? Thus we find that familiar movement descriptions, particularly those met in dance, are in many circumstances quite inappropriate and even misleading, hence the need to develop an analysis and terminology applicable to all situations and all types of movement.

FOUR

Constituents of stylized movement

What are the main changes that take place in turning ordinary movement into stylized forms required by dance? What resulting nuances must a good notation system be able to cope with?

Exaggeration of one kind or another is an obvious device, and may be in:

(a) unusual timing (abnormally slow or fast) for common, familiar actions;

(b) isolated movement of a part of the body (hand, foot, knee, etc.), which normally does not move in total isolation, or special emphasis placed on a part (elbow, shoulder, hip, etc.);

(c) variation in spatial pattern: a design or pathway which is 'larger (or smaller) than life', or body shapes related to known poses but performed with sufficient modification to cause them to depart from the norm;

(d) unusual quality of movement: exaggerated strength, smoothness, limpness, heightened tenseness, etc.

Timing

Actors on stage are already one step away from portrayal of ordinary everyday activities. Timing is a significant part of the effect that is achieved and contributes to the general 'pace' of the performance. Directors of plays often give timing instructions in terms of beats. 'Let two beats go by before replying', or 'Take six slow beats to walk from the door to the table'. In opera actions are set on the accompanying music.

Dance relies strongly on music, the choreography usually being composed to an established musical piece. When no music is used, as in Jerome Robbins' ballet *Moves*, dancers count strict beats to keep together or take visual cues from each other. A solo dancer moving in silence can use intervals of time freely, each interval being relative to the others. Most music used for choreography has a clear pulse or beat, though some modern pieces use sounds of all kinds, such as electronic effects in which no regular pulse can be detected. In learning to move to such pieces a dancer usually sets a basic inner pulse and then determines how many go by before another main identifying sound occurs. Thus we see that, whether modern music is judged by seconds (stop watches) or by a pulse created in the mover or listener, we come in most cases back to a basic pulse. Important for the audience as well as for the dancer is the feel of this pulse and the awareness

(instinctive if not overt) of the passage of time, of when a dancer's movements fall on the strong beats, and when they fall off the beat. In dance
notation allowance must be made for all such variations in timing, whether
they occur within the actual movement of the dancer's body – or in the
relationship of the movement to the accompanying music.

Overlapping of actions creates further variations in the timing of movements. For example, in a formal bow, the interrelated timing of the head
movement and the accompanying torso bend will provide a very different
message according to whether the actions occur completely simultaneously,
or whether there is only a slight overlap. The head may start first and the
body later, or the head participation may come throughout the torso bend
or only near the end. With each such variation the expressive effect is subtly
altered.

Fig. 4.1 illustrates five possible timing variations in combining a torso and
head inclination. Several other variations in overlapping are possible. In the
diagrams below T = torso and H = head, while for this purpose ↑
represents bending (inclining) forward.

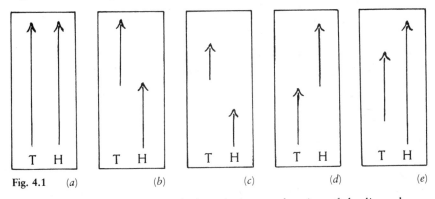

Fig. 4.1   (*a*)   (*b*)   (*c*)   (*d*)   (*e*)

Reading each diagram upward, the relative overlapping of the lines shows
clearly how much of the available time is spent with a single action occurring and how much with both. In Fig. 4.1 (*a*) torso (T) and head (H) bend
forward simultaneously, a gracious bow. In (*b*) the head starts first, then the
torso. The delayed torso tilt may suggest uncertainty. In (*c*) the head bends
forward rather abruptly, then there is a gap before the torso bend suggesting
a resentful or mechanical bowing to a superior. In (*d*) the torso bends by
itself, the head inclines after. This can express a reluctance to bow, a lack of
true respect. In (*e*) the head bows first and is continuing even after the torso
has stopped, suggesting a servile attitude, self effacing. Perhaps from this
sampling can be seen the many variations possible in the overlapping timing
of just two separate actions. Notation systems must be able to cope with
such variations in overlapping of two, three or more actions.

Focus on parts of the body

The manner in which parts of the body are used can produce stylized
movement. Focus can be on actions of isolated body parts or on two parts

21

moving simultaneously which are not so linked in everyday life. The point at which an action is initiated can change both the expression of a simple unadorned movement and the effect it produces. In the case of a walk, does the movement start in the torso or at the extremity, the foot? Is one part of the leg initiating the action, i.e. is the knee or the thigh leading in preparation for a step forward? In rising from a seated position, is it the top of the head or the chest which leads the rising movement? An arm gesture may be performed in a variety of ways. Does the limb move in one piece or in sections? Does initiation within one movement change from one part to another, as when shoulder initiation of an arm gesture changes to finger tip guidance? When is one part included in the movement of another part? For example, is the hip included in a leg gesture at the start or only at the end? All such variations in the manner of performing a movement must be indicated in the notation when these details are significant.

Spatial variation

Subtle changes in space patterns may involve slight displacements from standard directional points, for example, the sideward horizontal arm in classical ballet is placed slightly lower and more forward; the overhead arm in Flamenco dance is placed slightly backward. Spatial variation may involve a slight deviation from the standard path of a movement, producing extra curves, or there may be a rigid adherence to a straight path for a gesture, the extremity of the limb following a beeline path rather than the curved paths which result naturally from the build of the body.

To illustrate some possible deviations, let us take a straight gestural path as in Fig. 4.2. In this path a deviation, a slight departure from the expected line, may occur at the beginning (*b*), in the middle (*c*), at the end (*d*), or all through (*e*). More than one deviation may occur, as in (*f*)–(*h*). Deviations may be two-dimensional, staying on the same plane, as do the lines on this paper, or they may be three-dimensional, as on a globe.

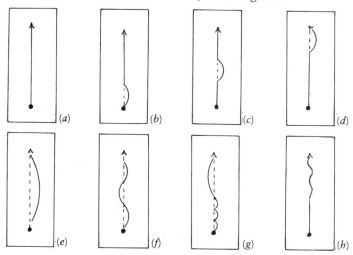

Fig. 4.2

A good way to explore the above variations in movement is to extend an arm forward from a starting position with the hand near the shoulder, as in Fig. 4.3. The hand can then describe all the spatial variations shown above, following the arrows as though they are drawn on the floor. Or the actions may be performed as in Fig. 4.3 (*b*) in which the arm is raised overhead; the paths shown in Fig. 4.2 (*b–h*) are then followed as though drawn on the wall in front of you. Though only a few spatial variations have been illustrated here, the potential range is not hard to imagine.

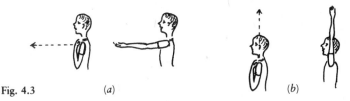

Fig. 4.3   (*a*)   (*b*)

Quality, variation in 'texture'

How a movement is performed is affected by the 'texture' or 'quality', that is, by the flow of energy which may initiate the movement, drive it, support it or control it. The use of energy more than anything else lifts an ordinary action onto another plane, and into a theatrical statement. The simplest such change occurs through use of emphasis. Placement of a slight stress (or even a lack of stress) in a movement changes the impact of the action. In a single gesture emphasis may be at the start, in the middle or at the end as in Fig. 4.4 (*a–c*), or several accents (stresses) may occur as in (*d*). Indeed there can be stresses (accents) regularly or irregularly placed.

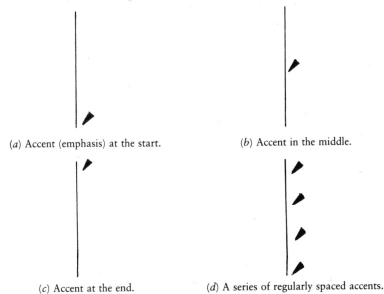

(*a*) Accent (emphasis) at the start.   (*b*) Accent in the middle.

(*c*) Accent at the end.   (*d*) A series of regularly spaced accents.

Fig. 4.4

A very simple analogy can be made with speech where placement of emphasis subtly changes the meaning. Take a simple sentence like 'Henry can sing.' Stressing the first word, the middle, the last, or all three will convey in each case a different meaning from that which the words themselves actually say. Established dance styles have their inherent dynamic patterns which the performer learns and then performs instinctively. As a result such dynamics are often not included in the dance notation of those forms. But in the studying process, in analysing the movements to understand and master the contents, variations in the use of dynamics should be analysed and faithfully recorded.

Movement changes which come under the general heading of dynamics include variations in the ebb and flow of energy, the releasing or holding of force, and how these combine with specific body/space patterns. Dynamics is the aspect of movement which is the most difficult to define, the one in which terminology is the least universally developed. Most notation systems ignore dynamics completely or fall back on music indications, pp, p, mp, mf, f, ff, which are only partially suitable for movement.

Of the notation systems which have developed through the ages most never reached the point of including the kind of detail we have explored here. It has been enough to be able to state 'step forward on the right foot on count 1', i.e. to provide the basic body/space/time structure without subtle details. As a notation system develops the question of where to draw the line on detail must constantly be faced. When a highly developed system is used the writer must make a decision on how much or how little to include.

FIVE

Degree of specification in movement description

It is only through investigating the different ways in which movement can be described as well as the reasons, intentions, motivations behind the movements, that we can understand what is important in any movement and therefore how notation should handle it. We must know which of the different components in a movement are essential and therefore must be included in the notation, and which are of varying degrees of significance, to be recorded according to need and/or intention. As mentioned before, the choice of description will largely be determined by the purpose for which the notation is being made. Let us consider levels and purposes of movement description in more detail.

Because recording movement is such an unfamiliar procedure to all but a few, some words on what it entails may be helpful. The most common form movement notation takes is that of selecting and describing key points through which the parts of the body pass or at which they come to rest. This is comparable to the technique used in cartoon animation in which the leading artist draws the key positions and assistants fill in the many frames required to produce the desired motion. In movement notation the reader fills in the linking movement passages between the stated points. If spatial key points are close enough, this is no problem, but too large a gap will leave the path to follow open to guesswork.

Chromaticism of movement

One aspect in which a direct comparison between music and dance fails is in changes of pitch in music and spatial level in movement. In music the transition from a low note to a high note can pass through all the notes between, the chromatic scale, or the high note can be reached directly with no intervening sound. In movement such interval 'leaps' are not physically possible, all movement on earth is chromatic by nature.

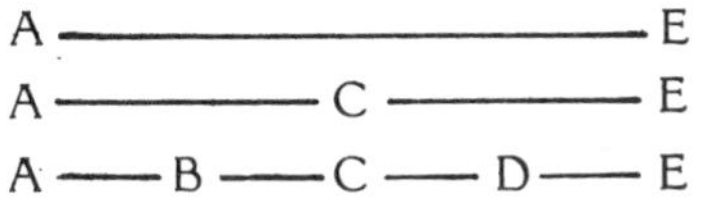

A ————————————— E
A ——————— C ——————— E
A —— B —— C —— D —— E

Fig. 5.1

One cannot get from point A to point E, Fig. 5.1, without travelling along the continuum between A and E.

Most forms of dance feature positions, clear destinations which are held for at least a fraction of a second, and/or given an accent, so that they register on the viewer's eye. The optical nerves welcome static poses after much continuous motion. In moving from point A to E, both performer and viewer may find their concentration is on the destination, even though the movement is reasonably slow. A slight emphasis, an appropriate variation in timing and energy, or a pause at point C would provide an awareness of that point on the path. In chromatic movement the performer is aware of and enjoys the passage through all intermediate points, B, C and D. When the path of the movement is direct and obvious, there is usually no need to mention the intermediate points, thus a simple description suffices for such travel.

In the process of analysing movement from film or video, the viewer with knowledge of that form of movement knows what is important in its execution and hence can select significant key moments.

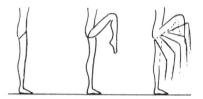

Fig. 5.2

For example in lifting a knee forward from the feet together parallel position, Fig. 5.2, there is only one direct pathway; thus only 'knee forward high' (the thigh slanting upward) needs to be described. Some movement research involves painstaking analysis of film, frame by frame, the results being plotted or fed into a computer. This method involves an enormous amount of data, most of which can be ignored for a particular investigation. A movement trained notator working with a flexible notation system can swiftly produce a record with the desired degree of detail based on the appropriate analysis required for the task in hand.

Degree of detail to be included

In recording movement the writer is faced with decisions concerning the degree of detail to be included. Let us start with an analogy – the description of a house. For many purposes it may be sufficient to say, 'Two storeys, three bedrooms, two bathrooms, living room, study, kitchen, single garage. Stucco exterior, shingled roof.' A description of the front exterior might be: 'Front door with porch off centre, two windows on the right of door, one on the left,' and so on. Not too much detail is needed before one can recognize the house when one sees it. On the other hand, to reproduce the same house in all detail requires a multitude of specifications concerning dimensions, materials used, colour of exterior and interior finishes, location of electric outlets, plumbing, and so on. Every detail must be indicated and specific plans provided if the replica is to conform identically to the original. And so it is with reproducing movement. Architects and builders know that time and patience are needed for detailed and accurate specifications. Recording and reproducing dance is comparatively new. Are complete specifications needed? Is the employer of the notator willing to pay for the time it takes to record all details? For any specific dance how much detail is enough? Doris Humphrey once instructed a notator 'Keep the notation simple, don't clutter with unnecessary detail.' A year later when the work was again being taught, Humphrey turned to the score for details she had forgotten, details which had, alas, been left out – at her request. It is not easy to know today what the needs of tomorrow will be. Hence many experienced notators include extensive detail in a score knowing that simplification is always possible. A skeleton score can always be extracted, but a detailed score cannot be built up from a bare outline description.

Describing movement is something which dancers seldom do, let alone non-dancers who may be reading this book; therefore it would seem worth while to take a moment to give an example of a dance step and illustrate the progression from the barest outline of the action to a detailed description of a final stylized version. We will take the very familiar process of a step, a single transference of weight from one foot to another.

1. The basic action: weight transference.
2. Parts of body involved: left foot to right foot.
3. Direction of movement: the weight moves forward as it is trans- ferred.
4. Duration, amount of time (here the disciplines of dance enter): the transference of weight takes two counts.
5. Placement of the timing in relation to musical counts: the step starts on count 4 and continues through to count 1 of the next measure (bar).
6. Use of level: the knee bends as the step starts but straightens halfway through, ending with normal standing (an under-curve during one step).
7. Specification concerning how the foot contacts the ground: as the step starts the foot slides as it moves forward, contact with the ground being on the whole foot. In an ordinary step the foot usually moves forward clear of the ground; here contact with the floor occurs from the start.
8. State of leg rotation: at the start of the step the leg is rotated inward 45°; as the leg straightens to normal standing level it rotates out 45° with the weight on the heel, toes just off the ground.
9. Dynamics of the action: as the low forward slide is taken, there is an emphasis, a 'digging' into the floor, i.e. pressure occurs which disappears on the rising.
10. Specific transference of weight: on the low part of the step onto the right foot, the left foot often remains on the ground, still sharing some weight, but on the rise with the outward rotation, all the weight is taken onto the right foot. (How much the weight is shared and what the free leg does when free of weight is usually left to the individual.)

11. Material which follows: this step is followed by a symmetrical stepping action for the left leg, and may be repeated, right, left, right, left.

The resulting walk is a well known step from the 30s called 'trucking.' No mention has been made of accompanying body and arm movements. Exactly what should happen with the rest of the body, the use of space and energy, could also be defined in great detail, if needed.

Redundancy avoidance

Following the dictum 'That which is known need not be mentioned', some systems of notation have aimed specifically at redundancy avoidance. If from two pieces of information a third can be known, then there is no need to write in that third piece of information. The Benesh system has operated on this basis, thus keeping indications to a minimum and the notation simple in appearance. Classical ballet the world over is so standardized that many details can be taken for granted in recording balletic compositions. It is comparable to letters between family members in which much information can be omitted since existing automatic understanding allows for abbreviations. The antithesis of this is the legal document where everything is spelled out with utmost clarity. As a result legal documents are lengthy and ponderous and only lawyers and those concerned with the outcome of such documents care that the details be there and that they be accurate.

In actual practice the inclusion in written movement of a certain number of details which appear redundant actually facilitates reading; not only is the reader reassured but the absence of having to 'figure it out', perhaps of making an educated guess, increases reading speed and reduces errors.

Because movement is complex and many subtle variations can occur, a full notation is desirable if the movement is to be faithfully reproduced by individuals quite unfamiliar with the original structure and style. Such detail is needed in three circumstances: first, during the initial learning of a movement style or technique (the period of disciplined training during which personal movement preferences must be overcome and the exact details of the dance form absorbed and understood mentally and physically); second, for comparative research into stylistic differences between 'schools' or cultures; and third, for content analysis and evaluation of a choreographic work.

Those fluent in a particular dance style do not want to read details they already know, hence the tendency to abbreviate, to omit details, and to prefer an outline of the sequence as an aide memoire. Most dance notation systems have aimed at such simplification from the start. In the case of systems capable of far greater detail – for example, the Stepanov system – the writers may not have had the time or incentive to record more than an outline because of the conditions prevailing when the notating took place.

Practical limitations

In the thirty scores recorded in the Stepanov notation several indicate that there was only time for sketchy notes – for example, floor plans with a few words alongside. In other cases only the ballerina's footwork is recorded. Occasionally arm movements are filled in, but rarely is there what one would consider a complete score. Fine details for head, hands, etc. are not included. Either there was not time or these details were considered unimportant.

In evaluating a score one must consider the experience of the notator. To become a professional notator requires many years of experience with movement and two years in mastering and gaining speed in the use of a system of notation (no matter which of the highly evolved notation systems is being used). Most notated scores from the past, for example those in Stepanov notation, would now be considered the work of an intermediate student. Lack of experience resulted in unreliable scores, as judged by present professional standards. There is not only the system itself to master, but also how to view movement. This requires a trained eye and judgment sharpened by experience.

When there are slight variations in the repeated performance of a gesture, what exactly should the notator write? Many minor decisions have to be made, thus putting the stamp of his judgment on the score. In the case of notating from film, the movement is always the same, but is it accurate? When several dancers are performing the same movement and slight differences are observed, who is right? If the notator knows the style of dance involved, or the intention of the choreographer, an educated guess can be made. Welcome the day when choreographers can record their own works and be responsible for all such decisions themselves! In the meantime each choreographer should have a personal amanuensis, a notator completely fluent in his style, his way of thinking and working, the kind of role which Janet Moekle fulfils for Paul Taylor and his company.

As can be seen, understanding movement is essential. In the case of complex or non-standardized movement, the notator has a great responsibility. A professional dance notator is not just a movement stenographer but a translator, a transliterator who expresses in one language the equivalent sense and meaning found in another.

Detailed observation and selection of facts

The recording of every detail of a dance sequence must be done if there is a real need for an exact copy of a particular performance. The mirror image in Bournonville's *La Ventana* comes to mind. For these passages the dancers must be carefully drilled. It is rare in dance, but such duplication of movement is illustrated in the work of impersonators who must study and master exact details of body stance, hand gestures and facial expressions in addition to the voice. In theory dances could be notated to this degree of detail; in practice it would be far too time-consuming and costly, and to what avail? Therefore every notator must make a selection. Is the selection totally up to the personal preference of the notator?

Margaret Morris (and others since and perhaps before) discovered that there is more than one way to write a movement or position. Morris's dictum: 'Use that description which is simplest to write', has been the clarion call for generations of notators who write it 'this way because it is easier.' A very different attitude is now taken by many notators. A Labanotator advises: 'Choose that description which most closely expresses the intent of the movement, even if it takes more writing.' In this century with no library of notated materials on which to bring up generations of readers, in each system the emphasis had at first to be on writing rather than on reading. The attitude was: 'Writing should be quick, easy, simple. If difficulties are met, no one will want to bother: it is all too much work.' Now there is a definite swing toward what is a fact of life in other fields. For every writer there will be thousands of readers. Book publishers are meticulous about how a work is written; spelling, punctuation, meaning, general impact, pleasing impression, etc. Much time and care is taken in the production of a book because it will be that much easier, pleasanter, more rewarding, enriching, etc. to the thousands of readers. But in dance notation the reader has, up to now, too often been given little consideration. Quick and easy may also mean sparse, arid, barren, an outline, a skeleton without flesh, sinews or muscle. Now that notation is being used for serious movement study, for research, for education, there is a greater need and hence a greater incentive for the writer to be painstaking in the movement description chosen.

Some systems make a clear arbitrary choice from the start. Pierre Conté, the French musician and dance teacher, developed his system for his own use and was not interested in the needs of others. Relationship of one hand to the other, as when held in front of the body, was not important to him, yet the positioning of one hand above the other was often a feature in Doris Humphrey's choreography. Who should determine the limits of what any system should encompass? The Eshkol-Wachmann system is concerned with the physical changes that take place (changes in spatial placement, body angles, etc.) and not with the dancer as a human being. Therefore dynamics, movement concepts and motivations for actions are not included in that system.

This question of what should be written for any given movement came up by chance during one of the experiments undertaken by William C Reynolds during his notation research project at Anstey College, England, a few years ago. A series of simple, basic actions were recorded on video and subsequently notated by leading experts in the Laban, Benesh, and Eshkol-Wachmann systems. In one example an arm was raised sideward. The performer, unaccustomed to such isolated actions, unconsciously included a minor shift in the shoulder alignment and a slight head adjustment. The Eshkol-Wachmann notators expected to record these adjustments as well as the main arm displacement. Others notating from the same video tape either did not observe these minor body adjustments or assumed correctly that they were not important, not intended to be recorded and therefore ignored them. In the case of the Benesh system, the notator asked to know the dance style from which the movement came in order to know how to write it.

The results of this particular experiment revealed not only the differences in understanding of movement built into a system but also differences in what the writer looks for and considers important.

SIX

Modes of movement description

To paraphrase Gertrude Stein it could be said that 'A movement is a movement is a movement,' but, just as a rose may signify different things to different people – a token of love, the product of a successful insecticide, an object to paint – so one simple action may have a range of meanings depending on by whom, for whom, and why it is performed. Therefore the sense of the movement must be captured by the writer if the reader is to have the key to understanding the movement, to know how to approach it, and hence how to re-create it. Although the act of writing movements on paper goes back centuries, it is only recently that efforts have been made to include concept and intention in the movement description. The following discussion is an attempt (without becoming technical) to give a clear idea of some of the possibilities.

1. Indication of movement concept

An outline description of the movement idea allows freedom in interpretation on the part of the performer. The choreographer indicates in general terms what he has in mind without stipulating the exact form this idea should take. Thus a framework is provided within which to improvise. How a particular dancer will realize the choreography is left open. If this is what the choreographer wants, then the notation must be capable of capturing the same brief, outline instructions. Such basic instructions are often given as primary dance exploration or as groundwork in choreography classes, but may also be chosen for the final form of the notation for a piece of choreography.

To cite a specific choreographic instance in a dance work which blended precisely structured movement with free passages, the choreographer, Forrest Coggan, called at one point for the following action: 'Lie on the ground and flutter the elbows.' Very clear instructions, but open to several interpretations. Should the lying be prone or supine? Or on the side? Where are the arms to be placed? Overhead? Out to the sides? In a symmetrical position? Asymmetrical? Pauses between the flutters? Simultaneous fluttering? A great deal of freedom exists, and, as the choreographer intended, no two performers would produce the same final result, though each is performing the same movement idea. Though Coggan had a film of the work, he did not want subsequent dancers to learn from it as they would then be imitating the previous dancer's interpretation instead of creating

31

their own from the basic movement ideas. Therefore he resorted to Motif Writing in recording this section of the piece.

A typical basic motif movement phrase might be: 'Small springs followed by a large energetic bursting leap, then low running steps accompanied by waving arm gestures concluding with a gathering movement.' Does this description seem far removed from the choreography seen on the stage? Several choreographers, Frederick Ashton for one, often work in just this way, giving the dancers movement ideas which they then try out, and, if the result hits the right note, the material is kept. Or minor modifications may be made before the movements are 'set'. Motif description may be only an interim stage, or it may indeed be the appropriate form in which to capture the choreographic ideas.

2. Specific shape produced

Another basic choreographic idea may be to produce a particular body shape or design. For example, the basic effect wanted may be of limbs producing a right angle. In Fig. 6.1 this is illustrated with gestures of the arm. Each arm position looks different because of a different spatial placement, but the basic shape produced by the limb itself is the same in each.

Fig. 6.1

The choreography may consist of rhythmic changes in placement of such shapes. Two performers may be using such material in unison or in sharp contrast. Statement of the shape without indicating any particular placement may be required in the notation.

3. Floor design

A choreographic work might feature a specific path on stage to be followed, the dancers being allowed to improvise as they wish while following the stated floor pattern (Fig. 6.2). This often occurs in group scenes where villagers play 'follow the leader' while enjoying themselves 'tripping the light fantastic toe.' For such instances stage plans are needed as well as indications of relationship to the path being travelled, i.e. facing the direction being travelled, having your back to it and so on.

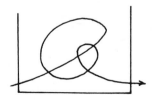

Fig. 6.2

4. Air design

Designs in the air are frequently performed by the arms or hands. A shape may be traced by a foot or even the head. In one East Indian dance a design is drawn by the chin. Air designs are frequently met in pantomimic gestures. We recognize the abstracted everyday gestures of Marcel Marceau even though he has no objects in his hands; the design of the movements gives the message. At one point in Leonide Massine's *Beau Danube* a line of boys at the back, using both arms, symmetrically draw with their hands the familiar design representing the outline of a girl, as in Fig. 6.3.

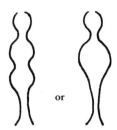

Fig. 6.3

The variety of possible designs may include writing letters or words. Many beautiful modern dance arm gestures, notably in Doris Humphrey's works and some of Ruth Currier's, are based on such designs. These may be as delicate as filigree and hence need to be notated in fine detail (subtle rotations, leading with the finger tips, etc.). However, statement of the basic idea, the trace form to be made, provides a direct indication of the meaning of the movement.

5. Directional points

Another form of design arises from movement between a series of directional points. An example might be: 'Starting up, go down, then to the left, then to the right, and finally up', as illustrated in Fig. 6.4 (*a*).

(*a*)   (*b*)   (*c*)

Fig. 6.4

This pattern may then be repeated indentically. When looked at obliquely, this example produces a design with two triangles apex to apex, which could be described as a simple drawing of a butterfly in flight, as in (*b*). But the performer may have no such idea in mind. It is quite possible that he is a musician conducting 4/4 time, or may even be a Christian making the sign of the cross. The exact size need not be significant; it is the points in space, their relation to each other and to gravity that matter. Observe how completely changed the 'message' is when the shape of (*a*) is placed horizontally, as in Fig. 6.4 (*c*). The shape is the same, but its placement changes its significance. The original basic concept rested on the relation of the initial movement to gravity, i.e. from up to down, the other directional points relating to this initial line of movement.

In dance a motif based on a directional pattern may be repeated many times but the manner of performance may vary. Directional patterns often appear in a jazz sequence, perhaps starting in a muted way and building up with each repeat until the gestures are filled with energy and spatially enlarged. The repetitions plus the personal variations in the group add to the impact. For such needs the notation must be able to show the basic directional points quite apart from the final form, the specific size, and other details incorporated in the final setting.

6. Time pattern

It is probable that the jazz motif mentioned above would also have a set rhythmic pattern to go with it. If a time pattern is evolved from a basic pulse, then it can usually be stated in music notation. But, particularly for a solo, the timing may be relative, it should not be counted. It should be felt as sustained movement stretching out in time, or as quick, sudden actions separated by various time lengths of stillness. For example: 'A very slow action immediately followed by a quick action, then a slight pause, another quick action, a longer pause, a quick action leading to another very sustained action, pause.' Such patterns often serve a dramatic purpose. There may be accompanying music, but the movements may ride over the music, having their own time pattern, or there may be no music at all. If, as we mentioned before, the dancer counts to himself, that fact is usually evident in the movement. Better to sense the spans of time being used without counting them. Though such time patterns are comparatively rare in most dance forms, in other movement fields the need also appears. Therefore indication of such use of time must be incorporated in any comprehensive system of movement notation.

7. Dynamic pattern

Quite in contrast to the movement ideas already stated, the choreographer might only establish the mood, the pattern of change in the dynamic qualities to be used. 'Drift, float like a cloud, then suspend. Three strong slashing movements. Arrest the last one, hold; then wilt, "dissolve", until resting on the floor.'

Patterns of energy may be the source of choreographic invention. Often these soon combine with rhythms so that a rhythmic-dynamic pattern is established which forms a rich basis for improvisation, calling on a wealth of spatial placements and involvements of parts of the body ranging from actions of isolated parts – hand, head, foot – to total involvement of the whole body.

8. Pattern in use of body parts

Use of body parts may be the focus of choreography. Abstract ideas may produce designs created by isolated changes in situation of hands, head, shoulder, hip, leg, elbow, etc. A stylized sequence expressing comedy or tragedy might be based on contact between hands, elbows, knees, hand and head, foot and knee, etc., or clapping and slapping may involve various parts, as in a Bavarian schuhplattler.

The eight categories outlined above illustrate the kinds of movement ideas with which a system of notation must be able to cope if it is to serve all needs. As instructions become more precise, room for invention and freedom in interpretation diminishes. There are many stages between such very general statements and a completely definitive score. The following is a typical mid-way description: 'Using either arm, make a sideward gesture which initiates a turn. Coming out of this turn run forward with forward gestures of the arms in any level.' Such instructions require notation statements in which choice of arm, of sideward direction, of turning direction and of level for the forward gestures are all left open.

As instructions for actions become more specific, precise use of parts of body, spatial directions, timing and dynamics all become clearly defined and recorded.

Choice of description for specific actions

A choreographer usually asks for specific, narrowly defined actions. These take many forms but might be as follows: 'Taking four counts (beats) lift the right elbow backward with a constant sustained pressure, the palm of the hand facing the floor. On count 5 allow a sudden relaxed downward drop of the elbow, at the same time bring the finger tips to just in front of the shoulder, the hand half closed. Without pausing at all, continue on through counts 6, 7, 8, the arm slowly rising, led first by the knuckles of the hand, then the tip of the index finger, which is joined by the other fingers, each in turn stretching upward. All during this extension the palm is facing backward. On count 8 the arm has arrived up. Slight pause. On 9 and 10, rotate the arm inward so that the palm faces forward and then out to the side; at the same time stretch the arm further upward, taking the shoulder and ribs with it. On count 11 and 12 swing the arm forward, down and back (the down direction coming right on count 11). On 13, 14 swing it down, forward and up again. During the swings hold the arm normally, but on count 14 return it to the twisted, reaching up position arrived at previously on count 10.'

The sequence just described gives specific details in use of time, space, dynamics, rotation, flexion, extension, parts of the body leading, parts included. Much may be happening at the same time with the legs, torso, head, and also the other arm, which, though not the focus of attention, may have a pattern which relates to and supports the main action. The above sequence could have been described through other words, the movement idea differently expressed. Seldom is there only one way to describe a movement, no matter how simple.

To make this fact clear we will take an isolated action. Fig. 6.5 (*a*) shows the starting position and (*b*) the end position resulting from the action. The starting position itself could be described in at least four ways. How would you describe the starting position? The action? Here are some possibilities.

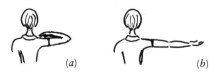

Fig 6.5 (*a*) (*b*)

Anatomical descriptions*

Starting position: right arm abducted 90°, elbow flexed 180°. Action: 'Extension 180° in the elbow joint.' Here emphasis of the movement is on the state of the joint. Having started completely closed (flexed), the elbow joint 'opens' completely. This is a physical (anatomical) description of the action focusing on awareness of the change in the state of the elbow, the flexion or extension being important. Note that, as far as the elbow is concerned, this same physical action could be performed with the arm forward, as in Fig. 6.6 (*a*) and (*b*), or in many other directions; the spatial placement does not change the elbow action.

Fig 6.6 (*a*) (*b*)

Spatial (directional) description

Starting position: upper arm (elbow) horizontally out to the side, lower arm to the opposite side (note arrows in Fig. 6.7 (*a*)). Action: 'The lower arm moves through the point vertically above the elbow (straight up) on its way out to the side horizontal point.' (Fig. 6.7 (*b*) and (*c*)).

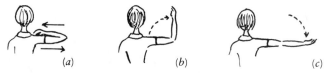

Fig. 6.7 (*a*) (*b*) (*c*)

Though there is no pause in the vertical situation, the performer is aware of passing through this direction on the way to side horizontal. The mental image of passing through points in space affects the manner of performance of a movement.

---

*The term 'anatomical' is used for description in which the emphasis is on the physical state, the flexion, extension, rotation, abduction, etc. resulting from movement in the various joints of the body. General rather than medical anatomical terminology is being used here.

It is interesting to note that, since the whole arm ends side horizontal, the description could have been in terms of a whole arm action instead of speaking only of the lower arm. The difference lies in whether the emphasis should be on an isolated movement of the lower arm, with no movement of the upper arm, or whether the emphasis is on unity of direction at the end for the arm as a whole. In the latter there will probably be a slight muscular change in the upper arm, a slight intensification, making the performer and the viewer aware of the limb being sensed as a whole unit at the end. Whichever performance is chosen, the hand should be carried as part of the arm, neither especially alive, nor forgotten.

Description of path
'The extremity of the hand (the finger tips) travels on a semi-circular path in the air.' In the chosen example this path is an upward semi-circle, the axis being at the elbow, Fig. 6.8. When the concept behind the movement is of the finger tips progressing on such a path (as if tracing the inside of a sphere), this description will provide the reader with the right image with which to produce the desired movement. There will be a slight heightening of energy in the finger tips; the fingers will probably be slightly more stretched and they will have a sensitivity, an awareness, which did not appear in performances based on the previous descriptions. Such slight differences in emphasis will produce physical and dynamic 'colouring' which could, of course, be described in great detail. However, understanding the concept behind the movement will produce the required subtle differences in performance, without the need to spell out such details.

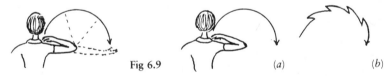

Fig 6.8   Fig 6.9   (a)   (b)

Design description
'Draw an arc, with the extremity of the arm.' Here the pattern, the design or shape being 'drawn' in the air, is of importance. Because of its simplicity this example, Fig. 6.9 (a), is very close to the path description discussed above. However, there is a major conceptual difference between travelling along a path where one is in the process of 'going' (motion) and may not know the destination, and progressing through space while knowing ahead the shape and limits of the design. It can be argued that the observer may not see a difference in performance; this may be true, but the performer derives inspiration from imagery, and so needs to know how to approach the movement in order to get the right sensation. The inner concentration of the performer is something the audience senses through the resulting move-ment.

When a more complex design is used, as in Fig. 6.9 (b), the difference in progression is more obvious. The same design can be drawn on planes in many different locations, e.g. as though on the floor, on the ceiling, on the wall in front, etc.

37

Relationship description

Starting position: hand above shoulder, elbow away from the side of the body. Action: 'gesture toward person (or object) G.' From relating to oneself, the gesture opens out toward a focal point G, and in so doing establishes a relationship between hand and person (or object) which will clearly be seen, as though connected by an electric current (the dancer's 'radar'), Fig 6.10 (*a*). The positiveness of this action is reinforced here by the sympathetic support of the gaze. Looking at the focal point emphasizes the action. Such a gesture often occurs in drama, for which such use of the head would be expected. However, depending on the situation, the relationship between the two people and the meaning of the gesture (a positive, negative or neutral statement), the head might be looking into another direction, perhaps at another person, while an arm is gesturing toward the chosen focal point, as in Fig. 6.10 (*b*). Here the statement is more likely to be 'Do I have to dance with *that* one?'

Fig. 6.10

A reverse relationship would be the action of the hand moving away from the shoulder. From the starting position of hand above shoulder, the movement idea could be that of putting distance between hand and shoulder by moving the hand away. Spatially this would be the same as Fig. 6.10 (*b*), but a specific destination for the 'away' need not be stated. However, the movement motivation is very clear. In performance one is aware of the 'spatial tension', the relationship, between hand and shoulder. The awareness of those two points can be felt by the performer and, when expressively performed, observed by the audience.

A more obvious version for 'hand away from the shoulder' could be a hillbilly pulling out his braces (suspenders) in a gesture of self assertion (drawing attention to himself, his importance), as in Fig. 6.11 (*a*) and (*b*). With his thumb under the top of a good flexible elastic brace, his gesture could follow the space pattern we have established. (If the elastic is too tight his elbow would have to drop to exert more pressure.)

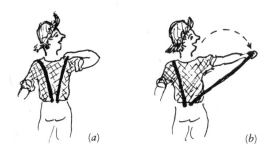

Fig. 6.11

Meaning of gestures – reason for choice of description

The purpose of this section is to convey the extent to which it is important to understand the movement one is writing in order to select the appropriate description. The notator needs to be well educated in movement analysis, in understanding what 'is going on'. As discussed elsewhere, the notator is a translator of the movement observed. It is not just a matter of writing the date, or other such information which has only one form and one meaning. As a model we will take a London policeman directing traffic and see to what extent his gestures need to be 'understood'. Action: starting as in Fig. 6.12 (*a*), he raises his right arm, (*b*). The drawing here tells us all we think we need to know about this simple movement.

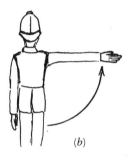

Fig. 6.12

Part of body – right arm.
Type of action – raising, lifting.
Direction – sideward (we know this from the picture).
Destination – side horizontal (also clear from the picture).
Reason (motivation, idea or cause of the action) – to stop traffic. How do
    we know? Only because it was stated that he was in traffic, and it is
    our common knowledge that the meaning of this gesture is 'STOP!'
The appropriate description of this action requires two vital additional details: palm intentionally facing forward, and the addressing, the relationship of the gesture to oncoming traffic.

Fig. 6.12

Now take another action: our English 'Bobby' has now moved only his lower arm (bending at the elbow). From being side horizontal, the lower arm is now vertically up, Fig. 6.12 (*c*). Meaning: because he is still looking

39

in the same direction and his palm is facing that direction, we take it to be the other version of 'stop'. But if the directions for face and palm change, as in (d), the motivation and hence meaning of that lower arm gesture are changed. Now he is addressing the traffic on his right, telling it to stop. If one saw only this drawing with no knowledge of the situation, one might think that the man is looking at the back of his hand – a quite different focus and relating situation.

(d)   *(e)*

Fig. 6.12

In Fig. 6.12 (e) he is gesturing to traffic at his right to come on; the change of palm facing has produced a beckoning movement, a motion to indicate the direction in which the traffic is to go. The addressing is still to the traffic on his right even though the gesture is away from it. This difference in purpose raises the point that if the intent is to be included, the action must be written differently from (c). The description should be: 'Addressing the car and, retaining this addressing, the hand (in fact the lower arm) moves toward the opposite direction.' Occasionally a policeman does use only his hand, but generally, to make the movement more visible, he moves both hand and lower arm. If the gesture had been bigger, as in Fig. 6.12 (f), the meaning would have been the same, so exact destination for this gesture is not important. However, if instead of (c) our man performed (g) to stop the traffic, his arm destination would have looked odd indeed, being one form of a salute! Thus we see that for some gestures destination matters and for others it does not.

(f)   *(g)*   *(h)*

Fig. 6.12

Now our officer is at the doctor's and is undergoing a test for 'tennis elbow'. The doctor asks him to flex his elbow to determine the degree of pain, the range and ease of movement. Here all emphasis is on the elbow joint, Fig. 6.12 (h).

Our man is now at home, painting his living room. The ceiling which has a curved arch requires his attention. He carefully brushes along the quarter circle curve, guiding the brush along the inside, by flexing his elbow, but the flexion is only incidental, his concentration is on the curve which the brush at the extremity of his arm is describing in Fig. 6.12 (*i*).

Fig. 6.12

Finally our man is showing off his muscles to his kids, (Fig. 6.12 (*j*)). Again the action is one of elbow flexion, but with the difference of a dynamic use of energy in bringing the antagonist muscles into play to make the muscles bulge. Here palm facing is not important: the hand will probably be clenched into a fist. Exact destination is not important and spatial placement is important only in that the arm should be seen to advantage. The only relating (addressing) that is going on is the rapt attention and adoring gaze of his two young children.

These examples have explored a range of possibilities as to how and why one or two simple gestures may occur; there are doubtless more. Perhaps only the main outline of the movement need be written, since everyone reading the material will know what it is all about. But unless he is certain to have knowledgeable readers, it is important for the notator to provide all the details necessary for the understanding and reproduction of the movements. In contemplating how the many complex movements which occur in a piece of choreography may need to be carefully and faithfully defined, one can see that the task of notating such a work in detail requires a carefully trained sensitive professional notator.

SEVEN

Historical development – letter codes

Many discourses on dance notation begin with Egyptian tomb paintings and Greek vases where delightful dancing figures are indeed to be found. But what substantial information do these drawings provide? No specific sequences 'spelled out', no dance compositions preserved. The Egyptians had three hieroglyphs for the act of dancing, but none with which to describe actual movements and steps. Though dance was part of life in these ancient cultures, it was not a serious art worthy of recording and preserving. Speaking of preserving, we must bear in mind that throughout the centuries dance notations were developed to meet only the needs of the moment, a form of memory aid for readers already knowledgeable in the style of the period. It is only now that concern for the enrichment of future generations exists and is a reason for undertaking the detailed work required for a faithful record of dance technique or choreography.

A historical survey of the development of dance notation systems in the western world* reveals incidentally the progression in the development of dance, physically and socially, and in changes of attitude toward the material of dance itself. What we know of dance in earlier centuries rests on pictures and word descriptions. These are coloured by the way society or the individual writer of that period viewed dance and chose to depict it. Although our concern with dance notation is focused on specific use of symbols or signs of some kind, pictures and word descriptions must also be given consideration since they provide a record through which much valuable information has been preserved. In addition, it is only through words and figure drawings that we have the key to the meanings and intentions of each notation system. Therefore books providing verbal descriptions will be mentioned as and when they illustrate a point or further the discussion in hand.

In general the presentation of historical systems will be chronological except where following through a particular aspect of recording movement provides a clearer picture of the ideas which emerged over the centuries, for example in the use of floor plans and the indication of relationship to music.

The earliest books on dance appeared in Italy in the fifteenth century. During the Renaissance, dance and correct social deportment became important as the many principalities vied with each other for supremacy in

---

*Consideration is not being given here to ancient oriental systems.

the noble arts. The need for magnificent display derived from the political ambition of the princes. Such display was a means of propaganda, finding its outlet in the splendour of pageants and 'balli'. There was no better way to display wealth and position than by giving balls at which, during the stately dances, elegance in dress and manner could be shown to advantage. Dancing masters, well conversed in the elaborate etiquette as well as the steps required on the ballroom floor, were both in demand and highly esteemed. The most famous of this period was Domenico da Piacenza, whose work *De arte saltandi et choreas ducendi* is the oldest known treatise on dance technique. Two of his students, Antonio Cornazano and Guglielmo Ebreo, both became famous in their own right and recorded their knowledge of the dance of that time. By present day standards the dances then popular at court were simple. Known as Basse Danses (low dances) because the dancers did not leave the ground, they contained five main basic movements or step patterns which were arranged in different sequences to form a variety of dances, each dance having a distinguishing name, for example the very popular *Filles à marier*. Since each basic movement had a name, spelling out a particular dance sequence was easily accomplished by listing the initial letter for each movement.

Fig. 7.1 'Filles à marier' from *L'Art et Instruction de Bien Dancer*. (A. H. Guest Collection)

The five movements and their letters in the time of Domenico and his followers were:

R – révérence, reverencia (the bow with which each dance began);

s – simple (a step forward followed by closing the feet together);

d – double (three forward steps followed by closing);

b – branle (a swaying step, sometimes indicated by c for conge, another name for the same movement, or by the sign **9**);

r – reprise, ripresa (a backward step).

Thus the dance *Filles à marier* is spelled out as: 'R b ss ddd ss rrr b ss d rrr b ss ddd ss rrr b ss d rrr b'. This dance was published in *L'Art et Instruction de Bien Dancer*, an anonymous book of the late fifteenth century, which is believed to be the first printed book extant devoted to the art of dancing.

The Letter System varied slightly but was used in many manuscripts of the time in Europe. The most magnificent collection of such dances, the Golden Manuscript, c. 1460, was written in gold and silver on a black background and belonged first to Marie de Bourgogne (it is often called the Burgundian Manuscript) and later to her daughter, Margaret of Austria, hence its application 'The Dance Book of Margaret of Austria'. The original is now in the Royal Library in Brussels. Fig. 7.2 shows the steps written under the music notes to which they should be performed; the name of the dance is written just above the letters. (Note that the 'r' is written to look like a 'z'.)

Fig. 7.2 The Dance Book of Margaret of Austria. (reprint, Library of Congress)

Since the Letter System was so simple and served its purpose well, it is amazing to discover that an unknown dancing master in Spain thought to turn the letters into signs. The existence of two Catalonian manuscripts using this device which are in the municipal archives in Cervera, near Barcelona, only came to light in 1931 when they were mentioned casually in a book on Spanish folklore and costumes. One of the manuscripts has the letter notations placed above the symbol notation, thus providing the key. Fig. 7.3 (*a*) spells out the popular 'Filles à marier'. Simple as it is, to our knowledge it is the first use of abstract signs to represent movement.

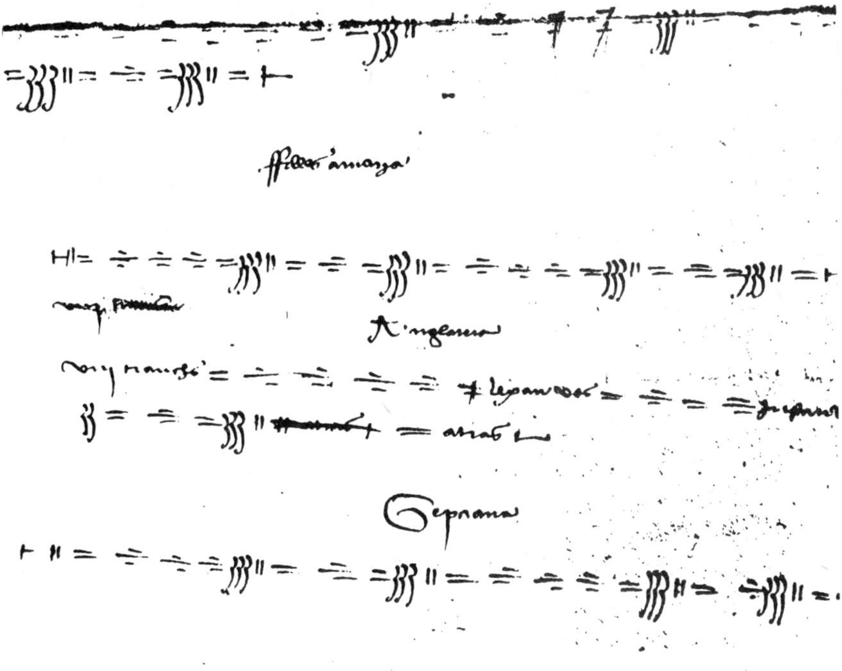

Fig. 7.3 (*a*) Cervera Manuscript: excerpt showing 'Filles à marier' in the second line of notation. (Biblioteca de Catalunya, Barcelona)

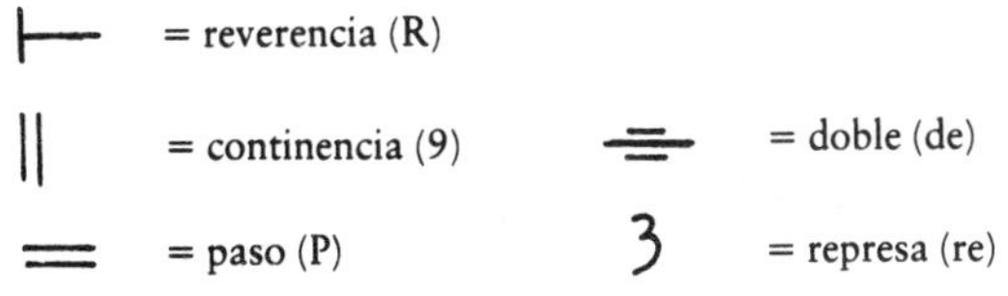

⊢—	= reverencia (R)		
‖	= continencia (9)	⩵	= doble (de)
⩵	= paso (P)	3	= represa (re)

Fig. 7.3 (*b*)

The signs have some pictorial relevance in suggesting the movements they represent. A horizontal stroke indicates a forward movement, a vertical stroke a step in place. Thus the reverence is a forward body movement in place; the branle (the continencia, swaying to one side then the other) is shown as two steps in place; two horizontal lines represent two simple (paso); three horizontal lines the double (doble), and the z sign the reprise (represa).

And what do 'R, s, d, b, r' mean to us today? It is only through books containing careful explanations of how each step should be performed that we can come close to the dance of that time. The best known such book, the most widely translated and reprinted, is *Orchesographie* by Thoinot

Arbeau, published in Langres in 1588. This book provides a delightful as well as a detailed and authentic record of sixteenth century dances, dance music and social mores, set forth as a dialogue between master and pupil, one Capriol who is desirous of learning all that is an essential part of the education of every well bred young man. Arbeau admonishes him: 'you have executed your steps and movements nicely and kept the rhythm well, but when you dance in company never look down at your feet to see whether you are performing the steps correctly. Keep your head and body erect and appear self-possessed. Spit and blow your nose sparingly, or if needs must turn your head away and use a fair white handkerchief. Converse affably in a low, modest voice, your hands at your sides, neither hanging limp nor moving nervously.'[1]

The careful verbal explanations of the steps are in many instances accompanied by woodcut illustrations, probably by Arbeau himself, Fig. 7.4.

Fig. 7.4 Illustrations from Arbeau's *Orchesographie*.
(Richardson Collection, Royal Academy of Dancing)

How precisely are these to be interpreted? For reconstruction today much needed detail is missing, and the resultant ambiguity leads to differences in interpretation. Arbeau spelled out the dances by placing the names of the steps next to the appropriate music note on the vertically placed music staff, read from the top of the page down. Fig. 7.5 illustrates the Gavotte.

It is interesting to note that Thoinot Arbeau was a pseudonym for Jehan Tabourot, a Jesuit priest who became Canon of Langres. He certainly was in favour of dancing, but perhaps it was unseemly for an ecclesiastic to write such a book. As we shall see later, Arbeau was not the only priest to be concerned with recording movement; indeed, inventors of systems of dance notation have come from many walks of life.

Before leaving the device of word abbreviations, it is worth noting that this idea is still employed for forms of dance which have an established vocabulary of steps. Although this chapter is concerned with the fifteenth to eighteenth centuries, reference will be made to later developments as and when a clear link exists which can best be followed in this chapter. In relation to word abbreviations, what ballet student has not jotted down: 'gl as en4 ss' for 'glissade, assemblé, entrechat quatre, sissonne' as a quick reminder? Most ballet teachers have tried quick abbreviated notes, or even longer verbal descriptions, only to find them unintelligible a year or so later. To establish some kind of system is essential, as did some ballet masters and choreographers, Bournonville for one (Fig. 7.6) from whose notes some degree of reconstruction of his works is possible; Harold Lander for another.[2]

Fig. 7.5 Arbeau: coordination of steps with music.
(Richardson Collection, Royal Academy of Dancing)

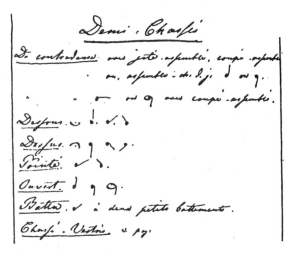

Fig. 7.6 Bournonville ballet shorthand.
(Royal Library, Copenhagen)

Antonine Meunier of the Paris Opéra published her ballet terminology shorthand in 1931 (Fig. 7.7). Despite the widespread use of ballet, even such a 'tailor-made' system, which would appear to have immediate appeal in ballet circles, did not overcome the dancers' reluctance to learn to read or write dance.

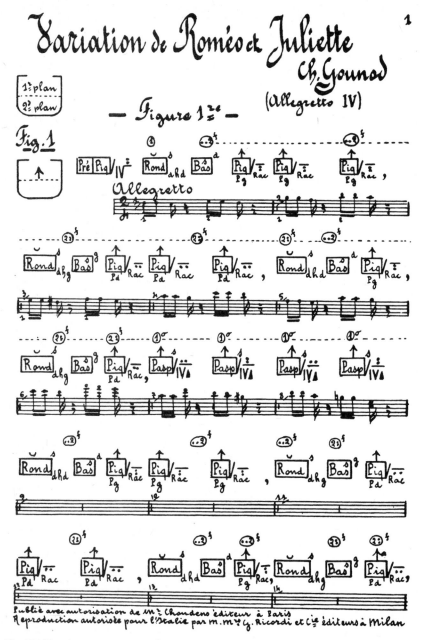

Fig. 7.7 Meunier system: excerpt from a score. (A. H. Guest Collection)

EIGHT

Historical development – floor plans

For the performance of the Basse Danses, where the dancers should stand in the room and where they should face were explained in the text as part of the correct conduct on the ballroom floor. In the Renaissance it was generally known whether a dance merely advanced and retreated, staying basically within the same area, or whether it progressed around the room; therefore this information was not stated in the notation. The development of intricate designs to be traced by the dancers as they traversed the floor led to indication of these on paper. The earliest illustration of such a plan is surely the rose design (Fig. 8.1) which Fabritio Caroso included in his book *Nobiltà di Dame*, published in Venice in 1600. This design is headed 'The Contrepasso according to the true mathematics after the verses of Ovid'. The intertwining of the paths for the Ladies and the Cavaliers suggests a 'hey', or 'grand right and left' without the taking of hands. When variations in floor designs began to be explored, the steps themselves were still simple, but by the Baroque period charming floor designs were being combined with intricate steps.

Fig. 8.1 Caroso: the Rose Pattern from *Nobiltà di Dame*. (Richardson Collection, Royal Academy of Dancing)

All floor plans use the obvious device of the 'bird's eye', or overhead view, with appropriate lines drawn to represent the paths taken. Indications for the performers show where they are placed in the dance area and where they face in relation to each other and to the front of the room. In the old days the front of the room was known as 'the presence', that part of the room where the king, prince, or noble lord and his entourage were seated. Today, on a proscenium stage, front is the audience. Excellent examples of variation in floor design are the horse ballets which were part of the luxurious entertainments arranged at the courts of Italy, France, Austria, and other European countries. Fig. 8.2 (a) shows one formation from a ballet on horseback which was part of *Il Mondo Festigiante*, a display given for a ducal wedding in Florence in 1661. In Menestrier's book *Des Ballets Anciens et Modernes* (1682) the horse formations are shown with stylized symbols, Fig. 8.2 (b). Many other examples exist. Today the performances of the Vienna Riding School may not be called 'ballet' or 'dance' but the movements and patterns come close to it.

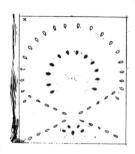

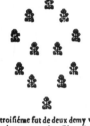

La troifiéme fut de deux demy voltes
à courbette pour les Chevaliers, &
pour les Efcuyers un tour au galop.

(a) Horse ballet: excerpt from *Il Mondo Festigiante*.
(Library of Congress)

(b) Menestrier: example of a horse ballet formation.
(Richardson Collection, Royal Academy of Dancing)

Fig. 8.2

John Playford's *The English Dancing Master*, first published in 1651, could be called a transition method of notating dances in that he used a few letter abbreviations: D – double; S – single; Wo – woman; We – women; cu – couple and Co – contrary. Simple signs were used for repeats, word descriptions gave the actual sequences, and in the basic floor plans for the starting positions for the dance, the symbol (a) represents a man and (b) a woman (though in the third and subsequent editions these were reversed), (Fig. 8.3). Eighteen editions of Playford's books of dance appeared, the last dated 1731.

Fig. 8.3 Playford: three examples of formations of dancers.
(Richardson Collection, Royal Academy of Dancing)

Many fanciful devices have been used to represent the dancers on the floor plans and we will digress a moment to consider how these evolved through the centuries. Fig. 8.4, presents a charming design, aesthetic in its own right, which is, in fact, part of a dance written in the Feuillet–Beauchamp system.*

---

*Commonly referred to simply as the Feuillet system.

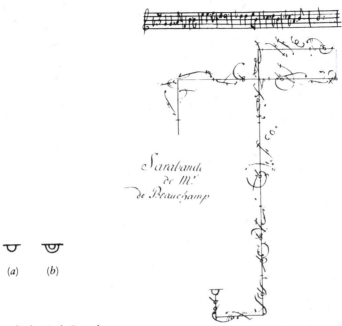

Fig. 8.4 Sarabande de M. de Beauchamp.
(Derra de Moroda Archives, University of Salzburg)

Much more will be said later about this system; for the moment it is enough to note that on the path across the floor are written the step variations to be performed on that path. The top of the page is the front of the room, and the indications Fig. 8.4 (*a*) or (*b*) show where the dancers start in the room and where they are facing, the flat side being the dancer's front.

Many dance books of the eighteenth and nineteenth centuries show floor plans with the accompanying music, the steps indicated briefly in words on a separate page. Such simplicity seemed to Landrin and later to Thomas Wilson and Lestienne-Dubois and others to be the most practical way of recording the popular contredances. These featured intricate floor designs and changing of partners for four or more dancers in contrast to the Baroque dances involving intricate steps for solo or duet performance. Surprisingly, Feuillet in his *Recüeil de Contredances* of 1706 explains his notation system briefly and then gives only floor plans for the dances with the accompanying melody line.

In De La Cuisse's books of contredances, 1762, his floor plans Fig. 8.5 (*a*) did not indicate clearly where the dancers faced. Later he added a small circle to show front, as in Fig. 8.5 (*b*).

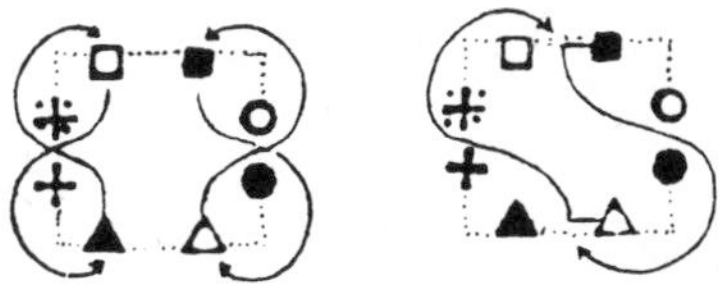

Fig. 8.5
(*a*) De La Cuisse: example of floor plans.
(Library of Congress)

Fig. 8.5
De La Cuisse

(*b*)

Facing direction added.

Despite the fact that Feuillet's 'track' system was such a success in its day, no other system has employed the device of combining path and step information; all others have kept indication of body movements and floor plans separate. Floor plans as we know them today were first published by Saint-Léon (Paris, 1852) (Fig. 8.6), and later by Zorn (Leipzig, 1887) (Fig. 8.7).

Fig. 8.6 Saint-Léon: floor plan.

Fig. 8.7 Zorn: floor plan.

Both showed the stage area from the audience's point of view. In Saint-Léon's score of the Pas de Six from *La Vivandiere* the girls are indicated by white pins, the man by a black pin, the point of the pin showing the facing direction. Some exotic signs have been devised to indicate the dancers.

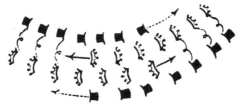

Fig. 8.8 Klemm.
(New York Library of the Performing Arts)

Man   Woman

Fig. 8.9 Roller.
(Bibliothèque de l'Opéra, Paris)

Fig. 8.10 Jolizza
(Library of Congress)

In Klemm's system (Leipzig, 1855), top hats were used for the gentlemen and crowns for the ladies Fig. 8.8. Roller (Weimar, 1843) shows couples by black and white hearts, diamonds, clubs and spades (Fig. 8.9), while somewhat later Jolizza (Vienna, 1907) provides a St John's Cross for the man and a fan for the lady (Fig. 8.10). Nijinsky, who also drew his floor plans from the audience's point of view (Fig. 8.11), considered separate symbols to indicate type of performer — tall, short, fat, thin, adult or child.

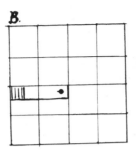

Fig. 8.11 Nijinsky system: floor plan from *L'Après Midi d'un Faune*. (British Library, courtesy Romola Nijinsky)

For intricate floor plans our admiration must focus on those written in colour by Manzotti for his epic productions of the 1880's, such as the one in Fig. 8.12. Reproduction of these works, for example his ballet *Excelsior*, in various capitals in Europe demanded some form of notation for the placement on stage of so many people.

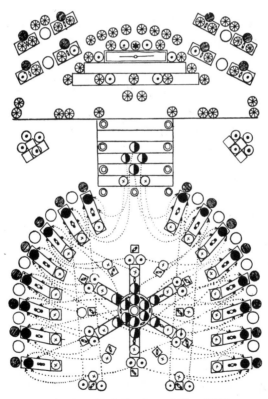

Fig. 8.12 Manzotti: Floor plan from his ballet *Amor*, Milan, 1886.

(La Scala Library, Milan)

Another choreographer of grand spectacles was Bolossy Kiralfy whose intricate coloured floor plans, c. 1894, sometimes included indication of the ballet steps to be performed.

Much simpler were the floor plans written in the Stepanov method, first used in Russia in 1892, in which crosses represent the men and circles the ladies (Fig. 8.13).

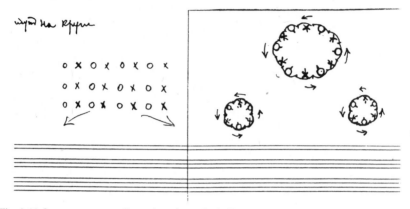

Fig. 8.13 Stepanov system: floor plans from the ballet *Raymonda*.

(Harvard Theatre Collection)

It is significant that until Laban's system (Vienna, 1928) all floor plans were written from the audience's point of view and not as experienced by the performers. It was as though the dancers were not to be involved, but only those watching them. Laban centred his system on the performer so that in the movement score all floor plans are written from the dancer's point of view (Fig. 8.14).

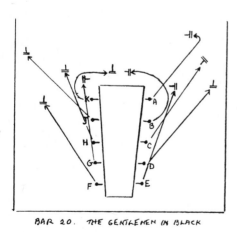

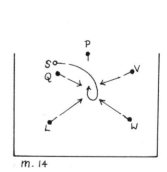

(a) Excerpt from *The Green Table*, 1939. (Courtesy Anna Jooss Markard)

(b) Excerpt from Ashton's *Illuminations*, 1982. (Courtesy Sir Frederick Ashton and the Dance Notation Bureau)

Fig. 8.14 Laban system: examples of floor plans.

54

In these plans a white pin represents a girl, a black pin a boy, the pin pointing into the direction faced. In a finished score a separate set of the whole series of floor plans is provided, drawn from the director's point of view for his benefit in checking correct placement of dancers and use of stage space. This concentrated set of floor plans also gives a quick overview of the development of the choreography in respect to entrances, exits, arrangements of dancers on stage, the interlacing of paths, and so on.

Some systems, for example the Eshkol-Wachmann (1958), do not use floor plans on the principle that if the movements, the travelling steps, are correctly written and performed, the desired floor design will result. This, in fact, was also Laban's original idea. He believed the dancer's actions were paramount and no 'outside' indications should intrude. This and other idealistic ideas had to give way to practical demands met in the professional situation. In the reconstruction of a work, floor plans give an immediate message and contain a surprising amount of immediately accessible information, easy for the uninitiated to understand. In the interest of keeping the notation score concise, Benesh (London, 1956) devised 'shorthand' signs which convey information on group pattern and location, and signs which combine direction faced and direction of travel. These are written where appropriate beneath the stave notation and have the advantage of being quick to write but require study to be understood. The additional use of floor plans has been found beneficial as a reading aid in some situations. The illustration in Fig. 8.15 summarizes the individual actions of twenty couples as they change formation. The standard indication of performers on the plans is black pins for women and white pins for men.

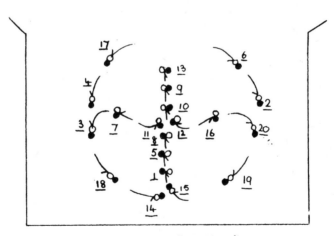

Excerpt from MacMillan's *Mayerling*.

Fig. 8.15 Benesh system: example of a floor plan.
(Courtesy Kenneth MacMillan and the Institute of Choreology)

Stage plans have been applied to drama, as when the Shakespearean authority, Margaret Webster, investigated the use of dance notation and, to save time in rehearsals for her repertory company, had her staging of *The*

Taming of the Shrew notated (Fig. 8.16). Pavis 1981, discusses the value of indicating stage movements for theatrical productions.

Pet. Go, rascals, go, and fetch my supper in..
            Exeunt Servants
(*singing*) Where is the life that late I led—
Where are those—Sit down, Kate, and welcome.— 130
Food, food, food, food I
       Re-enter Servants with supper
Why, when, I say ? Nay, good sweet Kate, be
   merry.
Off with my boots, you rogues I you villains, when ?
(*sings*) It was the friar of orders grey,
    As he forth walked on his way :—

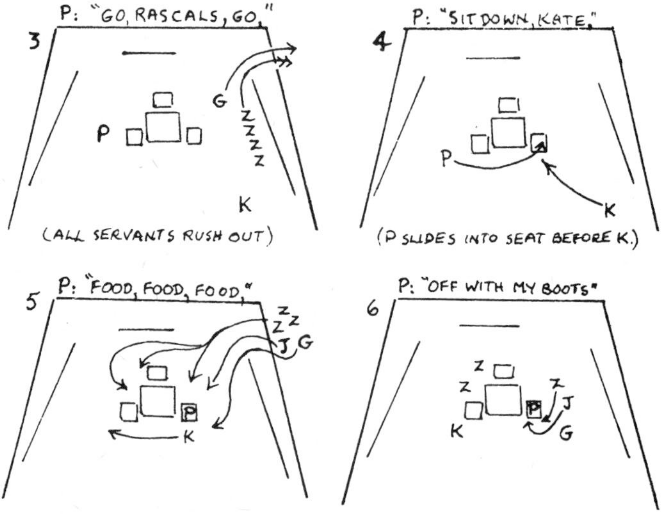

Fig. 8.16 Excerpt from *The Taming of the Shrew*, Margaret Webster production.
(Dance Notation Bureau Library)

For television programmes floor plans have facilitated production. In 1965 for the filming of *USA: Dance – Four Pioneers* the floor plans for Doris Humphrey's *Passacaglia* were handed to the lighting director who used the sheets to mark his cues for the different sections of the dance, these sections and the arrangements of dancers being very clear from the notated plans.[1]

Writing floor plans requires no special training. It is tantalizing, therefore, to realize how much valuable information concerning ballets now lost could have been recorded had someone taken the trouble. It would have been a minor matter for each dancer to indicate his or her path and position in relation to other dancers, adding, as one sees in many of the Stepanov scores, a few word notes at the side as a general guide to the steps used. Today we see dance researchers piecing together whatever fragments they can find to reconstruct dances of the past. How woefully negligent dancers and choreographers of bygone eras have been!

NINE

Historical development – music, timing

Until recently dances were always performed to some musical accompaniment, therefore placement of the step indication under the appropriate music note sufficed to indicate timing, i.e. when a step occurred. As we have seen, this was true of the early letter systems; it is also true of the stick-figure-based systems, those which visually represent a dancing figure, or an abstraction of it. Such placement in relation to the music was used by Saint-Léon (France, 1852), Zorn (Germany, 1887), Lissitzian (Russia, 1940), Misslitz (Germany, 1950), Jay (U.S.A., 1955), Benesh (England, 1956) and more recently Sutton (U.S.A., 1973). Saint-Leon, however, went one step further by providing the possibility of combining the appropriate music note-head and tail with the movement indication to give precise time value to each part of a step (Fig. 9.1).

Fig. 9.1

Saint-Léon system: timing.
(A. H. Guest Collection)

His concern with timing is not surprising since he was a musician as well as a dancer. Another musician who became fascinated with the problem of writing dance, Sol Babitz (U.S.A. 1939), incorporated signs for time values in his stick-figure-based indications. As dancers frequently count while learning sequences placement of the appropriate counts above the notated steps was and still is frequently used in lieu of writing out the music notes. The need for greater precision led Benesh to devise special timing signs to spell out on which beat or subdivision of a beat a position should be achieved (Fig. 9.2). The number of beats in a bar is indicated and each movement falls on a beat unless a specific time sign appears.

Fig. 9.2 Benesh system: timing (A. H. Guest Collection)

For most systems timing is an additional indication, not an integral part of the movement notation. The first system to incorporate an indication of timing into the notation itself was that of Feuillet (1700). The path taken by the dancer is indicated by a centre line. Bar lines across this line relate to the bar lines of the music written at the top of the page, thus indicating which steps occur within which measure (Fig. 9.3).

Fig. 9.3

Feuillet system:
timing.
(Glasgow University Library)

This simple device is easy to follow when, for example, three steps occur within a bar of three beats; but when two, or perhaps four steps occur within a bar of three beats, how are they to be proportioned in the time available? Improvements in indicating timing, treatises on cadence, were introduced later as the system developed, but for many of the dances the reader of today must try out the different possibilities and make decisions based on knowledge of the style of the period and on what physically feels right.

Since time, duration, is an element common to both music and dance, it was inevitable that at some point music notes would be chosen as the basic signs for dance notation, retaining their time significance and being modified in some way to indicate direction or part of the body used. Klemm (Germany, 1855) was the first with this idea, making use of some notated indications to clarify his descriptions of the correct performance of dance steps. Placement of the note stem on right or left indicated right or left foot; double stems signified both feet. In Figure 9.4 the movement notation is placed under the music.

Fig. 9.4 Klemm: use of music notes for timing.
(New York Library of the Performing Arts)

But it was Stepanov (Russia, 1892) who devised a full system for notating ballets based on music notes (Fig. 9.5).

Fig. 9.5 Stepanov system: timing. (Harvard Theatre Collection)

Since then others have tried the same idea, notably those with a strong musical background, such as Conté (France, 1931), Nikolais (U.S.A., 1945) and McCraw (U.S.A., 1958). What appears at first to be an obvious solution to indicate timing for movement proves in the long run to be a handicap, since music notes are not flexible when fine variations in timing must be expressed. Among those who used music notes there is an ambiguity as to how duration for slow movements is to be written and interpreted. Does a semi-breve (whole note) mean that the stated destination (position) is held for four beats, or that it takes four beats to arrive at that destination? Adhering to established music notation rules compounds the problem since movement has, in fact, such very different requirements.

A sophisticated, versatile approach to timing had to wait for the twentieth century, when the idea of length on paper to indicate length of time (duration) was established. By selecting a standard unit, e.g. half an inch, for each regular pulse – be it in relation to music or to seconds and subdivisions of seconds – the writer can show clearly the duration of the action (its extension in time) by the length of the movement indication. This device frees movement notation from its bondage to music notation while at the same time providing direct correlation to any accompanying music through the use of bar lines. Though music notes are not needed to indicate movement rhythms, for a full, archival dance score the accompanying music score can be placed alongside, parallel with the dance notation.

The first system to employ this device was that of Laban (Vienna, 1928). A vertical centre time line is marked off into regular beats and the movement symbols drawn shorter or longer according to the amount of time required for each action, the symbols being designed to allow for variation in length (Fig. 9.6).

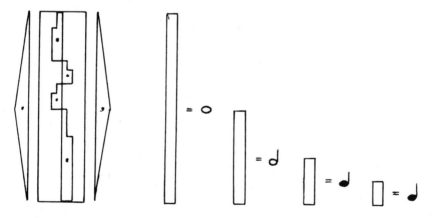

Fig. 9.6 Laban system: timing.

Quite independently and for another purpose, New York musician and mathematician Joseph Schillinger, whose system of movement notation was never completed because of his early death, used the device of lengths on graph paper to indicate time values in teaching complex rhythms to music students in the 1930s and 40s.[1] Regular divisions of the staff, a regular grid to indicate on paper the regular beats, is also a feature of the Loring system (U.S.A. 1955) and of the Eshkol-Wachmann (Israel, 1958). In these two systems flexibility in length of symbol does not exist; instead a stated action is placed in the time space where it starts and is understood to take the time available, i.e. the blank spaces which follow, until another action is written. If a pause is to follow an action, Loring inserts the sign for 'hold' which subsequently is cancelled; Eshkol-Wachmann draws a thick line at the point where the previously stated action is to be completed (Fig. 9.7).

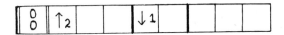

Fig. 9.7 Eshkol-Wachmann system: timing.

For many systems general timing is considered sufficient and the need to indicate intricate overlapping durations does not arise. This is particularly true of many folk dance systems. The Proca-Ciortea system (Fig. 9.8) used by the Rumanian Folklore Institute, provides the device of modifying the letters D (for the right foot) and S (for the left foot) to indicate the time value.

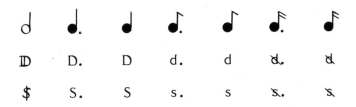

Fig. 9.8 The Proca-Ciortea system: timing

Greater distinctions than these are usually not needed in folk dances.

TEN

Historical development – eighteenth century

The Feuillet Era

Long was the Dancing Art unfix'd and free;
Hence lost in Error and Uncertainty:
No Precepts did it mind, or Rules obey,
But ev'ry Master taught a different way:
Hence, ere each newborn Dance was fully try'd,
The lovely Product, ev'n in blooming dy'd:
Thr' various Hands in wild Confusion toss'd,
Its Steps were alter'd, and its Beauties lost;
'Till Feuillet, at length, Great Name, arose,
And did the Dance in Characters compose:
Each lovely Grace by certain Mark he taught,
And ev'ry Step in Lasting Volumes wrote.
Hence o'er the World this pleasing Art shall spread,
And ev'ry Dance in ev'ry Clime be read.
By distant Masters shall each Step be seen,
Tho' Mountains rise, and Oceans roar between.
Hence with her Sister Arts shall dancing claim
An equal Right to Universal Fame,
And Isaac's Rigadoon* shall last as long,
As Raphael's Painting, or Virgil's Song.

Canto II, 25 from *The Art of Dancing*, a poem in three cantos by Soame Jenyns,
London, 1729.

Such appreciation for dance notation has indeed been rare, but Jenyns had good reason to praise the Feuillet notation. Over the centuries the idea of dance notation and its practical use has gone in and out of favour. The greatest flowering followed the establishment in 1661 of the Académie Royale de la Danse in Paris by Louis XIV who, by his own example of excellence as a performer, set a high standard in dance as a required social grace. The need for instruction at court and for the educated classes, the importance of dancing masters, and the desire for new dances provided the climate in which a practical system of notation could flourish. An ingenious

---

*The Rigadoon (Rigaudon) as composed by Mr Isaac, famous French Dancing Master active in London, was recorded by John Weaver.

system called *Chorégraphie ou l'Art de Décrire la Danse* which suited admirably the needs of the day was published in 1700 by Raoul Auger Feuillet, but there is little doubt that the system was in fact originated by the famous ballet-master, Pierre Beauchamps, who, one can surmise, was tardy in completing his work and publishing the results and so was outstripped by the younger, ambitious Feuillet.[1] Whatever the details of its 'birth', the system commands respect for the information it conveyed in a compara-

Fig. 10.1 Feuillet system: example of a dance.

tively simple way and for the degree to which its publication and use spread throughout Europe.

A second edition of the initial book appeared in 1701. By 1706 both John Weaver and Paul Siris had produced English translations in London, to be followed in 1710 by another by John Essex. Gottfried Taubert published his German translation in 1717, and so the list grew. Recüeils, collections of dances, were published almost yearly from 1700 until 1722, making available the latest compositions by famous teachers to all who could read. Dance literacy was an expected skill in an educated man. Indeed, one reads of complaints from the clergy of ladies having books of dances instead of Bibles on their bedside tables.

An amusing illustration of the practical, daily use of the notation is the following excerpt from *The Tatler*, 1709, written by Joseph Addison:

'I was awakened this morning by a sudden shake of the house; and as soon as I had got a little out of my consternation, I felt another, which was followed by two or three repetitions of the same convulsion. I got up as fast as possible, girt on my rapier, and snatched up my hat, when my landlady came up to see me, and told me that the gentlewoman of the next house begged me to step thither, for that a lodger she had taken in was mad. . . . I looked in at the keyhole, and there I saw a well-made man look with great attention on a book, and on a sudden jump into the air so high, that his head almost touched the ceiling. He came down safe on his right foot, and again flew up, alighting on his left; then looked again at his book, and holding out his right leg, put it into such a quivering motion, that I thought he would have shaken it off. He used the left after the same manner when on a sudden, to my great surprise, he stooped himself incredibly low, and turned gently on his toes. After this circular motion, he continued bent in that humble posture for some time, looking on his book.'

Addison finally learned that the gentleman was a dancing master who 'had been reading a dance or two before he went out, which had been written by one who taught in an academy in France.' The dancing master informed him 'that there is nothing so common as to communicate a dance by letter.'[2]

Feuillet's system is based on a centre line which traces the dancer's path across the floor and hence it is referred to as a 'track' system. It could be said that the step indications are modified footprints. Fig. 10.2 (*a*) shows a step forward on the right foot, (*b*) a step forward on the left. The black dot indicates the start and the angular line at the end represents the foot. Fig. 10.2 (*c*) is a step to the right on the right foot, (*d*) a step to the left on the left foot.

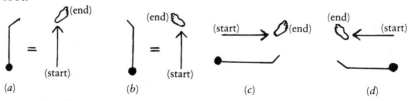

Fig. 10.2 Feuillet system: indication of step direction.

Strokes and symbols added to the basic step line allowed ornamentation in stepping to be shown, a few of the possibilities being: Fig. 10.3 (*a*) a bending of the knee during the step; (*b*) a rise on half toe during the step; (*c*) a springing step; (*d*) a gliding step, and so on.

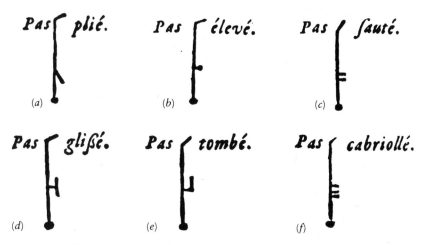

Fig. 10.3 Feuillet system: step embellishments.

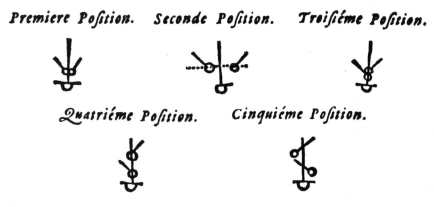

Fig. 10.4 Feuillet system: positions of the feet.

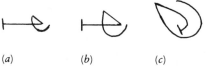

Fig. 10.5 Feuillet system: arm movements.

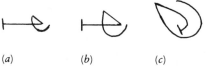

Fig. 10.6 Feuillet system: taking and releasing hands.

Many dances were written without indication of arm gestures, emphasis being concentrated on the intricate footwork; elegant carriage and graceful use of the arms were taken for granted.

Feuillet's abstraction of the 'footprint' idea was later reversed in 1843 when Franz Anton Roller adopted the same idea but put a foot at the end of the symbol (Fig. 10.7).

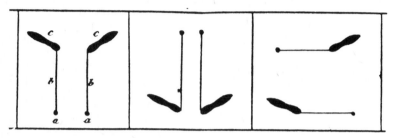

Fig. 10.7 Roller: adaption of Feuillet signs.
(Bibliothèque de l'Opéra, Paris)

Use of footprints for ballroom dance has been a common practice; it is immediately visual, but lacks any movement indications. Some ballroom steps have been illustrated through photographs of empty shoes, a man's pair and a lady's, arranged to indicate the next foot placement – not exactly a dance notation method but nevertheless a device to add to the list.

As Feuillet's system spread later writers made improvements, adding more detail, but essentially the system remained the same, lasting for nearly a hundred years. Why did it decline and fall into disuse? Two main factors are evident. First, following the French Revolution and the decline of the old régime, dance for the new middle class evolved into simpler forms. Contre-danses (country dances) brought over from England emphasized dances for several couples using intricate floor patterns but simpler steps. These led to the nineteenth century quadrilles, waltzes, etc. This break from older forms meant also a break with the written forms of the dances. While social dances became simpler, theatrical dance, which in the beginning of the eighteenth century had been basically of the same form as that danced at court, had developed a much more demanding technique, a greater range of movement and an enlarged dance vocabulary. Feuillet's notation did not provide for separate indication of steps (transference of weight) and of leg gestures, nor could the level of the leg raised off the floor be shown, let alone other newly developed details of footwork. No provision had been made in his system for a greater range of arm gestures, both ornamental and pantomimic, nor for use of the torso and head. Theatrical ballet productions also often involved a large cast requiring path indications for many dancers moving simultaneously, for which the track notation of the Feuillet system was quite unsuited. It became obvious that for professional dance a new approach to recording movement was needed. By the turn of the century Feuillet's notation was in decline.

There were those who regretted its neglect and the fact that famous teachers of the time were discouraging the use of it. Even in its hey-day not everyone was in favour of notation. Noverre, the great dance reformer whose writings on mid-eighteenth century dance are still highly respected, was prejudiced against notation.[3] On the other hand Gaspare Angiolini, famous ballet-master and contemporary of Noverre, found Feuillet's system quite satisfactory as it contained all principles of the ballet of the period. In Angiolini's opinion, Feuillet did more for the future by recording some of the dances in notation than Noverre, who failed to do so.[4]

The second factor in the decline of the system was the shift in performance of dance, both theatrical and social, from the educated classes to the general populace. Thus the traditions of dance literacy were broken and dance moved again into the still prevalent oral-visual tradition. Dancers were trained and choreographic works were handed on merely by watching others and being told what to do. Books were no longer connected with the physical activity of dancing, and the advantages of written dance were totally lost. Even today this lack of literacy in dance education is inherited with the art itself, a disadvantage which is difficult to overcome.

The system which bears Feuillet's name may have been put on the shelf, but there it has not remained, for in this century dance historians such as Shirley Wynne and Wendy Hilton have in increasing numbers turned to the wealth of materials recorded in it, a rich heritage from the past that offers valuable knowledge of dances of the period and the rewarding experience of re-creating them with as much authenticity as research can provide. Even today the system commands our respect and admiration for the tremendous amount it accomplished.

ELEVEN

Historical development – nineteenth century

Théleur

The next big surge of interest in dance notation centred on stick-figure based systems, but before that an isolated system appeared as though from nowhere, enjoyed a brief success and then vanished. This was the system devised by E. A. Théleur, an English dancing master, whose book *Letters on Dancing* was published in London in 1831. Little is known about Théleur. It is likely that his real name was Taylor and that, on his return from studying in Paris, he felt the French spelling would provide him with more authority as a dance master in London. Despite competition in the form of publication in 1830 of *The Code of Terpsichore* by the eminent dancer, teacher and choreographer, Carlo Blasis, Théleur's book received a good press, judging by the quotes cited in the 1832 edition. His system of notation, which he called *Chirography*, is of interest to us since it is based on abstract signs and includes indications for basic movements, not just positions. He lists seven such basic movements and 'spells out' the various steps through appropriate signs, the first so-called 'alphabet system.' For present-day needs of reconstruction he does not provide enough detail, but we are the richer for his inclusion of the *Gavotte de Vestris* (Fig. 11.1), as an illustration of his system – a small part of the dance heritage which has been made more available to dance students of today through Mary Jane Warner's research and transcription of it.

Théleur provided two versions of his system, a detailed version and a simplified, memory-aid version for those who were already familiar with the steps. This was the first instance of the introduction of a 'shorthand', an idea which Zorn also introduced, possibly quite independently.

Saint-Léon

No system of notation emerges full blown out of a vacuum. Many dance teachers experimented with ideas and no doubt the undeveloped jottings of the distinguished French teacher, Albert, were the basis of the system which his ex-pupil, Arthur Saint-Léon, published in Paris in 1852. This notation, called *Sténochorégraphie*, was the first to use modified stick figures. Why had it taken so long for this very obvious device to be used? Perhaps the changes in stage costume which revealed more of the body led to the idea of a more direct representation of the figure.

Fig. 11.1 Théleur system: first part of the *Gavotte de Vestris*.

In his time Saint-Léon was a famous dancer and choreographer; today he is probably best known as the original choreographer of *Coppélia*, the 1870 version still preserved at the Paris Opéra. Perhaps his familiarity with music notation – he was a child prodigy on the violin, and the only performer known to have danced a variation immediately after playing a violin solo – helped him overcome the general reluctance on the part of dancers to be concerned with dance literacy. His book *Sténochorégraphie*, published in Paris in 1852, presented his notation system through the standard ballet steps. He does not include verbal discourses on how to dance, as did Théleur, but presents his notation system with explanations and examples.

What features in the Saint-Léon system are of particular interest? As we survey the systems of notation evolved through the centuries, it is tempting to go into detail to explain how each one works, but such detail must wait for another book. For our purposes here, it is of interest to know what new ideas and points of view were put forward with each new system.

Mention has been made earlier of Saint-Léon's integration of specific time values. He also introduced a feature which has been common to almost all stick-figure based systems; that of indicating the figure as seen by the audience. The reader has therefore to reverse right and left sides of the body.

The exception is the visually-based Benesh system (1956) which did not incorporate this drawback, the movement being seen as if from directly behind the dancer. For indication of footwork Saint-Léon uses a five-line staff* which loosely represents the stage as seen by the audience in that progression of the symbols down the staff indicates advancing toward the audience, and vice versa. A thick line is used for the supporting leg, a thinner one for the leg in the air. Placement of leg symbols on a staff line indicates supporting, and between the lines shows springing into the air. The arms, head and body are written on a separate line above the rest of the staff. Saint-Léon is the first to introduce indications for 'épaulement' (slight turning of the upper body). The leg indications are stylized, and signs are added to provide further information. Upper body indications are more pictorial. Fig. 11.2.

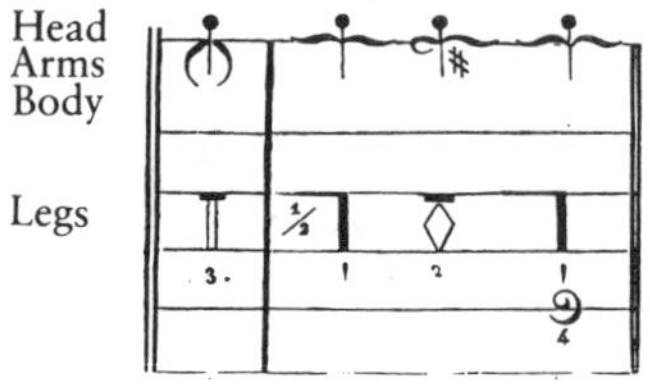

Fig. 11.2 Saint-Léon system:
staff showing preparation for
pirouette in 2nd on the left foot.

Saint-Léon's greatest gift to future generations was the inclusion in his book of the notated score of the Pas de Six from his ballet, *La Vivandière*, as performed in Paris in 1848 (fig. 11.3).

Fig. 11.3 Saint-Léon system: excerpt from the Pas de Six from *La Vivandière*.
(A. H. Guest Collection)

---

*Favier (1751) was in fact the first to use the five-line music staff, he also modified the basic sign for the dancer to show the time value.

Neglected for over a century, it was first reconstructed in 1974 by me at the Royal Academy of Dancing in London. Since then performances of the work have taken place in Paris, in New York where it is performed by the Joffrey Ballet, and in London where it is danced by Sadler's Wells Royal ballet. In this score Saint-Léon gives detailed description of the footwork, but only general arm positions and few head and torso indications. One might assume that, since it is the nature of classical ballet to be concerned first with footwork, the established correlations of arms and head to the footwork were to be added by the performer. However, the Bournonville heritage from the same period, which has been handed down from person to person to the present day, reveals that it was indeed the style of that time to keep the arms simple so as to set off the brilliant footwork.

It is our loss that Saint-Léon had no time during his busy professional career, travelling all over Europe mounting his ballets, to record further works. Only a few jottings in his system have so far turned up. Alas that no devotee of the master took up the notator's pen to capture his ballets for us!

Zorn

Dance notation is concerned with movement, and through its various signs and indications important details concerning the correct way of performing exercises and steps can be spelled out. A book which includes notated material is usually taken to be a book expounding a particular notation system, but may in fact be about dance, the notation being used only to clarify performance details. Such a book was *Grammatik der Tanzkunst* published in Leipzig in 1887 by Friedrich Albert Zorn. An English translation, *Grammar of the Art of Dancing* appeared in Boston, Mass., in 1905. The book does indeed explain the system, but primarily it is a most informative text on the basic exercises required in dance training and the correct performance of the various ballet steps of that period – a researcher's paradise if one is interested in the teaching methods and technical performance of steps of the mid and late nineteenth century.

Zorn was a highly respected ballet master who held consultations with Paul Taglioni, Saint-Léon and other noted choreographers, examining all obtainable books on dancing to understand what had been done previously and what remained to be done. He was a member of the Association of Dance Teachers in Germany, which advocated widespread use of the system. From the Boston edition we know of the interest of the American National Association of Masters of Dancing which also advocated its use. What happened? No further material in the system has turned up and there is no evidence that others became fluent in reading and writing this method.

Zorn acknowledges Saint-Léon's system and compares the writing of the positions of the feet, etc. in both systems. It is interesting to note that Zorn's figure drawings (Fig. 11.4) are less abstract and more directly pictorial than Saint-Léon's. There is no staff; a base line is drawn for the floor and it is clear from the figure itself whether it is standing on the line or is in the air above. The whole figure may be drawn, or only the legs. Perspective is attempted, but is not always clear. Movement indications include inturned legs, standing on the heels and other actions needed for character or national dances.

Fig. 11.4 Zorn system: pictorial indications.
(A. H. Guest Collection)

Zorn was thoughtful enough to include a selection of dances in his book, the most important of which was the solo dance, the *Cachucha* (Fig. 11.5), which the ballerina of the Romantic period, Fanny Elssler, had made so famous. This is another gem from the past which present and future generations can enjoy since a professional performance of the dance based on my research and reconstruction has been filmed and a book published which presents the background history together with the Labanotation score.

Fig. 11.5 Zorn system: extracts from the score of Fanny Elssler's *Cachucha*.
(A. H. Guest Collection)

Stepanov

Of the systems of the past, only those which have left a record of dances and an analysis of dance steps are now worth the trouble of mastering, unless, of course, one is making a detailed study of systems of notation for their own sake. A system which will always evoke interest is that devised by Vladimir Ivanovich Stepanov, a dancer of the Imperial Ballet in St Petersburg, whose book *L'Alphabet des Mouvements du Corps Humain* was published in Paris in 1892. Stepanov became involved in the study of anatomy and concerned with the idea of writing down movement. By 1891 he had formulated a system of notation and, as a result of a successful demonstration to the authorities, was given assistance to go to Paris for further anatomical studies. In 1893 the system passed an elaborate trial and was adopted as a required course of study at the Theatre School, Stepanov being given the title 'Instructor of Theory and Notation of Dance.'[1] Pupils of the time, such as Tamara Karsavina, referred to it as 'black magic.'[2] She writes in her biography: 'Lessons of notation were unpopular with pupils. We called them abracadabra and cabalistics. That did not prevent my taking an interest in the subject.'[3] Balanchine, however, recollects that he found the method of great use as an aid to studying ballet technique.[4] In time a few mastered it enough to take part in notating the current repertoire.

Stepanov was the first to base a movement notation system on the anatomical structure of the human body. A good portion of his book concentrates on anatomical diagrams and the notation is presented as for movement in general, not only for ballet. Using music notes as the basic signs for dance notation had been first introduced in a casual way by Bernard Klemm, whose *Katechismus der Tanzkunst* was published in Leipzig in 1855, but Stepanov's was the first full system based on this device, the time value of the note being the same as in music. A modified music staff provides sections in which to place indications for the legs, arms, and whole torso. Direction and level for movements of the main limbs (whole leg, whole arm, whole torso) are indicated by placing the music notes on the lines and spaces of the staff (Fig. 11.6 (*a*)).

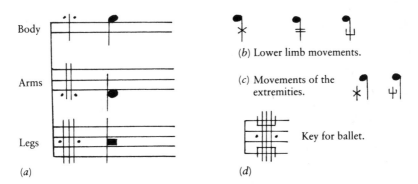

(*b*) Lower limb movements.

(*c*) Movements of the extremities.

Key for ballet.

Fig. 11.6 Stepanov system: staff; movements of parts.

Movements of secondary parts (lower leg, lower arm, chest) are indicated as flexions of the knee, elbow and waist. Indications for such flexions and for rotations of these parts are written on the stem of the music note (Fig. 11.6 (*b*)). Movements of the extremities (foot, hand and head) are written as flexions of the ankle, wrist and neck, the signs for flexion and rotation being placed on a small vertical line adjacent to the main music note. This organization works when major and minor parts move simultaneously and arrive together at a destinational pose, but proves awkward when individual parts overlap in timing. No independent signs exist for the specific parts of the body – an essential element in any system of movement notation.

Stepanov's system provides several innovations: the idea of a clef or key for the different parts of the staff to indicate the normal situation for that part; the statement of balletic turnout in the key for the legs (Fig. 11.6 (*d*)); use of

(*a*) Contact with ground.   In the air.   (*b*) Limbs – right or left.

Fig. 11.7 Stepanov system: additional indications.

square-headed music notes for contacting the ground and round-headed notes for gestures (Fig. 11.7 (*a*)); placement of the stem of the note to indicate right and left sides for legs and arms (*b*).

In 1895 Stepanov was sent to Moscow to introduce the system at the Bolshoi Theatre School, but died soon after at the age of 29. His associate, Alexander Alexeievitch Gorsky, a noted dancer and later choreographer, undertook the responsibility of continuing the work and published a Russian manual on the system in 1899. This incorporated a few modifications and placed more emphasis on the notating of ballet material. In 1897 Gorsky was provided with an assistant, Nicolai Grigorevich Sergeyev, who was to be the person most responsible for putting the system to use. In 1903 Sergeyev was made regisseur of the company and was placed in charge of notating the major works in the repertoire.[5]

Here we see a system officially accepted and being put to practical use, yet before long completely abandoned. The foremost reason is that it had been used for the classical vocabulary and so became a casualty when the new ideas of Fokine and his followers resulted in changes in choreographic taste and in the emergence of freer, more flowing movements. These freer movements were not easy to write; the blame lies somewhat on the notation system, but also on a lack of training in writing more than one style. Sergeyev was very much part of the old régime; unable to adapt to the new trends he probably took a rigid stance regarding possible modifications of the system to meet any new needs. Certainly when the parting of the ways came, he left for western Europe taking the scores with him, thus leaving no sources for future revivals or research in Russia. His memory, bolstered by the scores, made it possible for him to revive full-length ballets such as *Giselle*, *Swan Lake*, and *Sleeping Beauty*, for leading companies, in particular the Vic-Wells Ballet (now the Royal Ballet) and the International Ballet.

Sergeyev was the first twentieth century professional dance notator. His work and the scores are therefore of special interest to us. How did he use the scores in rehearsals? How much did his way of working vary from present-day reconstructions based on current scores? Many stories abound. Bridget Kelly Espinosa recalls his rehearsing with the score on the floor, turning the pages with his stick. She spoke of different versions emerging from the same scores.[6] The fact that his productions of the same ballet for different companies varied did not bother the dance world, though it raises eyebrows amongst conscientious dance notators. Comparable differences met in the playing of a Beethoven symphony would be quite unacceptable to the music world. It is probable that he remembered different versions from the past and brought out whichever best suited the dancer at hand.[7]

Adjusting steps to suit particular performers was an established practice, the idea of choreography being sacrosanct not yet having arrived. Yet at other times he would adamantly insist on sticking exactly to the score.

Ninette de Valois recalls that he did his homework the night before, coming ready to teach by personal demonstration, but always with the score on hand for an occasional glance at it to confirm a detail.[8] From his days working with the International Ballet there is a story of a prank being played on him during a rehearsal. While his attention was elsewhere, the pages of the score were turned forward. When Sergeyev returned to the score, he pondered a moment while reading the page and then continued straight on with the rehearsal.[9] Was looking at the score sometimes a ploy to gain a few moments in which to organize his thoughts? Both Margot Fonteyn and Ninette de Valois speak of his being unmusical and having difficulty fitting the dance steps to the music score. This must have been a personal defect since the Stepanov system was based on music notes and this aspect should have been no problem. On the other hand the passage may have been incorrectly written in the first place.

The so-called Sergeyev scores, now at the Harvard Theatre Collection in Cambridge, Mass., range from complete works, neatly copied (Fig. 11.8) to

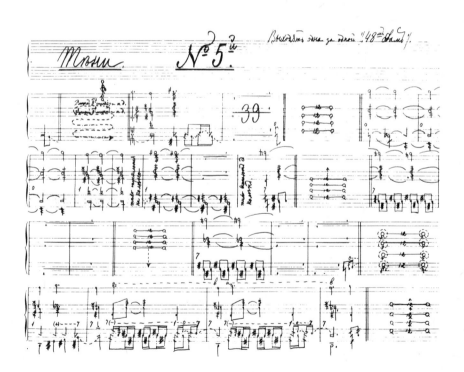

*Translation: They enter one by one / 48 ladies /

Fig. 11.8 Stepanov system: The Shades from *La Bayadère*. (Harvard Theatre Library)

rough notes, obviously hurriedly written. Many contain only floor plans with a few verbal descriptions alongside, such as 'maidens kneeling.'

Those who anticipate a detailed study of the style of the period through these scores are heading for disappointment. Although the system allowed for considerable detail to be written, the writers were only concerned with – or only had time for – a memory aid. Despite this the scores still provide much valuable material for comparative research.

The Stepanov method deserves attention for two other reasons – its use by Vaslav Nijinsky and by Leonide Massine.

Nijinsky

The Nijinsky system has long intrigued all interested in the subject. It was never published and little is known of it. In 1956 the British Dance and Movement Notation Society in London sponsored a series of lectures, one of which featured the Nijinsky system presented by Madame Nicolaeva Legat, in whose possession were transcriptions in French of Nijinsky's original 1918 notes, which were at that time deposited in a bank vault. Mme Legat presented the basic facts as she knew them, but, never having used the system herself, was unable to answer simple questions concerning how to indicate walking steps or a simple arm circle. At a loss to know what to do next regarding the system, she invited me to work with her in sorting out and making sense of the accumulation of notes. The results of many meetings indicated that Nijinsky had two or three different ideas in hand and apparently had not decided which version to select. All were based on the same general idea as Stepanov's system which, of course, as a student, Nijinsky had learned.

With these notes in hand, I then sought permission from Nijinsky's wife, Romola, to have a copy of the score of Nijinsky's *L'Après midi d'un Faune* (Fig. 11.9) which is in the British Library.

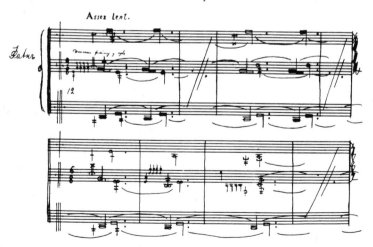

Fig. 11.9 Nijinsky system: opening bars of *L'Après Midi d'un Faune*. (British Library, courtesy Romola Nijinsky)

It soon became clear that the notation in this score, painstakingly written by Nijinsky himself in 1915, did not incorporate any of the ideas I had met through Mme Legat, nor did it follow precisely Stepanov's system. In my effort to decipher the score, questions arose such as how to interpret directional indications, what cancellation rules were used, and so on. Some phrases made sense; many were impenetrable. The hope that a functioning, easily read transcription could be produced soon faded. Fresh attempts over the years on my part and also the painstaking work by Claudia Jeschke brought no further solutions. Nijinsky's lack of practical experience in using notation and the absence of colleagues at hand to try out and proofread what he had written were obvious handicaps.

Massine

Leonide Massine retained an interest in the Stepanov notation from his early student days in Russia. He was firmly convinced that music notes were the only suitable symbols for recording dance, and thus adhered to Stepanov's system, making only a few modifications to serve his own needs. As with Saint-Léon, Massine's professional life as a dancer and later as a choreographer absorbed all his time, and he was too busy mounting his ballets around the world to devote much time to notation. Thus through lack of practice his speed in writing and reading notation was painfully slow. Concentration on practical application of the notation came in the last decade of his life when he experimented with and prepared for publication his theories on choreography. Realizing years before that the classical ballet vocabulary was, in fact, a stumbling block to creative thinking and the development of new choreographic ideas, he sought a totally fresh approach based on the basic movements of which the human body is capable, thus reverting to Stepanov's original idea, the anatomical approach. Massine developed his choreographic course using the notation as an integral part. One wonders how much his ideas would have been affected had he not worked in such self-imposed isolation, out of touch with others exploring choreographic ideas and unaware of how other systems of movement notation viewed movement. During his last years he had the experience of having his ballet *Le Tricorne* recorded in the contemporary system of Labanotation while the ballet was taught to the London Festival Ballet, and subsequently of seeing the score put to use in rehearsing the work in Dusseldorf. His amazement at the detailed description in the score of the handling of props and of the quality and dynamics of the movements led him to acknowledge the superiority of the Laban system and the limitations of the Stepanov in which such specific details could not be indicated.[10]

TWELVE

Historical development – twentieth century

The twentieth century, certainly from 1928 on, provides a very different picture. Since then, on average, a new system has appeared every four years. Many inventors have made no study of old or contemporary systems, often out of ignorance, sometimes intentionally.

The whole 'modern', 'contemporary' development with its tremendous changes in dance technique has meant that every possible kind of movement might need to be recorded. Inventors of systems of notation as well as prospective students of notation have to consider whether a shorthand memory aid is the answer, or whether time and energy should be invested in a detailed system capable of recording everything. Modern technology appears to make written movement notation obsolete. Advances in the use of computers in the last decade provide a challenge to notation systems. One has to think beyond the scribe in the rehearsal studio. Yet the successful reconstructions of works from dance scores, the practical and functional use of notation, the surge of interest in historical and 'period' dances recorded in notation, all go to prove the value of a good dance notation system and the rewards obtained from its functional use. The idea that notation is solely a means of recording a work for future reference is giving way to the daily use of notation as a research tool and also as an educational aid in understanding and mastering movement.

As might be expected, the twentieth century ushered in the concept of a system of notation concerned with all forms of human movement, not only with dance, and based on a more scientific approach than heretofore. Stepanov basically belongs in this group, though, as we have seen, the use of his system was such that its potential was limited. Despite the twentieth century emphasis on universality, new systems continue to appear employing former ideas, some systems being concerned primarily with one form of dance, and some being designed as a quick and easy device for those seeking a memory aid.

In covering twentieth century systems we meet a few which, though they seem to have passed quietly out of the mainstream, yet have something of particular interest for us in our investigation into notation ideas. We also meet systems which are very much alive and widely used. Obviously these latter deserve special attention, yet the line must be drawn in going into their background, mode of operation, extent of use, etc. since these facts can easily be discovered by contacting the centres established to promote these systems. (*See* Appendix E.) Discussion of each system will centre on the features which were new or significantly different from those that had appeared previously.

In the case of twentieth century systems, much more information is available concerning the inventor, the purpose for which the system was devised and the problems met in its use. Growing interest in the leading contemporary systems prompts the desire to make direct comparisons between them. Such comparisons will not be made here; other books may deal with this interesting investigation.

The first two fully-fledged systems of this century, both published in 1928, were widely different in form, yet the originators – Margaret Morris and Rudolf von Laban – had much in common in their breadth of vision and concern with the phenomenon of movement.

Morris

Margaret Morris was a performer, teacher, choreographer and movement therapist who began her career in the early 1900s. She was the product of no one school of dance, was largely self-taught and was a free seeker after truths about movement. Her background and attitude coloured her approach to teaching and stage production. Her attitude toward notation, cited in the preface of her 1928 publication, *The Notation of Movement*, is interesting: 'It is comparatively easy to invent a system for recording any one method of dancing, whatever that may be, as single signs can be used to mean an elaborate movement, the pupils who understand the technique know already the step the sign stands for. But I have always had in mind the *future* development of dancing, there must be progress and variation, to prevent stagnation.' She describes how she became involved with notation: 'The idea of writing down dances first came to me from Raymond Duncan ... who recorded the Greek positions ... with lines giving a diagrammatic representation ... My own method only began to be practical when I ceased to make signs to *resemble* the positions they stood for; the mind quickly learns to visualize the position from the symbols written.'

As a result of her work in the medical field she approached movement notation from the broad base of anatomical possibilities. From its first beginnings in 1913 the method was based on the idea that all human movements take place around an imaginary central axis, thus the limit of movement of the limbs can only be in circles around the joints to which they are attached. One senses immediately ideas similar to those behind Stepanov's system, but Morris incorporated a great deal more detail, including breathing, facial expression, muscular tension and relaxation, etc. Her system is comparable to Stepanov's in that spatial placement for the limb as a whole is written on the staff, and movements of the lesser parts are written on or next to the main indications.

The staff in the Morris system originally consisted of six lines (Fig. 12.1 (*a*)). Later this was changed to four lines (*b*). Direction is shown by the signs illustrated in (*c*). A vertical stroke for the vertical situation (as in the normal standing position) is logical and could be guessed, but why the slanting stroke:∕ for forward? The reason she gave at our 1954 meeting was that forward is the direction most commonly used and the stroke∕is the most easily drawn by the hand. The sign for backward: — is also non-pictorial, though ⟋ , the sign for sideward, has the logic of being a combination of the forward and backward signs, i.e. the direction between. Side is understood to be the open sideward direction, a minor indication being added to show crossing to the opposite side. Level is indicated by placing the direction sign on the staff combined with the addition of a stroke or dot (Fig. 12.2).

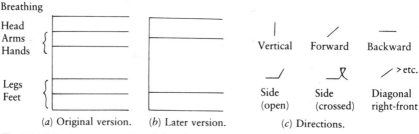

Breathing

Head
Arms
Hands

Legs
Feet

	Vertical	Forward	Backward
	Side (open)	Side (crossed)	Diagonal right-front

(a) Original version. (b) Later version. (c) Directions.

Fig. 12.1 Morris system: staff and directions.

Degrees in lifting the left leg sideward.

Fig. 12.2 Morris system: levels.

Movements for the right limbs are written on a line, those for the left below the line. This, then, was the first system (but not the last) in which a symmetrical position or movement does not appear as symmetrical signs on paper. There are no specific signs for parts of the body, but different signs are provided for all possible movements of the shoulders, hips, feet, fingers, etc. (Fig. 12.3).

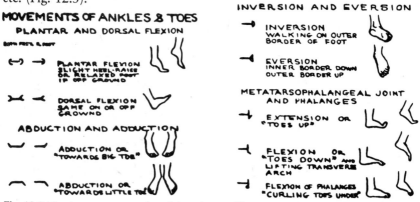

Fig. 12.3 Morris system: examples of signs for specific movements.

(A. H. Guest Collection)

80

For timing bar lines are used and dots placed between them for each beat in the bar. Appropriate placement of the movement indications thus states when each occurs (Fig. 12.4). Fig. 12.5 is an example of a score.

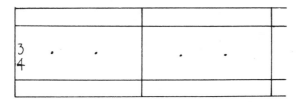

Fig. 12.4 Morris system: timing.

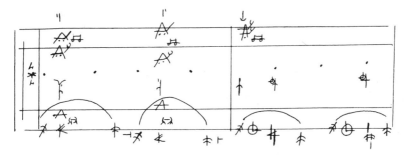

Fig. 12.5 Morris system: excerpt from *Peer Gynt*.
(A. H. Guest Collection, Courtesy Margaret Morris)

Morris was a pioneer, combining a dance career with the new approaches in movement therapy and in pre-natal care. Her Margaret Morris Movement (M.M.M.) schools flourished in England and abroad. That she had time to create and publish a system of notation was remarkable. No further materials were published and among her followers none continued to develop the system. The recent revival of interest in her work at the Margaret Morris Centre in Biggin Hill, is already including work with the notation and has resulted in a new publication. There is also a centre in Glasgow (*see* Appendix E).

Laban

Though widely different in temperament, in spheres of activity and in style of movement, Margaret Morris and Rudolf Laban had much in common in their interest in movement of all kinds and their open, unbiased attitude toward the work of others. During his early travels Laban became fascinated by differences in movement between peoples of different cultures, long before he focused his observations on dance. It was to his advantage not to have been moulded by years of academic dance training: his mind was open to all possibilities and to searching for new ways of looking at and experiencing movement.

Laban's first jottings were a shorthand for the space harmony progressions he had formulated. Later he sought to record movement basic to all forms of dance. From this work grew the ideas which formed the foundation of the present Laban movement notation system.

In evolving the third and final version of his notation, Laban admittedly took two ideas from Feuillet – the centre line dividing right and left sides of the body, and placement of bar lines on this centre line to coordinate with the music bars. Laban was the first to adopt a vertical staff,* thus departing from the idea that some sort of music-based staff should be used, or at least that dance writing should progress from left to right, as do all European languages.

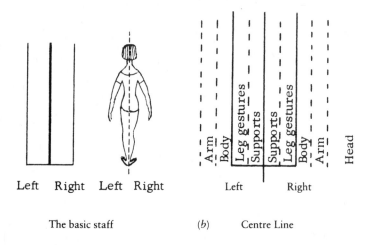

The basic staff   (b)   Centre Line

Fig. 12.6 Laban system: staff.

The vertical staff representing the body (Fig. 12.6 (a)), which is read from the bottom up, combines the vertical physical image which we have of ourselves with continuity in indicating movement. Other vertical image systems are read horizontally, and thus indication of continuous movement must be broken into segments on the page. Another innovation, which seems self-evident, but which, interestingly, has not been followed in other recent symbol notation systems, is that of a symmetrical staff representing the symmetricality of the body. In Labanotation symmetrical positions and movements appear as symmetrical designs on paper. The main parts of the body are represented by columns on the staff (Fig. 12.6 (b)).

Specific parts – limbs, joints, areas, surfaces – are shown by 'families' of symbols, (Fig. 12.7). Numbers are reserved for music measures, counts, numbers of people, etc.

---

*In Laban's 1928 and 1930 publications the staff was printed horizontally on the page, it was nevertheless intended to be read vertically.

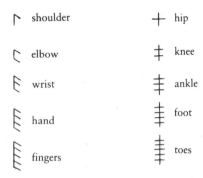

Fig. 12.7 Laban system:
      examples of parts of the body.

shoulder   hip

elbow   knee

wrist   ankle

hand   foot

fingers   toes

Pictorial representation of direction by symbols which 'point' into the direction they indicate can be traced back to Feuillet, but drawing them as a block shape, (Fig. 12.8 (*a*)) so that the third dimension – level – could be included by the shading of the symbol, was new (Fig. 12.8 (*b*)).

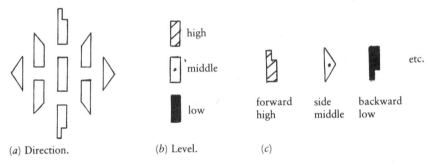

high

middle

low

forward   side   backward   etc.
high   middle   low

(*a*) Direction.   (*b*) Level.   (*c*)

Fig. 12.8 Laban system: direction.

Also new was the idea of lengthening the signs to indicate duration of movement, the start of a symbol showing the moment when a movement begins and the end of the symbol the moment when it terminates. The longer the symbol, the slower the movement; the shorter, the quicker (Fig. 12.9 (*a*)). For metric (measured) time, units of equal length marked off on the staff represent the regular pulse or beat, (*b*).

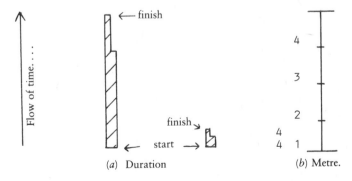

Flow of time....

← finish

finish ↘

← start →

4
4

4

3

2

1

(*a*) Duration   (*b*) Metre.

Fig. 12.9 Laban system: timing.

83

Labanotation is the only system in which four factors are combined into one symbol: direction of the action (shown by the shape of the symbol), level (shown by the shading), timing (shown by the length of the symbol), and the part of the body moving (shown by its placement on the staff). Because timing is built into the movement symbols themselves, the system is self-sufficient and not dependent on the notated sequences being placed next to a music staff. However, in published dance scores which include music, the music is placed vertically alongside the Labanotation to provide correlation. Since the pianist will have his own music score, such placement in the dance score is for reference only.

Fig. 12.10 illustrates an excerpt from a historically significant Labanotation score written in 1939. Not only was *The Green Table* by Kurt Jooss the first detailed score of a major ballet ever to be written (details included descriptions of hand, finger and head movements, dynamics, parts of the foot, successions, deviations, part leading, etc.) but it was to become the first widely travelled score since it was used repeatedly by the choreographer to mount the ballet around the world. In addition it featured as the deciding evidence in an important court case involving plagiarism.

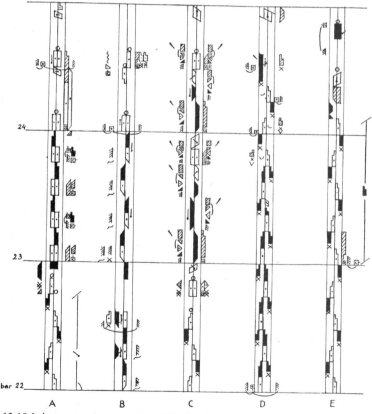

Fig. 12.10 Laban system: excerpt from 'The Gentleman in Black' from the ballet *The Green Table* by Kurt Jooss. Notated by Ann Hutchinson, 1939.
(From *The New Ballet* by A. V. Coton, A. H. Guest Collection)

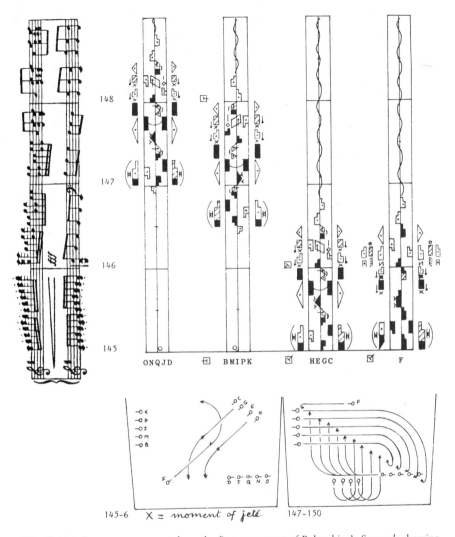

Fig. 12.11 Laban system: excerpt from the first movement of Balanchine's *Serenade* showing addition of music when melody line needs to be followed.

(Courtesy George Balanchine)

Criticism of the system has often been levelled at Laban's use of block symbols; they are thought to be clumsy and time-consuming to draw. In fact they can be quickly scribbled and still be legible. Despite several attempts over the years to modify the block symbols into pins and other single line symbols, they have remained because of their visuality, their flexibility in length to show timing, and the easily recognized designs they produce which can be read at a glance rather than 'deciphered.' They provide the basic structure of the movement which is then modified by lesser signs, pins, hooks, etc. to specify detail. Shorthand devices used by professional notators for speed have not been taught as part of the standard notation and all scores are written out fully in 'longhand.'

From his early studies of architecture Laban evolved an awareness of space which architects were later to rediscover — that buildings should be designed to enclose spaces of varying shapes and sizes, an idea comparable, one might say, to the 'white space' surrounding text and drawings on the page of a book or poster. For movement Laban made space alive and tangible. He added new dimensions to movement concepts and fostered the desire to translate those concepts into signs on paper. It remained for others to develop ways in which many of these concepts as well as other modes of movement analysis would be expressed in the notation.

Before Laban, every system had described directions — up, down, forward, backward, etc. — from the build of the body, that is, a body-based system of directional reference. Thus, even when lying on the ground, prone, supine, on the side, or even upside-down, 'up' is always 'overhead', i.e. the headward extension of the spine. Laban was the first to establish a set of directions based on the vertical line of gravity, the constant up and down, with forward being the direction into which the dancer is facing while standing. In the 1940s in research sessions at the Dance Notation Bureau in New York my colleagues and I discovered the need for keys to specify directional description, e.g. 'raise the arm toward the audience', or 'travel toward stage right', such orientation being more important than direction from the dancer's body. Thus keys somewhat comparable to music keys were evolved to inform the reader which directional system of reference is being used. As described, a choice of directional description sounds theoretically complicated and far from the everyday needs of dancers let alone people taking general keep-fit classes. It comes, therefore, as a surprise to realize that switching from one key to another is a very common occurrence in all forms of movement study and often occurs within one exercise. Because verbal instructions in movement classes are accompanied by visual demonstration, neither student nor teacher is aware of the switch from one key to another. However, on paper one must know to what the symbol for 'up' refers when one is off the vertical and also what is meant by 'forward' when twists occur in the body.

Laban was deeply concerned with shapes in movement. He wrote of the content of movement becoming understandable through its shape and rhythm and the relationship between shapes as they follow one another. He considered movement-shapes to be dynamic in themselves, they differ from the fixed shapes of objects which we see in our surroundings; it is only if the movement stops that one can observe body-shapes which are, however, always the result of a preceding movement. Laban was intrigued with trace forms, designs drawn in the air, such as have been captured on film in more recent years by attaching a light at the end of a limb and photographing the movement in the dark, an idea first tried out by Louis Soret in the 1880s. For gestures most notation systems provided only a description of destination, movement being the understood path from one position to the next. Such destinational description was used at first in the Laban system; only later were the more intangible movement descriptions introduced to record Laban's flexible spatial ideas, such as motion toward or away from a directional point, a person or object. These and many other concepts needed to be captured on paper. Laban was ever embarking on exploring new territory, leaving to others the task of carrying on what he had started. Movement concepts from other teachers, and ideas from choreographers working in a wide range of styles needed also to be transferred to paper. Gradually logical ways of writing these were evolved by the many people who were making practical use of the notation and who contributed significantly to the system which Laban had originated.

Laban was the first to stress the importance of aspects of movement which related performer to performer or performer to objects, for example, addressing a person, close proximity, contact, touch, etc. Albrecht Knust, who made the notation his life's work, contributed to finding ways of expressing these in notation. Knust also evolved practical indications for group formations and the many different shapes and changes which can take place when large numbers of performers are involved – wheeling, following the leader, canon form, etc. Initiation of a movement (where it originated and how it flowed from one part of the body to another), was a feature of the Jooss-Leeder modern dance technique, an aspect which Sigurd Leeder developed to a high degree and for which he evolved logical signs.

Laban's contribution in the area of dynamics, an aspect of movement neglected by most systems of movement notation, was his codification of 'Effort', an analysis which has enriched all forms of movement study, in particular physiotherapy, anthropology, and personnel assessment. This study of how a movement is performed, of its quality, of the kind of ebb and flow of energy in the body, has been given practical application by specialists such as Irmgard Bartenieff in the U.S.A. and Warren Lamb in the U.K. Application of Laban's spatial ideas, particularly spatial tensions, has facilitated expressive movement and the mastering of dance techniques.

In writing about a system of notation, the background of the inventor, and the state of development of the system, one is aware of the need to be unbiased and fair in every respect, including the amount of space devoted to describing each system. In the case of the Laban system much new ground was covered and many new ideas put forward by the many people who contributed to its development; hence the space given the system here. In most cases a system has been the result of the work of one person who retained control. As we saw with the Feuillet system, which lasted for nearly a hundred years, many other people became involved and contributed to its use and development. Laban intentionally inspired others to carry his work further. This was especially true of the notation system bearing his name. From the beginning he gave credit to the people who contributed ideas. Later contributors have included people who never met Laban and knew nothing of his developments in Space Harmony or Effort.

Laban 'gave his system to the world' in the sense that he did not insist on personal, single-handed control. Freedom to carry on inspired many to make practical use of the system, a healthy development which prompted its use by different people in a variety of fields. However, the isolation caused by World War II produced local 'dialects' in England, Germany and the U.S.A. Unified development has been guided by the establishment in 1959 of the International Council of Kinetography Laban (I.C.K.L.) which meets biennially to present new ideas and iron out differences. Centres which specialize in the system exist in several countries. (*See* Appendix E.) The notation has been applied to many fields of movement study, and professional training and qualifications have been established. Trained notators work with professional dance companies, while professional reconstructors revive works from scores in the U.S.A. and abroad. Publications include textbooks in several languages, dance scores and other notated materials.

Conté

After Stepanov's system went into decline four other systems of notation emerged using the idea of music notes as symbols for movement. The originators were Pierre Conté, Antonio Chiesa, Alwin Nikolais, and Charles McCraw.

Conté's first publication, *Traité d'Ecriture de la Danse*, appeared in 1931. From 1933 to 1938 he published a periodical, *Arts et Mouvement*, a total of sixteen issues which contained *Le Guide Chorégraphique* in which steps were analysed and different dances presented and discussed. He established an Institution also called 'Arts et Mouvement' which included a High School of Dance. In 1952 his book *La Danse et ses Lois* was published and in 1955 his work *Technique Générale*, which had taken many years of preparation, finally saw the light of day. His system was brought to the public's attention mainly through a film made about it by Jean Painlevé in 1946. Although it was considered by the authorities at the Paris Opéra, his system was not adopted. When I visited him in 1956 he showed me an entire music bookcase full of leather-bound copies of his notated dance scores. Who was this man who worked with such diligence and dedication for so many years, producing an impressive amount of materials, and who yet seems, in terms of world recognition, to have achieved so little?

Pierre Conté came to dance after many years as a musician and a soldier. By chance he became involved in gymnastics and sport and began to realize the importance of rhythm for success in athletics. This realization led to an analysis of movement and eventually to involvement with dance. He started writing rhythms on the board in music notes to improve performance. When he learned that no established notation existed for dance, that dancers worked by imitation, he determined to develop a system based on music notes. He then undertook an intensive study of different styles of dance, and gradually built up a company of dancers, a group mainly of amateurs for whom he created choreographic works.[1] Three main factors contributed to his lack of public success. First, in dance terms he was an amateur. Second, the dance profession in France was, and still is, sadly lacking in interest in the intellectual and cultural aspects of dance including concern with both the past and the future. Third, the system itself had obvious limitations, though no more than many other systems. Interestingly, most limitations were self-imposed. Conté developed a tool for the kind of choreography he devised. When I asked about how to show the relationship of one hand placed above the other, I was told that this was not important. My suggestion that a relationship of this kind was very important to choreographers such as Doris Humphrey, was brushed aside. Though he claimed that his system was not ballet-based, many details in it indicate otherwise: for example, the pictorial signs for retiré, développé, and the use of 'CP' for cou-de-pied, a position known only to ballet-trained readers.

A modified music staff (the standard five lines plus four extra lines above) provides spaces and lines on which movements of the parts of the body are written (Fig. 12.12).

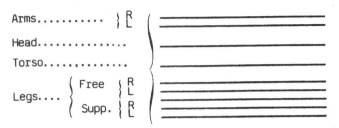

Fig. 12.12 Conté system: staff.

The two bottom spaces between the five lines are for supports on the left and right feet, and the two upper spaces for left and right leg gestures. Supporting on the arms is written on the lines of this staff, and the leger line for middle C is used for supporting on the head. The upper part of the staff provides four more lines on which are placed indications for movements of the torso, head, and at the top, arms. One innovation is the use of a single sign to indicate both arms performing a symmetrical movement.

Direction is shown by numbers, 0 being downward, 1 forward, 2 sideward, 3 backward, and 5 upward. Number 4 represents a twist of the torso or head. The reason 5 represents upward is that overhead is the direction for 5th position of the arms in ballet. Intermediate directions are indicated by combined numbers (Fig. 12.13).

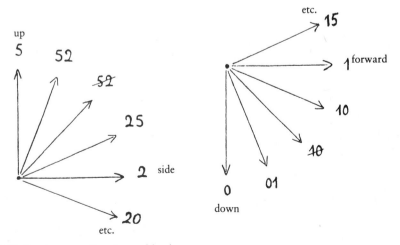

Fig. 12.13 Conté system: direction and level.

Letters or pictorially based signs are added for degrees of bending the limbs, for turning, ronds de jambe, parts of the foot supporting, etc. (Fig. 12.14).

Degrees of bending   demi-pointe   pointe   heel

retiré   en dehors   en dedans

ronds

Fig. 12.14 Conté system: examples of signs used.

Fig. 12.15 shows an example of Conté's system. Conté's work is being carried on by a few devoted followers at the Association Ecriture du Mouvement in Paris. (*See* Appendix E.)

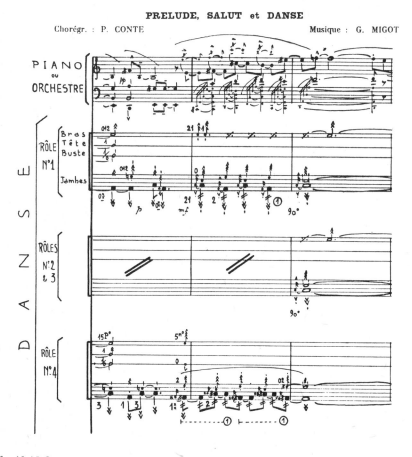

PRELUDE, SALUT et DANSE

Chorégr. : P. CONTE   Musique : G. MIGOT

Fig. 12.15 Conté system: excerpt from one of his choreographies.

(A. H. Guest Collection)

Chiesa

Much less is known about Antonio Chiesa whose system 'Motografia' was published in 1934, in Milan, Italy. Chiesa, a lieutenant in the Italian Military Aviation Corps, seems to have been interested in music, mathematics and dance. Starting work on his system in 1922, he used the bass clef for movements of the lower part of the body, the treble clef for the upper body. The shape of the music note head is changed to show direction (Fig. 12.16).

Use of the right or left side of the body is shown by placement of the note stem. Level (height and depth) is shown by sharps and flats, a return to normal by the natural sign. Directions refer to stage directions. Specific signs are used to indicate tilting, shifting, turning. Though intended for any form of movement, Chiesa's system was concerned specifically with ballet, the predominant form of dance in Italy.

| forward | backward | right side | left side | high | low | return to normal |

Fig. 12.16 Chiesa: directions.

Fig. 12.16 (*b*) Chiesa: extract from a score.

Nikolais

Two music note systems were directly inspired by the Laban system. The first, Choroscript, was invented by Alwin Nikolais, a name immediately associated with his choreographic creations in which he so imaginatively blends movement, sound, colour, light and the inventive manipulation of objects. That he worked on a system of dance notation may come as a surprise to many. Notators are often taken to be dull people who could not make the grade in the field of dance in any other way. However, all through history we see examples which contradict this belief.

Nikolais' dance training stemmed mainly from the Wigman line, in particular through his study with Hanya Holm, whose assistant he became. While a sergeant in the army in 1944 he took a crash course in the Laban system and, perhaps because of his extensive musical training, decided to replace the block symbols with music notes. These retained their time significance, the tails being turned to indicate the desired direction – a visual and easily read device (Fig. 12.17). Level is added by a small stroke attached above or below the head of the note.

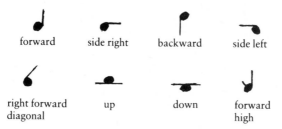

forward   side right   backward   side left

right forward diagonal   up   down   forward high

Fig. 12.17 Nikolais system: direction symbols

Nikolais also separated Laban's vertical staff representing the body into two staves of five lines,[*] loosely comparable to the treble and bass staves in music (Fig. 12.18). The arms, legs and supports were written in the left hand staff, torso and head in the centre and parts of the torso on the right.

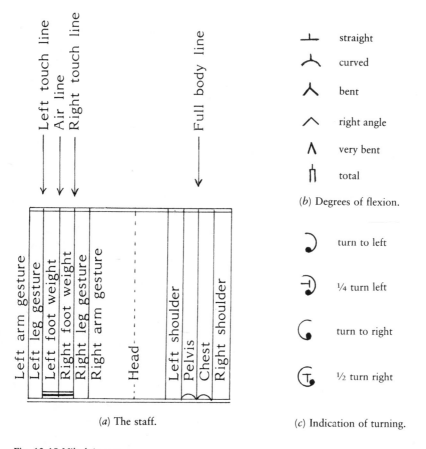

(a) The staff.

(b) Degrees of flexion.

⊥ straight
人 curved
人 bent
⌒ right angle
Λ very bent
∏ total

(c) Indication of turning.

turn to left

¼ turn left

turn to right

½ turn right

Fig. 12.18 Nikolais system.

---

[*]The Laban staff originally consisted of five lines. The second and fourth lines were soon dropped for visual clarity.

Fig. 12.19 Nikolais system: example of a score.
(A. H. Guest Collection)

For many years his system was included in the curriculum at the Henry Street Playhouse in New York, where he taught and choreographed, and rough notes of many scores were taken, but no book was ever published. He and his colleagues were too engrossed in providing the dance world with something far more precious – inventive choreographies and exciting performances.

McCraw

While playing the piano for my Labanotation classes at the School of American Ballet in New York, Charles McCraw conceived the idea of devising a method of dance notation based on music. The system, called 'Scoreography', was published in 1964. Apart from the bass clef representing the lower part of the body, and the treble clef the upper, McCraw tried to link dance to music notation even more than his predecessors. Notes placed on the lines and spaces which, in music, are called 'A', 'B', 'C', 'D', etc. represent directions in the following novel way (Fig. 12.20).

A-right (à droit)	**E**-up (élevation)	○	horizontal
B-back	**F**-forward	△	upward
C-centre (place)	**G**-left (gauche)	▢	downward
D-down			

Fig. 12.20 McCraw system: direction

Diagonal directions are indicated by use of sharps and flats (a device also used by Saint-Léon). Level is indicated by the shape of the note head. Placement of the note stem indicates right or left side of the body.

In following the explanations of the McCraw system one needs to have a background in music notation. As Walter Paul Misslitz, an inventor of a dance notation based on stick figures, wrote: 'It is much easier to invent a dance notation than to notate the dances exactly in direction, time and space.'[2] Like many others, McCraw provides signs for parts of the feet and many other details, but omits graded reading material to demonstrate the practical application of the system. His ideas were not put through the rigours of daily use and trial in 'live' situations prior to publication.

Zadra

Inventors of notation systems have come from all walks of life. No two people could have been more different than Zadra and Ruskaja, both of whom devoted time to evolving systems based on abstract signs.

In about 1935 the Revd Remy Zadra published in Boston, Mass. four volumes on the *Method Zadra: Music Appreciation for Children, Physical Education and Classical Dancing, and Graduated Daily Exercises*. Zadra was an amateur gymnast who took degrees in Sacred Theology and Music in Rome. Rhythmic gymnastics and music visualization led to his desire to provide the students with an aesthetic experience through music and movement. His system of notation arose from practical needs in the classroom. Through signs which were somewhat pictorial, somewhat abstract, he was able to provide general movement descriptions. An interesting innovation was his use of symbols with straight lines for gymnastic exercises, but with curved lines for artistic movement (Fig. 12.21). Sequences were written on large wall charts so students could read and perform the exercises at the same time. Zadra claimed to have translated the complete course of the Swedish method of physical culture and also the physical training of the U.S. Army, as well as the fundamentals of classical ballet. A tremendously enthusiastic, energetic man, he found it difficult to understand why his system was too elementary to meet the needs of professional dance.[3]

Fig. 12.21 Zadra system: example of his artistic gymnastics.

(A. H. Guest Collection)

Ruskaja

A very different point of view and personality lay behind the system developed by Jia Ruskaja (a pseudonym meaning 'I am Russian', her real name was Eugénie Borissenko), who began working on it in 1940 while a dancer in a Milan nightclub. By 1957 she had risen to a position of power in Italy, having high political connections. Her position provided her with the authority to establish and control the licensing of dance teachers in Italy. Such activities together with the directorship of the Academia Nazionale della Danza in Rome, a dance 'finishing school' for young ladies, left her no time to develop her system further or to record any complete ballets. For her system Ruskaja adopted the five line staff and an anatomical analysis of movement. The lines and spaces on the staff represent the different parts of the body from the audience's point of view. Movement symbols are strokes, diamonds, triangles, dots and a few curved signs (Fig. 12.22).

Fig. 12.22 Ruskaja system: an example of a balletic sequence in *Semiografia Coreutica*.
(A. H. Guest Collection)

Ruskaja was concerned with positions, movement being a passage from one position to the next. Indications are placed above the music to show timing. Her movement description is still 'outline' with, for example, the same kind of limitation met in the Stepanov system, in that to write a step (a transference of weight) one has first to indicate the leg gesture into the appropriate direction (let us say forward) and then show that weight is taken on that leg.[4] Such emphasis on the preparatory leg gesture makes it impossible to write casual, unemphasized walking where there is no thought of a preparatory leg extension before each step but merely a transference of weight forward. In several systems the design and movement analysis result in unimportant actions being given emphasis. Shifting the weight (consciousness of the centre of weight in the body and of its movements) has been a very rare item in the ingredients of notation systems. Placement of weight is basic, yet most inventors concentrate on arms and legs, movements of the extremities, and write the outer, visual picture rather than what is activating the change.

Loring-Canna

Eugene Loring came from a ballet background. He was a member of the American Ballet, a soloist and choreographer for Ballet Caravan, and director of his own company, Dance Players, in the early 1940s, and later of his own school, the American School of Dance, in California. His best known ballet is *Billy the Kid*. In this and other of his works he showed an instinctive feeling for movement which was closely related to modern dance. To settle a controversy over whether he or Ballet Theatre owned the rights to *Billy the Kid*, he had the work recorded in Labanotation, but never himself studied the system. Years later, when he became interested in evolving a system of dance notation, he joined the ranks of innovators who purposely avoided exploring the work of others, preferring to develop his ideas uninfluenced by other lines of thought. The result, *Kinesiography*, which he published in 1955 with D. J. Canna as co-author, is a very different and highly personal system. Fig. 12.23 is an extract from his score of *Billy the Kid*.

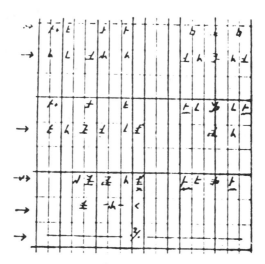

Fig. 12.23 Loring-Canna system: excerpt from the opening march from *Billy the Kid*. (A. H. Guest Collection)

In the Loring-Canna system the vertical staff, read from the top down, provides columns for each segment of the body, thus eliminating the need for signs for these parts. The result is a broad staff usually occupying a full page. Within the staff columns for the parts of the arms and legs are symmetrically arranged (Fig. 12.24). Loring was the first to use a staff which provided a column for each body segment.

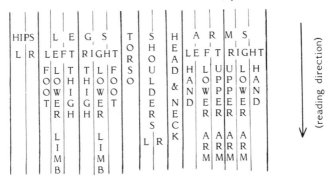

Fig. 12.24 Loring-Canna system: staff.

In his analysis all movement is divided into four categories, and it is in this analysis that his system is unique. The categories are:

1. *Emotion:* the character of the move. This category includes the Normal position; 'Extravert' (sic) positions which are open, turned out, or express confidence (e.g. outturned legs and arms, lowered shoulders, expanded chest, etc.), and 'Intravert' (sic) positions that are closed, turned in, or are lacking in confidence (e.g. inturned legs and arms, raised shoulders, concave torso and chest, etc.).
2. *Direction:* front, back, side (the open side unless otherwise indicated), front-side (diagonal), back-side (diagonal).
3. *Degree:* the amount of directional displacement from normal (i.e. level) and degrees for other actions.
4. *Special:* a category for a few positions that cannot be placed in any of the previous three categories, e.g. pivoting (right or left), pronation (toward or away from plumb).

The signs Loring uses are based on the sign for 'one', the symbol of unity. In actual practice this vertical line becomes slanted slightly to the right. Strokes placed at the lower left, lower right, upper left or upper right of this vertical line indicate material in the four categories (Fig. 12.25).

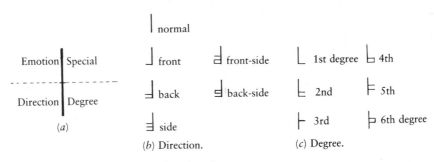

Fig. 12.25 Loring-Canna system: direction; degree.

Signs are combined as needed, degree strokes being added to directional or other indications.

Also unique to Loring is the introduction of spoken language to aid communication in teaching. This uses letters (upper and lower case) and numbers as a kind of code to represent the written symbols. For example, 'B' is extravert, '3' is the direction back, 'a' is first degree, 'R' is pivot right and so on. As was explained in Chapter Seven, timing for Loring is indicated by marking lines on the staff at regular intervals to represent the regular basic beats.

Loring appears to have searched for meaning in movement, not merely for cold, abstract facts. As with other teacher/choreographers, it appears that he did not have the time to devote to the completion of his system. The promised second book has not, to my knowledge, been published.

Benesh

Through its practical application in the field of classical ballet, the system devised by Joan and Rudolf Benesh has become one of the leading systems of the second half of the twentieth century. Rudolf Benesh, an artist and an accountant, became intrigued by the idea of notation when watching his wife Joan, a dancer with the Sadler's Wells Ballet in London (now the Royal Ballet) trying to jot down balletic sequences. Unaware of the existence of other systems, Benesh took an artist's point of view, believing that because dance (movement) is visual (perceived through the eyes) the form of notation representing it should also be visual and based on the logical structure of visual perception. All stick figure systems are, of course, visual representation. Benesh took the idea a step further by not drawing in the figure itself, but by plotting the position and movements of key points in the body (the extremities and centre joints of the limbs). These are drawn on a staff as though the writer is standing directly behind the dancer.

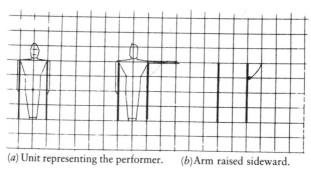

(*a*) Unit representing the performer.   (*b*) Arm raised sideward.

Fig. 12.26 Babitz system: staff.
(A. H. Guest Collection)

Without knowing it, Benesh had started off with very much the same idea as Sol Babitz, the brother of a dancer in Martha Graham's company. In 1939 Babitz had evolved an abstract 'stick figure' system. Using graph paper he provided a 'matrix' to represent the body, (Fig. 12.26 (*a*)). The figure was imagined and he drew only the indication of the movement itself, (*b*). In the Benesh system the 'matrix' is a section of a horizontal staff derived from music notation, (Fig. 12.27). Benesh believed that the five lines provide an ergonomically perfect and ideal matrix to represent the human figure. The top line represents the top of the head, the next line the shoulder, the third line represents the waist, the fourth line the knees and the bottom line the floor line. A support sign written under the floor line means supporting on the whole foot, on the line shows half toe, and above the line means supporting on *pointe*.

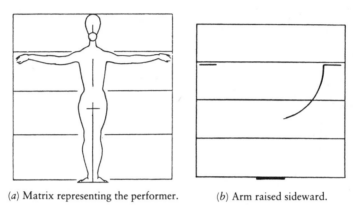

(*a*) Matrix representing the performer.   (*b*) Arm raised sideward.

Fig. 12.27 Benesh system: staff.

Benesh avoided several drawbacks built into earlier visual systems, for example, reversal of right and left sides of the body, and the need to turn the figure to clarify the position because of the missing third dimension. This missing dimension (the sagittal, forward-backward direction) is indicated by special signs. The basic direction signs which are used for placement of the extremities (feet and hands) are modified to indicate placement of elbow or knee when the limb is bent. 'Level' refers to a situation in the lateral plane of the body.

Fig. 12.28 Benesh system: placement (directions)

Thus by plotting the placement of the extremities of the arms and legs and of the elbows and knees when a limb is bent, various positions can be indicated. Movement lines are added to link starting and finishing positions, thus giving a more visual picture of the line of movement. A new idea was that of indicating the dancer leaving the floor when jumping by drawing a movement-line under the floor line, as if dancing on a mirror. In stepping the line curves upward; in jumping it curves downward. Fig. 12.29 shows a step–hop–hop pattern.

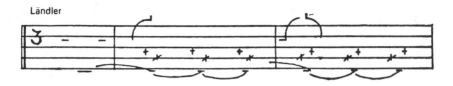

Ländler

Fig. 12.29

Information which cannot be written by visual means on the five-line staff is placed above it. For this purpose additional signs are used consisting mainly of letters of the alphabet, numbers and a few abstract signs. Signs under the staff indicate stage direction faced, turning, stage location, and direction travelled, (Fig. 12.30).

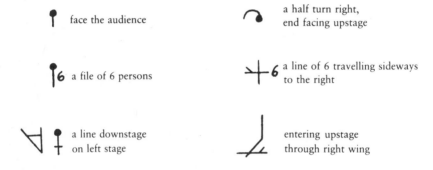

face the audience

a half turn right,
end facing upstage

a file of 6 persons

a line of 6 travelling sideways
to the right

a line downstage
on left stage

entering upstage
through right wing

Fig. 12.30 Benesh system: examples of signs placed under the staff.

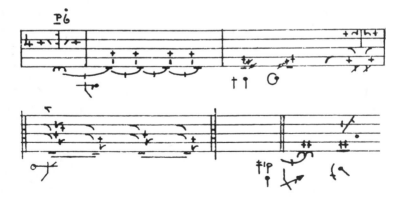

Fig. 12.31 Benesh system: example of a modern dance style.

An example of a classical pas de deux written in Benesh notation is the 'Grand Pas de Deux' from the third act of the ballet *Sleeping Beauty* (Fig. 12.32).

Fig. 12.32 Benesh system: Grand Pas de Deux from *Sleeping Beauty*.
(Courtesy Institute of Choreology)

Benesh was tremendously inventive in finding a few simple lines to express complex formations. He was concerned with a purely visual tool, embodying no theories.[5] As he pointed out:

> Movement of a human body is ... complex ... and signs used for plotting positions ... must therefore be capable of considerable manipulation according to certain concepts. .... The first concept is that a cross equals a bend, and by extension of the idea, a tilt. Thus we get the signs for bent elbows and knees and also body bends. Two further concepts arise from the simple manipulation of the basic 'level' sign, namely that a sloping sign means contact and that a tilt to the left means left and vice versa. By curving these sloping signs either upwards or

101

downwards we obtain the concept of supporting and supported respectively.

By manipulation of the basic three signs on the basis of these four concepts, the resulting number of signs is close to one hundred, each one giving different information. . . . A great deal more information is then added according to where they are placed on the stave: what part of the anatomy, or whereabouts in space, the stave serving as a matrix for both.[6]

The new ideas which were Benesh's particular contribution to the notation field were:

(a) simple signs which convey several items of information, comparable to speed writing;

(b) the concept of redundancy avoidance;

(c) his concept of the development of movement 'languages'.

Notable examples of (a) are the set of signs for stage location, direction faced and direction travelled.

Concerning redundancy avoidance Benesh writes:

One analyses and writes down a step in notation. On scanning this it will be found that much of the information is duplicated for various reasons. One can then eliminate some of the signs. Then perhaps by rewriting or analysing in a different way, reduce the total number of signs used. Ultimately one could arrive at the simplest in terms of the number of signs used. Generally speaking, this is the aim, as the result will be a simple and recognizable pattern. But there is a limit. A certain amount of redundancy must be included as a safeguard, especially against bad writing or errors.[7]

Benesh's philosophy and concepts of how the notation related to and served dance and other forms of movement are best described in his own words. He writes of the need to put into perspective the processes in the birth and upbringing of a movement language. Two stages in particular are described:

Stage I is the notation evolving stage, the end product being an alphabet.

Stage II is the practical application of notation and the evolving of languages.

Stage I is by nature mathematical and has been likened to Euclid. It commences with Axioms and Premises which are manipulated according to certain concepts. The means is the strict application of logic. The result is a basic alphabet.

Stage II. Choreology is the evolving of languages out of the basic alphabet . . . for example, Ballet, Modern Dance, Jazz, Indian Dance or application to medical, scientific or industrial use. . . .

Between Stages I and II there is a barrier. This barrier is a formidable one and unless a notation is capable of breaking through it, Stage II will never come into existence. . . .

The key to the break-through is simplicity. That is to say, the arriving at simplicity through complication. This is the pre-requisite to all creative thinking and applies equally to all works of art. On analysis a work of art is found to be extremely complex, yet to be successful it must appear simple. . . .

Simplicity does not necessarily mean omitting and reducing the value of things, it means the embracing of everything necessary into a simple unified theory or concept. . . .

Flexibility is another important factor throughout. The end product of Stage I, the notation, must clearly be flexible in the extreme. So also must the end product of Stage II if the language is to be alive and continue to grow. Hence the danger of rules. . . . A language depends for its universal comprehension upon the consistent use of rules. . . .

These languages must be allowed to grow naturally but . . . certainly nurtured with understanding and experience. The linguistic laws governing this stage are not fully understood. They are certainly not logical in the ordinary sense. It takes several years of working in the particular dance style before its language is fully understood in terms of notation.[8]

Modern contemporary dance has set a style of performance based on a discipline different from that of classical ballet. Disciplines or techniques are called language in choreology, and each one has its own grammar, or in other words, its own do's and don'ts.[9]

This brings us to the dictates of a particular language. What is it that makes one style of dance or kind of movement different from another from a linguistic point of view? The difference is the scale of values which differ in each case and the conventions or rules which arise from these. What is important in one case will not be in another, and vice versa. Notation presupposes a convention meaning that notation cannot be used abstractly but only as applied to a particular movement language. . . .

It is therefore essential for all concerned to know the language of a particular dance style. . . otherwise the eye would not know what to look for and what to discard out of the enormous visual information. The choreologist learns what to leave out rather than what to put in. It therefore follows that the notation not only presupposes the art convention but must also disregard certain details. . . . The answer lies in the correct analysis and knowing what to leave out, and the result must arrive again at a simplicity after having gone through so much complexity.[10]

From the above extracts it can be seen that Benesh is unique in this idea of 'language' and of a breakthrough between Stage I and Stage II. All systems have some form of basic 'alphabet', and there is a need in each case to learn and experience the practical application of this alphabet to different forms of movement. The degree of ease in application depends on the particular system and the style of movement being recorded. At different times the term 'language' has been used in connection with dance by many people, usually as a loose reference to the fact that dance is a means of communication. However, for the past twenty years and more the term 'Language of Dance'* has come to mean a deep understanding of movement

---

*In 1958 the term was registered in the U.S.A. as a service mark (trademark). In 1967 the Language of Dance Centre was registered in England as a business name.

through analysis of its basic content illuminated and reinforced by the use of the Laban system of movement notation.

Movement has its own logic. The natural language of dance stems from the movement itself, that is, from the physical 'syntax', the intent of the movement and the form that intention takes – all the aspects which contribute to a particular action, simple or complex.

From the physical movement alphabet, from the various 'parts of speech', each form of dance makes its own particular selection, the 'recipe' for that form. No notation is in itself the language; it is only a representation on paper of the kinetic language. This kinetic language has its own laws, the laws of physics and of anatomy which combine with the human element. As can be seen, in comparison with Benesh's ideas, this kinetic language is a very different concept of what 'language' means for dance. Benesh's 'languages' allow the notation to be kept simple because writer and reader know the movement style and hence the understood but unwritten details of performance.

In 1956, soon after its early stages of evolution, the Benesh system was adopted by the Royal Ballet for its particular needs. The establishment of a notator on the staff set an example later followed by many other ballet companies. The original textbook, published in London in 1956, presented the basis of the system. Subsequent publications have given some indication of its use in fields other than ballet. With the ballet system launched, Benesh turned his inventive genius to applying the system to other forms of movement. The analysis of movement has, however, remained the same: all movement is seen as visual in nature and therefore is recorded through a visual image.

In 1962 the Institute of Choreology (*see* Appendix E) was founded and training courses started. Dance scores of many styles have been notated. The system has been applied to several different fields of movement study. Reconstructions of ballets from the scores, usually carried out by the notator of the work or a dancer familiar with the work, have facilitated the teaching of these works in companies around the world.

Benesh maintained careful control over the system. All decisions concerning the development of the system were his. Since his death a Technical Committee has been established to solve questions of usage as they arise.

Lissitzian; Misslitz

Other twentieth century visual (stick figure) systems include that by Srbui Lissitzian, whose book *The Notation of Movement*, published in Leningrad in 1940, contains a generous introduction to other systems, historical and contemporary as well as the basics and examples of her own system. Many folk dances were recorded, in particular dances of the Armenian people, of which two large volumes were published.

Walter Paul Misslitz's system *Tanzfigurenschrift*, first published in 1954, is noteworthy for being printed in red and black to distinguish between right and left sides of the body. Misslitz also included a historical section presenting information on other systems. However, he also saw figure drawings as the only means of representing movement. In 1960 he published *Ballett-lehre*, introducing the basics of ballet technique, and also *Gymnastiklehre*, illustrating use of his system for gymnastics.

Jay

Letitia Jay, a New Yorker specializing in East Indian dance, invented a stick figure system which she presented in 1956. Several of her ideas were new. She provides a choice in viewing movement. The relationship of the 'stick-man' to the reader can be 'back reader', 'mirror image reader', 'upstage reader' or 'audience reader'. Direction faced on stage is indicated by attaching the letters F (front), B (back), R (right), or L (left) to the spine of the stickman. Height of jumps is shown by placing bubbles between the figure and the ground line – the more bubbles the higher the jump.

When the figure is facing away from the reader, the head is understood to be transparent so that facial expression can be drawn. It is understandable that Jay coming from an Asian dance background would be concerned with facial expression, a part of the body usually neglected by other dance notation systems.

To distinguish between different dancers in a group work, each is represented by a different hat. Abbreviations such as 'pu' (palm up) provide information which cannot readily be drawn. Despite great activity on her part for many years, the Jay system was never commercially published and no centre to promote it was established.

Sutton

A very new system, invented by a young, enthusiastic and energetic ballet dancer, is that of Valerie Sutton, who in a short span of time has left no stone unturned to put her system on the map.

Because Sutton's notation is based on a recognizable stick figure it has an immediate appeal to those who like to see the whole figure representing the dance movement (Fig. 12.33).

The Lilac Fairy Solo From Sleeping Beauty

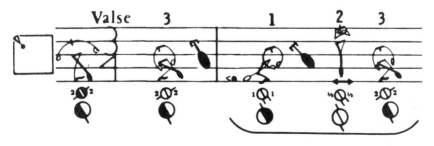

Fig. 12.33 Sutton system: excerpts from classical ballet.

(Courtesy Valerie Sutton)

Using a five-line music staff, Sutton provides an audience view of the figure which changes in perspective as the performer faces into different room directions. A new idea presented by Sutton is that of identifying a back view by drawing braces (suspenders) on the figure (Fig. 12.34).

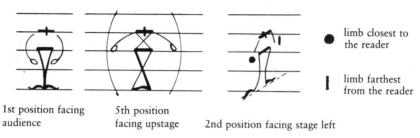

1st position facing audience	5th position facing upstage	2nd position facing stage left

● limb closest to the reader

❚ limb farthest from the reader

Fig. 12.34 Sutton system: perspective.

To overcome visual and perspective problems twenty-five writing rules are provided for drawing the stick figure. Among these are rules for when to use straight lines and when curved to represent a straight leg. Templates with parts of the body correctly drawn facilitate writing the figure in full script. For further clarification of what she terms the 'film-like script' (the figure drawings) a symbol script called 'position symbols' or '3-D symbols' is added beneath the staff. These additional signs indicate where the figure is facing and the relation of one limb to another (in front or behind, etc.), position details not always clear from the figure drawing. The 'in-out symbols' show whether a limb is close to the centre of the body or far, while the 'up-down position symbols' indicate vertical depth. Within the staff itself signs are added to show travelling, walking, jumping, etc. (Fig. 12.35). Fig. 12.36 illustrates a few of these signs.

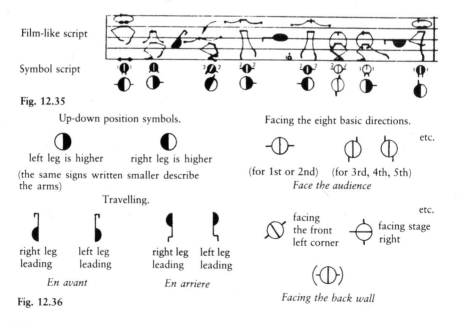

Film-like script

Symbol script

Fig. 12.35

Up-down position symbols.

left leg is higher   right leg is higher

(the same signs written smaller describe the arms)

Travelling.

right leg leading   left leg leading   right leg leading   left leg leading

En avant   *En arriere*

Fig. 12.36

Facing the eight basic directions.

(for 1st or 2nd)   (for 3rd, 4th, 5th)
Face the audience

etc.

facing the front left corner   facing stage right

etc.

Facing the back wall

Signs provided include those showing a relaxed hand, a flat hand, the classical hand, or a fisted hand. Sutton includes a variety of signs for facial expression, including variations such as 'listening', 'tasting', 'smelling', 'air bloating out cheeks', 'fish mouth', 'crying', etc. shown through drawings which are as pictorial as possible.

The system, first published in 1973, as *Sutton Movement Shorthand, Book One, The Classical Ballet Key,* by the newly established Movement Shorthand Society in California, was followed in 1975 and again in 1977 by publication of books of amendments. Adaption of the system for all forms of dance and the addition of textbooks on Sign Writing® for the recording of sign language used by the deaf (Fig. 12.37), followed the initial ballet-based book.

Fig. 12.37 Sutton system: written sign language for the deaf.
(A. H. Guest Collection)

Though Sutton calls her method 'Sutton Movement Writing and Short-hand', and speed and ease in writing are stressed, there is still the need for correct drawing of the figure and for addition of the position symbols. To overcome the time these take Sutton has introduced an abbreviated, quick writing, giving the minimum lines needed to suggest a movement or position (Fig. 12.38).

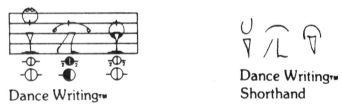

Dance Writing™

Dance Writing™
Shorthand

Fig. 12.38

With this 'skeleton' writing, the notator can, it is claimed, write down a dance as fast as it is performed. What is not clear is what is meant here by 'write down a dance.' Is the level of such writing hurried memory-aid notes or are we to expect a finished product, an organized, detailed record from which the dance can be faithfully revived?

The Movement Shorthand Society provides a newsletter for its membership and publications of materials such as excerpts from the Bournonville School which Sutton studied and notated during a stay in Copenhagen. A quarterly newspaper, *The Sign Writer*™, which features her notation for deaf sign language and spoken language has been established and teachers are certified in Sutton Movement Writing and in Sign Writing®. (*See* Appendix E.)

Eshkol-Wachmann

In the late 1940s the choreographer and teacher, Nadia Chilkovsky, predicted that one day dance might be composed in a manner similar to the composition of music. The idea then seemed far away indeed. But it was very much in the mind of Noa Eshkol in the 1950s as she sought to free dance from its old choreographic 'habits' and to experiment with compositions based on a series of progressions in spatial intervals comparable to intervals in music. Such intervals of movement of one basic form or another (rotation, rising, sinking, etc.) need not focus on the usual, familiar destinational points around the body. It would be, she found, possible to compose a whole dance based on a simple formula, a short series of moves, which, never coming back to the original starting point, could move on and on, the basic actions always being the same, but their occurrence in relation to the space around the body changing on each repeat of the formula. Eshkol's choreography has been very much bound up with the notation system which she and Abraham Wachmann evolved. By using the notation as a tool Eshkol has composed sequences of movement which would not otherwise have come to mind – or should one say, to body. Movement which evolves from the body, i.e. from a physical source, has a certain kinetic logic, no matter what the style or culture. Movement composed cerebrally imposes quite other demands on the body and can produce unusual sequences and positions. In watching the performance given by Eshkol's group, I found her use of body and space fascinating, my appreciation of the movement content of her compositions sharpened by the advantage of knowing her system and having a trained eye in notation/movement observation. The undancelike performance, the lack of dynamics, and the absence of the human element left most members of the audience cold. To them the performers were mere 'auto-mobiles' rather than personalities involved with dance. Had the performance been labelled 'motion' rather than 'dance', there might have been a greater appreciation of what Eshkol was striving for.

Noa Eshkol, daughter of a former prime minister of Israel, studied dance gymnastics with Tille Rössler before enrolling in 1948 in the Sigurd Leeder Dance School in London where she was exposed to his creative use of the Laban system. Eshkol wanted something more scientific and together with Abraham Wachmann, an architect who contributed to the early stages in the development of the system, produced the first movement notation based primarily on numbers. Fig. 12.39 is an example of Eshkol-Wachmann notation applied to ballet.

The approach to movement is mathematical and logical. There are three features which are new or differently handled from what went before: choice of unit of measurement; analysis of movement; indication of position or motion.

The standard unit for movement displacement, $1 = 45°$ (which is also the standard unit used in other analytical, non-visual systems) can, when needed, be changed to $1 = 30°$, $1 = 10°$, or even $1 = 5°$. Statement of unit is given at the start of a score. The choice of unit for time duration can, as in the Laban system, also be as small or as large as needed.

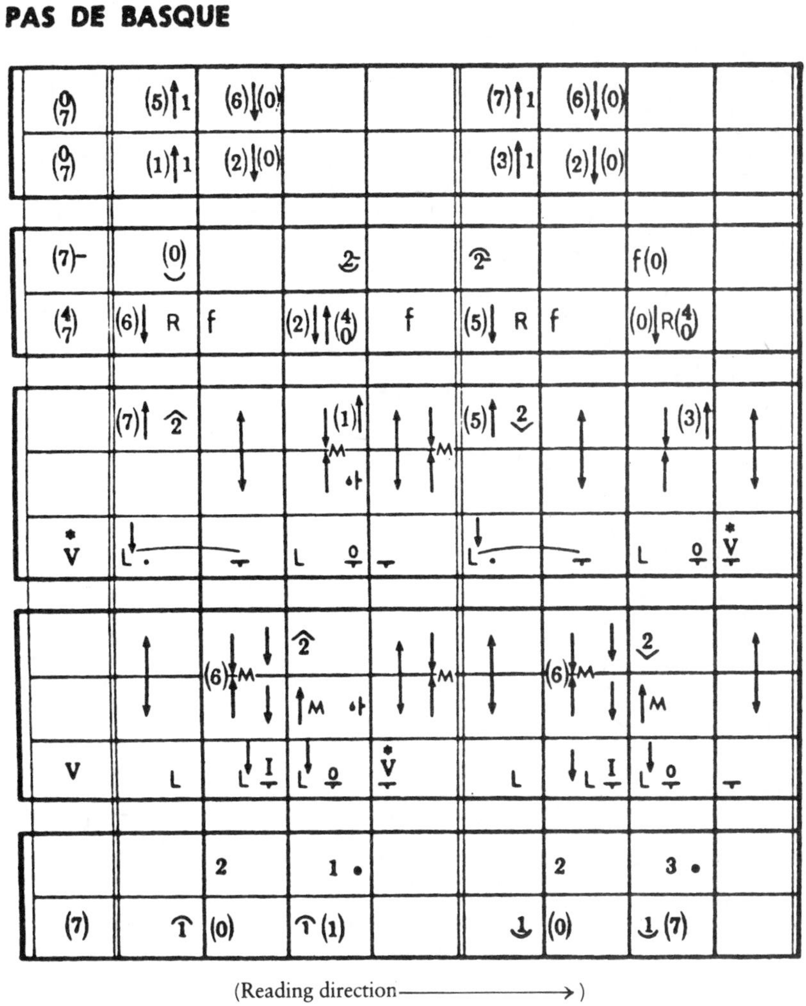

PAS DE BASQUE

Fig. 12.39 Eshkol-Wachmann system: example of its application to ballet. (A H Guest Collection)

(Reading direction ⟶)

The analysis of movement is based on the fact that the structure of the joints of the body dictates that every movement is circular in nature, taking place within a sphere. The three types of spherical movement are: rotary (around the axis of the limb); planal (the limb moves in a plane, the axis of the limb being at right angles to the axis of the movement); conical (the limb moves in a cone). Each of these has the possibility of movement in a positive or negative sense. Between pure rotation and planal movement lie the conical shapes. Analysis in terms of cones had not previously existed in dance circles nor in movement analysis used in connection with movement notation. Awareness was directed to the path in space of the extremity of the limb rather than the 'carving' of a cone shape made by the limb as a whole.

109

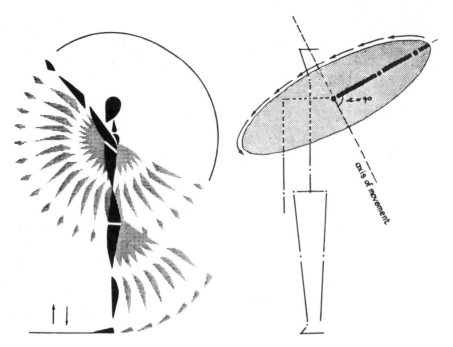

Fig. 12.41 Eshkol-Wachmann:
plane movement.

Fig. 12.40 Eshkol-Wachmann system:
axis of plane movement.

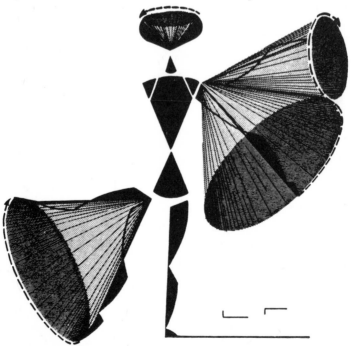

Fig. 12.42 Eshkol-Wachmann: conical movement.

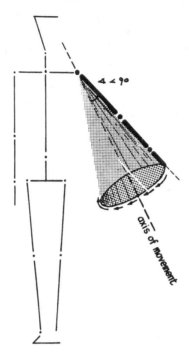

Fig. 12.43 Eshkol-Wachman: axis of conical movement.

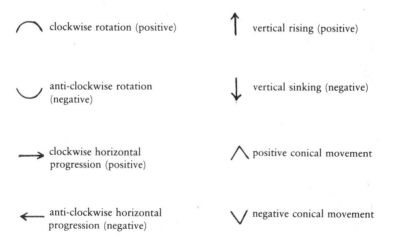

⌒ clockwise rotation (positive)   ↑ vertical rising (positive)

⌣ anti-clockwise rotation (negative)   ↓ vertical sinking (negative)

→ clockwise horizontal progression (positive)   ∧ positive conical movement

← anti-clockwise horizontal progression (negative) ∨ negative conical movement

Fig. 12.44 Eshkol-Wachmann: signs for motion.

Numbers are added to each of the signs for motion (Fig. 12.44) to state the degree of displacement (Fig. 12.45).

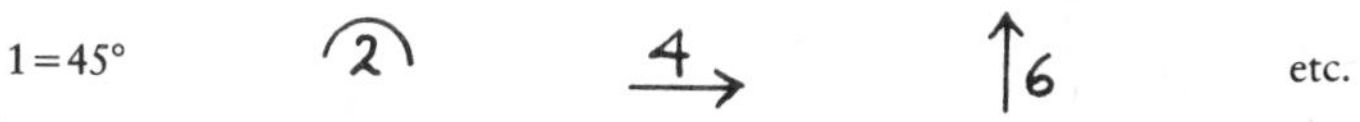

1 = 45°   ⌒2   →4   ↑6   etc.

Fig. 12.45

111

A position in the movement space is indicated through the establishment of a system of spatial references to which can be related the situation of a limb (position) and its change of place (motion). By a system of coordinates movement can be described in three ways: transition from one point to another; indication of the character of the path, the sense, and the amount of movement; statement of the position of the axis of the limb and axis of the movement. For the horizontal, 'Y' coordinates, zero is usually taken from where the performer is facing (Fig. 12.46); for the vertical, 'X' coordinates, zero is down (Fig. 12.47).

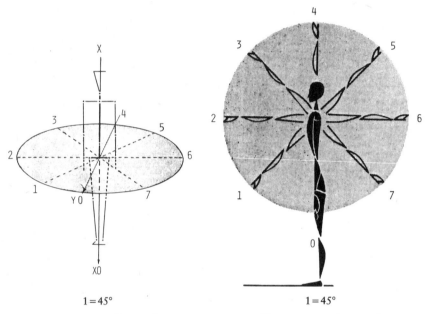

$1 = 45°$

Fig. 12.46 Coordinates of the horizontal plane.

$1 = 45°$

Fig. 12.47 Coordinates of the vertical plane.

A directional destination is shown by stating the two coordinates within brackets. Thus the point backward horizontal (2 in the vertical, 4 in the horizontal) is written as $(\frac{2}{4})$. The position right side high (3 in the vertical and 2 in the horizontal is $(\frac{3}{2})$.

The system is concerned very much with the shape of movement, though in quite a different way from that of Laban. Despite some basic differences in presentation of movement analysis, in actual practice the two systems are closer than would at first appear. For example, Eshkol-Wachmann also provides keys for different systems of reference. Several concepts which lie at the heart of the Eshkol-Wachmann system, such as circular paths for gestures, have existed in the Laban system but were not included or expressed as such in the standard textbooks.

The horizontal Eshkol-Wachmann staff, Fig. 12.48, provides spaces for each part of the body in a way comparable to Loring's system, but lacking his inner symmetricality in arrangement of spaces. When only part of the staff is needed only those spaces are drawn, identification of the parts of the body being written in words or word abbreviations at the start.

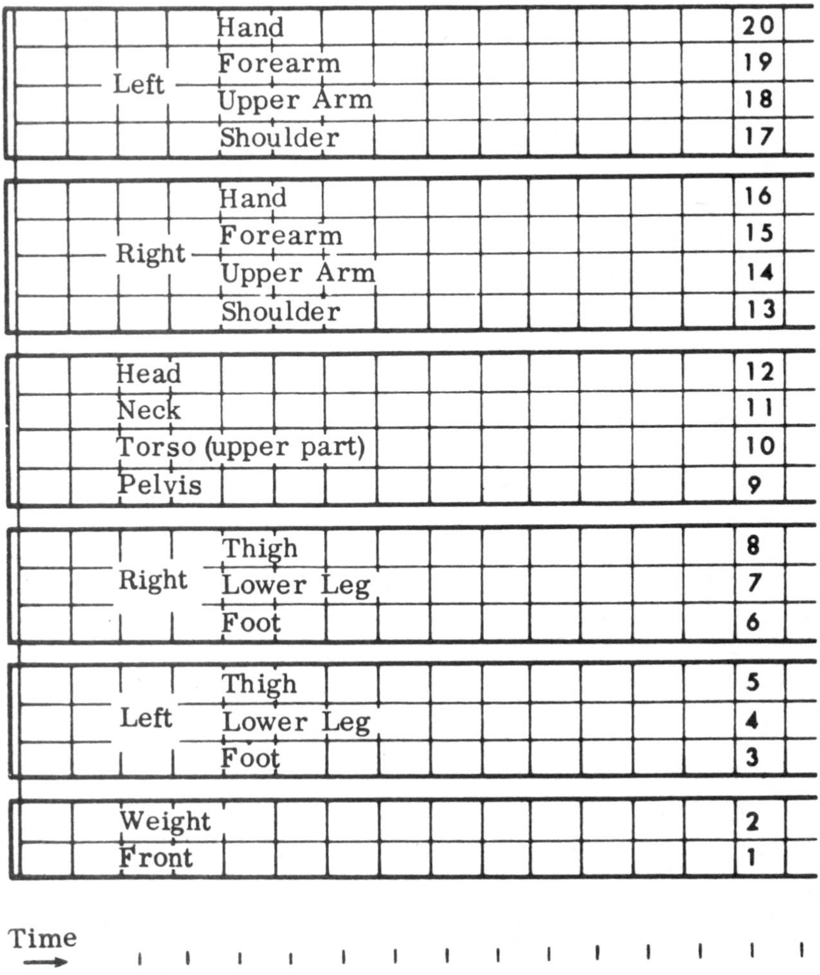

			Hand												20
		Left	Forearm												19
			Upper Arm												18
			Shoulder												17
			Hand												16
		Right	Forearm												15
			Upper Arm												14
			Shoulder												13
	Head														12
	Neck														11
	Torso (upper part)														10
	Pelvis														9
			Thigh												8
		Right	Lower Leg												7
			Foot												6
			Thigh												5
		Left	Lower Leg												4
			Foot												3
	Weight														2
	Front														1

Time
→

Fig. 12.48 Eshkol-Wachmann system: staff.

Use of numbers for the parts of the hands, feet, etc. establishes a logic which is carried throughout the system, though it results in a non-symmetrical representation of symmetrical body parts. At present there are twenty signs apart from numerals and a few letters such as M for maximum, m for minimum, R for reverse, i.e. retracing the path of the movement just performed – an idea which first appeared in Sol Babitz's 1939 system.

---

*English is used as the most universal language.

The original book, entitled *Movement Notation,* published in London in 1958, showed all movement in great detail, including the complex action of walking. No sign existed for contact (touch) since this was regarded as the result of some form of action and not an action in itself. Since then books geared to specific movement styles have been published and abbreviations and conventions introduced to serve the needs of each particular form of movement. For example, Roman numerals are now used for the positions of the feet in ballet where before they were precisely 'spelled out' in great detail.

In recording movement the Eshkol-Wachmann system considers the human body as a moving instrument and is concerned only with the changes which take place in the body's configuration. Any analysis or indication based on human expression or motivation is avoided, therefore dynamics are not included, other than time-influenced dynamics.

Apart from recording human movement, the Eshkol-Wachmann notation has also been used for recording animal movement in the book *The Golden Jackal* and also in a book *Shapes of Movement,* by John G. Harries, whose fascinating sculptural drawings bear some resemblance to those produced in the 1940s by the mathematician-musician, Joseph Schillinger.[11] The important difference is that Harries' shapes are also spelled out in Eshkol-Wachmann notation.

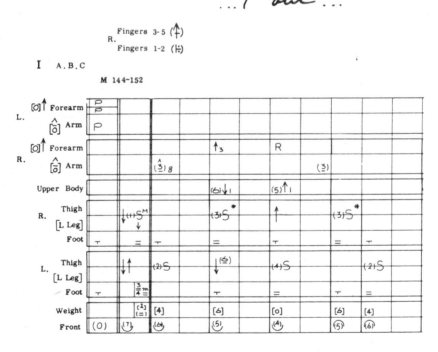

Fig. 12.49 Eshkol-Wachmann system: excerpt from Eshkol's *Diminishing Series Dance Suite,* 1978.

(A. H. Guest Collection)

The Movement Notation Society in Holon, Israel, which controls the development of the system, was established in 1968, and in 1973 a Centre for Movement Notation Research was established at the Faculty of Fine Arts in the University of Tel-Aviv. Because of its numerical basis the system has aroused interest in computer circles in the U.S.A., but it is mainly used in Israel. Information on courses, publications, etc. is available from The Movement Notation Society. (*See* Appendix E.) Eshkol is probably the only choreographer – or certainly the first – to compose completely on paper, her works being performed by The Chamber Dance Group.

Saunders – a return to words

To conclude this historical survey, we find that in the twentieth century recording movement appears to have come full circle with the introduction of Richard Drake Saunders' *Danscore – The Easy Way to Write a Dance*, published in Hollywood in 1946. Saunders' prepared sheets provided space for the accompanying music notes, a stage plan, and a large selection of words appropriate to the form of dance involved. By circling the appropriate words one could indicate that the right arm moves up while the left leg steps forward, and so on (Fig. 12.50). Special sheets were prepared for ballet, modern dance, jazz, etc.; even skating routines could be recorded through the Skatiscore sheets.

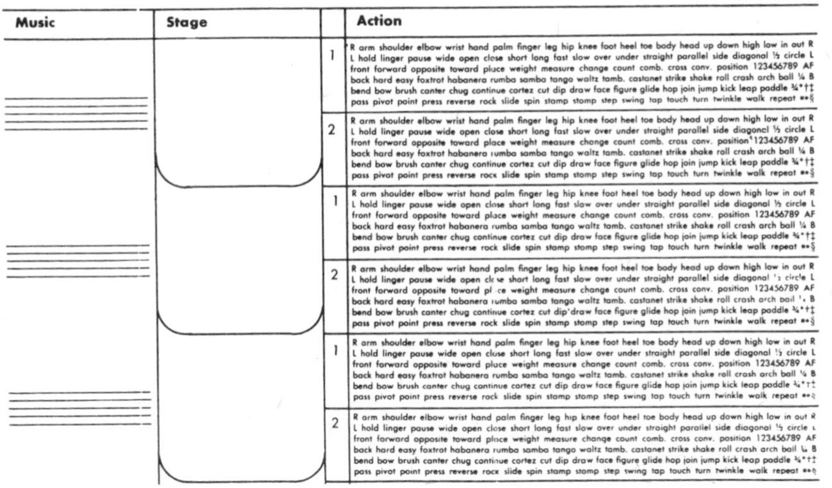

Fig. 12.50 Saunders system: sample page designed for Ballroom Dance.
(Dance Notation Bureau Collection, Ohio State University)

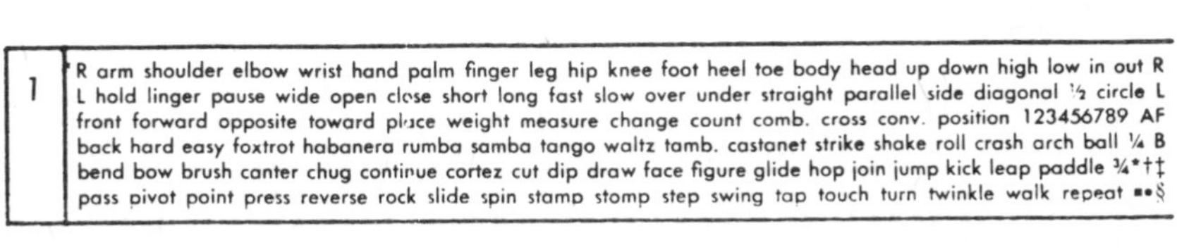

Fig. 12.51 Example of Saunders' choice of words.

Conclusion

Every system, regardless of its basis, needs trial under many different conditions. Each of the systems currently in use (other than 'closed' systems such as Feuillet and Stepanov) is constantly being proved and improved. Even those which are already highly developed need further work to cover in the most practical and satisfactory way the needs and demands of the many present-day fields of movement study, research and recording. No system is perfect, though some have claimed to be. No system can perform miracles, such as recording movement as fast as it is performed, or allowing it to be read back at performance speed, though such claims have been made.

Each person's attitude toward movement, the degree of awareness and comprehension of what takes place, the reason for recording or reading movement notation – all will vary, and one type of notation system will appeal to one type of mentality and not to another. The variety of needs which notation must fill may not be satisfied by one system or by another. There is an automatic visual response to certain types of systems, a response for which there may be no accounting. One system is spurned as 'chicken scratchings', another because 'I never could stand numbers', and so on. Personal prejudices are hard to overcome. 'We want a British system', or 'The symbols look so Chinese, and everyone knows that's an impossible language!'

Many of the nineteenth and twentieth century inventors of notation systems include in their books a historical survey of previous methods, usually taking pains to point out the weaknesses of these systems, where each one failed or why it was abandoned; in so doing they reveal how little investigation actually took place. Inaccurate statements on how other systems work prove that the writer has given only a cursory glance at the explanations of other systems, no sustained study of, or practice in, the subject having been undertaken. To embark on a systematic investigation of systems of movement notation requires an open mind, a broad, unbiased understanding of movement, an appreciation of semiotics, of symbology, of sign logic and linguistics. To these must be added years of patient study and trial, the actual practical use of systems. Who has the incentive, the time, the patience to undertake such a study? One must start by mastering one system, and then study others in depth. Only then is one equipped to make comparisons and arrive at certain conclusions based on fact and experience rather than on hearsay, partisanship, or emotional reaction.

THIRTEEN

Practical use of a system – some problems met

No matter how well a system is constructed, how highly flexible and versatile it is, the final proof of the pudding is in the eating: in the end a system's value will be determined by how faithfully the movement is recorded and the ease with which scores written in it can be read.

Writing errors

There must always be margin for error on the part of both writer and reader. The reader can repeatedly refer to the score to check his rendition of 'what the score states', and others can check the score to verify his results, but if the writer has made an error or left out important structural facts, the reconstructor of the work can only surmise what was intended and compose a logical movement phrase in the style of the piece.[*] The Feuillet system was so widely used that both skilled writers and readers emerged, and it can be assumed that, before printing, the notation was carefully checked by another reader. Certainly one finds few ambiguous passages in reading dances published in that system. In translating the *Chaconne for Harlequin* score I found one passage which was puzzling; after a certain point it no longer made sense. Referring to an earlier, less neat copy of the dance score, I found the correct information – a quarter turn had been written in the wrong direction.

In the case of Arthur Saint-Léon's Pas de Six from *La Vivandière*, working with the score gave the impression that Saint-Léon did not use his system daily and that the score had not been carefully proofread. In some cases it was easy to see what was intended: for example, the missing dots on a repeat sign ⁒; in other cases one could find out what was intended from the repetition of the same step later in the score. In certain passages the instructions were ambiguous or even unworkable, with the result that the reconstructor needed to exercise artistic judgment in the process of arriving at a suitable solution.

This was also true of Zorn's *Cachucha*. Though a simpler dance in several respects, some transitions were very awkward. Although the stick figures were carefully placed below the appropriate music notes, at times strict adherence to the timing indicated produced awkward, artificial movement. When the passages were performed to the music and the actions allowed to

---

[*]See Chapter 17, Revivals – The Dance Director

fall where kinetic logic dictated, a timing pattern – not far off what was written but far more danceable – emerged and was established for the performance of these steps.

Errors in movement description

A system often has far greater potential for accuracy than its users realize. Let us take two simple examples from the Stepanov scores in which the notator based his description on a movement analysis different from the true facts. In ballet an assemblé is a step in which the dancer springs off the ground from one foot, the other shooting out into the air (to help lift the body), while in the air the legs assemble (come together) and the landing is on both feet. Before this step actually starts (Fig. 13.1), the weight is usually on both feet: then, as one leg shoots out, all weight is transferred to the other foot so that in fact the actual spring is off one foot only. In the Stepanov scores one meets this step spelled out as though the dancer springs up from both feet and lands on both feet. While in the air, one leg remains down toward the ground while the other shoots out, usually to the side, as illustrated in Fig. 13.2. Such a jump is possible, but is not in the standard balletic vocabulary. (Read the figures from left to right.)

Fig. 13.1 Sequence of an assemblé.

Fig. 13.2 As written in Stepanov.

Another incorrect analysis is the step described in Stepanov notation as Fig. 13.1 above. This step, appearing as it does just before a misspelt assemblé, was obviously intended to be a preparation for the assemblé itself. Without doubt this was meant to be a glissade, illustrated in Fig. 13.3, a very common preparation for an assemblé.

Fig. 13.3 Sequence of a glissade.

A glissade starts with weight on both feet; the leading foot slides out (glissade means sliding) and the other pushes off so that there is a moment when both legs are stretched, just off the floor. The dancer lands on the leading foot, then slides the other foot in, thus ending with weight again on both feet. Although landing and closing are two separate movements, the closing usually comes so quickly after the landing that many dancers (and even some teachers) are unaware that they are not simultaneous. This obviously was the case with the Stepanov notators. They wrote an assemblé (Fig. 13.1) when they wanted a glissade (Fig. 13.3). What serious notators of today would call poor movement analysis was to them a convenient shorthand. Such a shorthand works only if the reader knows he is dealing with ballet and is conversant with ballet technique. What is not exactly stated can then be guessed.

The writers of the Stepanov scores recorded what they considered to be important at that moment. In the case of a pas de deux indications were usually given only for the girl, a fact illustrating the unimportance of the man's role. Although in ballets of this period the man was little more than a glorified porter of the beautiful ballerina, he was visible and had to take suitable poses, positions which would blend harmoniously with the ballerina's. Perhaps each gallant escort chose his own transitional movements and poses, but if nothing is written, how is a dance researcher to know what were the range and style of movements suitable for a man to perform in such a setting?

Some of the Stepanov scores in the Sergeyev collection are complete, neatly copied out and include head and body indications as well as arms. Unfortunately these are rare. To learn why so many scores were left in an incomplete state the reader is referred to Chapter 15, Stages in shaping up a score.

Degree of detail included

Laban always advised: 'Write more than seems necessary; better to have too much detail than not enough.' If the information is not there on paper, the reader cannot know it. In direct contrast to this approach Benesh preached redundancy avoidance: 'Eliminate everything you possibly can.' The general dance public, who have no experience in gleaning information from a movement score, cry 'Keep it simple! Don't clutter with unnecessary details!' Who is to say what is unnecessary? Because of the general belief that dance notation should be simple, the notator often takes the easy way out and writes as little as possible, only to find when the day of reckoning comes the omitted details are needed. There have been instances where a ballet recorded at memory-aid level could not be reconstructed, the process of reading back did not work. Some professional notators have shorthanded and have devised personal notes to the point where only they can mount the work from their scores. In any notating process it is the reader and the reconstructor who matter. Their needs must be anticipated.

How many times have dance directors, working from scores, pored over notated movement sequences searching the symbols to squeeze out a scrap more information which would make the sequence more logical, more comprehensive, or would give an indication of the desired style! At such moments we agree with Laban. Memory aid is fine if one is sure the readers will always be people 'in the know.' On hearing about the many scores written in the Stepanov system, people exclaim with delight 'How wonderful! How does the style of the turn of the century compare with the present day?' They are in for a disappointment, for the notators of that time were providing only a sketchy memory aid. Too often the parts of the body which contribute so much to style – torso, head, hands – were not included, nor were subtleties of timing or any dynamic content.

Over-analysis

The question of how much to write is always in the notator's mind. In analysing any complex movement there is the danger that if the notator slows down the movement too much, it will take on a different character and exaggerations will appear which cannot possibly occur at the proper speed. Good examples of such exaggeration are to be found in Saint-Léon's Pas de Six from *La Vivandière*. He frequently over-analyses – another indication that his system was not widely used by others or even frequently used by himself.

In several passages in Saint-Léon's score the dancers circle with forward travelling steps, down, up, up. On each step Saint-Léon has indicated a gesture for the free leg, rather high off the ground, as illustrated in Fig. 13.4.

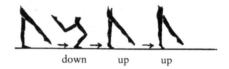

down   up   up

Fig. 13.4 Forward travelling steps (Saint-Léon score).

When these steps are performed up to tempo there is no time for these gestures and they impede the flow necessary for travelling. To retard the tempo would be musically wrong. It might be possible to perform the leg gestures if the pattern were sprung instead of stepped, but then the style would be wrong. According to the stage plans the dancers have to cover a great deal of ground in a short time; therefore in actual practice simple steps must be used to make the travelling possible and the fancy footwork has to go by the board. In this section the leg gestures in the original score were only at low level; in some places there are examples of piqué-glissades written with leg gestures up to hip level, a total impossibility!

Safeguarding uniform development

In the development of a system it is all too easy for notators to make up a new sign or usage on the spur of the moment to fill an immediate need. If there is not a central body keeping in touch with all notators through publication of new ideas, decisions reached, new symbols on trial, etc., such independent invention can get out of hand to the point where notators can no longer read each other's scores. Certain types of dance, mime, or stylized movement call for special usages. A glossary of such special usages or of abbreviations must be given for each score. If a new idea put forward in this way is found to have universal merit, it may later be adopted as universal standard practice.

FOURTEEN

The notating process

What is it like to be a dance notator? As more and more people in the dance world come to accept, understand, appreciate and make use of notation, professional dance notators are gaining recognition and respect, and receiving more opportunies to use their skills.

How does a notator go about his work? The following descriptions are based on my own experiences as well as on those of colleagues; similar experiences have been met by Benesh notators, and indeed would be met regardless of the system used.

Access to the choreography

To notate a ballet the notator must first, of course, have access to the choreography, i.e. the information to be notated. Access may be gained in any one or more of the following situations:

(a) being present during rehearsals when a new work is created;
(b) attending rehearsals when an established work is taught to an entirely new company;
(c) notating from film or video;
(d) interviewing the dancers to find out what each does. This last method is usually combined with attending brush-up and run-through rehearsals and performances.

(a) Recording of a new work

Since most choreographers do not work from notes and do little actual planning ahead, much of their time in rehearsals is spent trying out movement ideas, seeing if they 'work', that is, whether the dancers can master the steps and produce the desired effect. It can take hours for a phrase of thirty-two bars to be choreographed. Many sequences are discarded or radically changed. Why, you may ask, does the notator waste so much time notating material that will not be used? Surely it would be better for him to come in after the choreographer has decided what he wants. Choreographers have also thought this. In starting work on a new ballet, they felt the time to call in the notator was when sequences had already shaped up. This was my experience in the notating of *Orpheus*, the first ballet to be recorded at the time of creation. Balanchine did not bother to inform me of the first rehearsals, thinking that I did not need to sit through the period of trial and error and decision-making. This was a great mistake; the notator should be in at the start for two reasons. First, because every word the choreographer speaks, every movement thrown out, sheds light on his thinking processes, on his attitude and approach, and on the concepts and motivations of the movements, thus helping the notator to know how best to record the resulting phrases. In working with Balanchine I found that I developed a sixth sense and could tell by his 'body language' whether a step would be stillborn or not. Most of the time I was right, I just observed and waited, though occasionally I misjudged the outcome, a sequence was kept and I had to catch up later.

Secondly, the notator should be in at the start because the choreographer may wish to use in a later ballet phrases that were thrown out. Through the notator he can collect a 'bank' of such material. As yet, to my knowledge, no major choreographer has reached the stage of using a private choreographic secretary in this way. Choreographers have a lot to gain when they do. With Janet Moekle as his personal resident company notator, Paul Taylor probably comes closest to deriving such benefits.

Recording a new work is a comfortable situation for a notator; despite having to rewrite material and throw sections away, by the time the company is ready for dress rehearsal the score is pulled together. Last minute changes are noted, as are post-opening night adjustments.

(b) Recording an established work as it is being taught

Being present when an established work is taught to a new company is, with a cooperative choreographer or ballet master, the most practical situation for recording a work with the least amount of time 'wasted.' I use the word 'cooperative' since the notator will frequently want to have short conferences with the person teaching the work to find out the idea behind the movement, what is important, how it should be understood and, therefore, how it should be written. If the notator is lucky, the ballet will be taught in sequence, from start to finish. As each dancer is told where to enter or to stand on stage, and as each step is demonstrated, each body position explained, so the notator gets it written down. When the sequences are 'polished' the notator adds these finer details to the score. Coordination with the music is easy with a cooperative pianist on hand (and it is very rare that pianists are not cooperative). Such was the situation when I was called in to notate *Night Shadow*, taught by John Taras to the New York City Ballet.

The difficulty that arises during the teaching of an old work is that often there is more than one rehearsal taking place at the same time, the soloists being rehearsed in one studio, the corps de ballet in another. Unable to be in two places at once, inevitably the notator must capture much material at a later time. Because this happens so often, it is necessary to have assistant notators. Notator-trainees can gain experience and be helpful in jotting down floor plans and marking the music score with key cues and plans.

(c) Notating from film or video

In the early days, unfortunately, devices for rapidly capturing a performance of a ballet did not exist. Latterly film and particularly video have been a tremendous aid in pinning down missing details or whole sections. But when given the choice of notating from film/video or from live dance, the notator will choose live dance every time. This choice may seem surprising. It is only when one has spent two hours watching a small box or screen, running the film/tape back and forth, that one realizes what an exhausting operation it is. Because notating under such circumstances is concentrated work and tiring on the eyes, it is difficult to function for more than two hours at a stretch. While working, one wonders which of the dancers is really accurate, and how many movement mistakes are being notated which will have to be changed later. There is no one on hand to answer the many questions which arise on unclear passages. An outsider automatically assumes film/video means beautifully executed movement in bright light with clear definition, running smoothly in a sufficiently darkened room, the notator seated comfortably with an angle-poise lamp on hand to shine just on his pad. Too often such conditions do not exist, and the strain resulting from poor lighting produces headaches and advances exhaustion. Machines often refuse to function properly, tape nervously 'jaggers' by, the picture won't come clear. One must rewind, play, rewind, play. For general checking of short sections, pinning down certain details, film has value. For notating an entire work – no. However, if film/video is the only source of information, then it is used with gratitude – gratitude that precious choreography is not lost and can be converted into a more readily accessible form.

(d) Interviewing the dancers

Many dancers are considerate, patient and helpful. If the questions asked by the notator concern only a short phrase, an occasional tricky step or bit of partnering, they are usually very willing to provide the answer during a coffee break, or even come in early or stay after rehearsals. But some are quite uncooperative. Such work with the notator is not in their contract and they do not want their usual routine disturbed. In some companies it is possible to schedule special sessions with the notator, but such sessions are rare and often attended with bad grace. Notators have learned to use shorthand, taking up as little of the dancers' time as possible, and filling in memorized details later. A senior notator who had never developed speed, recorded the ballets he was commissioned to write by having each dancer come, one at a time, to his office. The dancer would show the first phrase and then wait patiently while he wrote in all the details with great neatness, producing a complete neat copy at the first draft. Thus the dance would be notated, phrase by phrase, dancer by dancer. This mode of working, while ideal for the notator, was agonizing for the dancers who, though they respected him and were keen to have the work preserved for posterity, disliked the boring inactivity of the sessions.

Speed of notating

How does a notator proceed in the task of writing down a ballet? How fast can a notator work? Can a notator get the movements written down by sitting in the audience during a performance? What actually does happen?

123

Questions such as these are often asked by the general public, indeed by anyone who has not studied and used a system of notation.

Only a camera can record a dance as fast as it is performed. There are several reasons why no notator, regardless of the system used, can notate merely from a performance. First, it must be remembered that the body of one dancer is like a small orchestra – two arms, two legs, torso, (pelvis, chest, shoulders), head and hands may all need to be taken care of. The rhythm of the movement must also be captured. Usually this information is added later. It is rare that only one part of the body is moving at one time. It is also rare that only one dancer is performing at one time. Second, the notator has to drop his eye to the paper to put the information down and, during those brief moments, the dancer will have performed several more movements which the notator will have missed. Only general notes on key moments can be taken during a performance, often just scribbled and then clarified immediately afterward. Third, it is dark in the auditorium of a theatre, so unless a special light is available for the notator, he cannot see the paper clearly. Use of a flashlight is extremely annoying to members of the audience sitting close by. As you will see from reading Chapter 14, capturing all the necessary information is a lengthy process. It is usually the process of *getting* the information, of determining what is to be recorded that takes time, not the actual process of writing it down in one or another system of notation. We have seen publicity sent out by originators of 'shorthand' systems which claims that, with their system, choreography can be recorded from the wings during a performance. This I would like to see! In my experience as a professional performer, the wings are usually too dark as well as too crowded with dancers waiting to make entrances or hurtling out on an exit. When questioned closely, the originator of one of these statements replied that it was not the full notation system that was used but a special 'speed writing' comparable, I gathered, to the kind of fast jottings which any of us make to capture a fragment here or there.[1] But catching scraps is not the impression given when speed in notating claims are made. The general public is still too uninformed about notation and how any system works to know what to believe.

How fast can dance steps be written down? I have usually given as a rule of thumb: 'as fast as the dancers can learn them.' There are a few exceptions arising from movements which are complex in nature yet easy to do. The dancers will be home and dry long before the notator has worked out the best way to write the passage down accurately. Conversely, there are movements which are much easier to notate than to perform, in which case, while the dancers are still struggling, the notator is sipping tea or stretching his legs.

How long does it take to write down a whole ballet? It is amazing the number of people who expect some miracle to occur with dance notation. Alas, a notator is not a Mary Poppins; there is no magic wand. Every detail that is important has to be decided on and included in the notation. We all know how long it takes to write a letter. We learned to write at an early age, and the words we write are usually familiar so that putting them on paper (spelling, punctuation, etc.) is no problem for most of us, and yet the process takes time. The general public does not see authors at work and so is unaware of how painfully slow the process can be. Much time is spent on rewriting and polishing. This is also true for the dance notator, who may find that the movement description first jotted down does not accurately represent the choreographer's wishes. The general public also does not see the composer of music battling with pencil and paper, painstakingly, note by note, putting down his musical ideas. It is a long drawn out job.

The most familiar image of the recording of information is the stenographer, who is writing down only what one person is saying, and that is usually dictated at a slower than normal speed. Courtroom stenographers have special machines with which to record what is said. Fortunately for them speech is usually punctuated by pauses.

To answer the question: "How long does it take to write down a ballet under average conditions?", it is easiest to cite circumstances in which an existing work is taught to a new company. The fastest I have ever worked was the five weeks in Paris when Una Kai, of the New York City Ballet, mounted Balanchine's *Concerto Barocco* and *Scotch Symphony*. Both are roughly thirty minute ballets involving around thirty dancers. Rehearsals took four to five hours a day, five days a week. At the end of the five weeks I had neat pencil copies of the two scores, ready to be microfilmed. The scores had not been checked, but even with the inevitable minor mistakes they were ready to be used for remounting the ballets at any time. For these two ballets the time factor worked out to two hours of work on the score for each hour of rehearsal time. This was achieved by working at a speed which could not be sustained over a longer period. Professional notators must have sensible working hours.

There are so many variables in the conditions under which a ballet is notated and in the time it takes the choreographer to impart his final decisions that it is very difficult to state a general formula for how long the notating process takes. Here are some of the variables: complex music which must be analysed for the dancers; complex movement coordination; dancers having difficulty with steps; partner work; use of props; complex group paths in which collisions occur and for which solutions take time; discarding of material on which much time has been spent. These are some familiar reasons why writing a score takes time. Recording exactly the right quality, the nuances, the details which are an integral part of the choreography, adds to the complexity of the notated score and hence to the time taken to complete it.

Monica Parker, director of the Benesh Institute, has provided the following formula as a guideline on the time it takes to record a ballet:

1 minute of choreography requires: 2 hours of rehearsal time,
6 hours for writing up notes
outside of rehearsal.

Thus one minute of choreography requires eight hours of work to produce the dance score. A ballet lasting thirty minutes would therefore take about 240 hours to notate. She suggests that the time factor is less affected by which notation system is employed than by which notator.[2] Murial Topaz, director of the Dance Notation Bureau, concurs. Labanotators have found it difficult to arrive at any precise formula, but agree with the Benesh figures, adding a bit more time for complex modern works using difficult music. Topaz makes the following significant comment: "I would add that the quality of the teaching and rehearsal conditions influence both the time it takes and the quality of the score produced".[3]

Perhaps a description of the step-by-step process in notating a ballet might clarify how notators work.

Organizing the work

As soon as the notator is informed that he is to start work on a ballet his first step is to obtain a copy of the piano score and to number the measures (bars). As soon as possible the pianist's copy is also numbered in order that, at any point in the rehearsals, the notator can correlate with the music. When the rehearsal director says "We'll start at ta-rum-ta-ta", or "at the repeat of the melody", time is wasted if the notator must then pick up his music score to locate these notes. Instead, a quick look at the pianist who whispers "Bar 104" and the notator is immediately cued in.

The notator arrives at the first rehearsal having become acquainted as much as possible with the music. If it is an older ballet, some research on its story, etc. enables the notator to know what it is all about and who the dancers are supposed to represent.

Where will he sit? Many notators like to sit at the back of the studio so that, seeing the dancers from the back, they can correctly identify the right and left sides of the body. There is also the advantage of being able to get up and unobtrusively learn a step which proves tricky to write; getting it into the body first can clarify the movement. Other notators prefer to be up front since they can hear better what the choreographer says, and also be nearer the piano to have a quick word with the pianist. In this situation the notator is facing the dancers and so, like a dance teacher who faces the class and says 'Right arm up' as she lifts her left, the notator must incorporate the inversion of right and left. Stage plans are drawn from the audience's point of view and changed later in the score to the practical dancer's point of view. As well as having a copy of the music at hand, the notator will have several pads of paper, since different sections may be worked on during one rehearsal and there will be a need to keep the papers separate. Often there is not time for labelling, sorting, organizing, etc. during a rehearsal; this must be done later when a ring binder and dividers are used.

What does the notator seek to get down first? That depends entirely on how the choreographer or ballet master proceeds. If it is a new work, some choreographers like to teach thematic material first, step sequences or movement patterns which later will be woven into the fabric of the chore-ography. Some like to place their dancers first, plan entrances and exits, sort out group arrangements, move the dancers around the stage, etc., and decide later what steps or movements will be used. In this case the notator will concentrate first on floor plans. Some choreographers put forward movement ideas and allow the dancers considerable latitude in shaping up these ideas into a setting most comfortable to them. For example: 'Travel along this stage diagonal doing jumping steps with a turn here or there', will be experimented with until the dancer decides on a favourite version which the choreographer accepts. Ashton took very much this approach in working out Nadia Nerina's variations in *La Fille Mal Gardée*. Working this way can be hard on the notator, for while one sequence is being figured out, the choreographer is off giving ideas to someone else for another sequence, and the notator is torn between finishing the first phrase or paying attention to the next. As is perhaps now clear, there is no one way to work: the notator gets what material is available. Rehearsals are not organized for the convenience of the notator, not perhaps because of a lack of appreciation for the notator's work but because of the inevitable pressure of time and the heavy financial cost of rehearsing a company.

Whether the ballet be a new one or an old, it is not unusual for the choreographer or ballet master to switch to different sections while teaching the material. A section from the middle of the first movement may be taught, then the beginning of the third movement, and so on, with no word to the notator as to where the pieces fit. If the choreographer is under pressure and the material is pouring out quickly, there is no time at that moment to ask 'What is going on, where are we now?' Missing material must be discovered later and the pieces identified and organized chronologically. Fig. 14.1 shows an example of rough notes taken during a professional rehearsal.

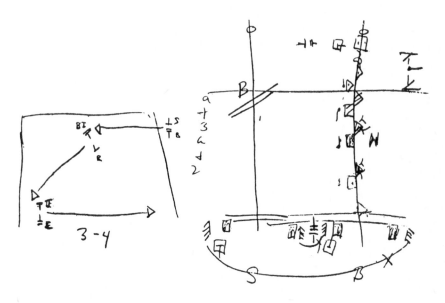

Fig. 14.1 Rough notes taken by Muriel Topaz during a rehearsal of *Lilac Garden*, choreography by Antony Tudor. (Courtesy Dance Notation Bureau)

If the notator finds that the performers already know the steps and the rehearsal period is devoted to polishing the material, he is at a great disadvantage and can only follow the music and place key indications above the appropriate notes – 'kneel', 'ara(besque)', 'pir(ouette)', and so on, written in notation or word abbreviations. Floor plans can also be written on the music page, pinning down on which measure a certain formation takes place or where a group starts to move across stage and where they finish. Being thrown into the above situation is becoming a thing of the past as choreographers have learned to appreciate and respect the work of the notator. However situations still occur where the notator has to piece the work together, catching what he can from rehearsals and filling in through checking the video.

Dancers are only allowed to rehearse a certain number of hours per day, but between and after rehearsals the notator may be hard at work. The scribbled notes of the day must be organized, put into chronological order, copied out and checked with the music to be sure that the dance movement fits the right number of music measures. Only through copying the material out soon after it is first written can sense be made of some of the deletions, the changes in counts, the scribbled notes which the choreographer's alterations have demanded. Only when each day's work is copied can the notator see what material is missing, what is not clear and what still needs to be 'captured' the next day. In the next day's rehearsal this same material will doubtless be gone over again, to reinforce the dancers' memory and to polish the sequences. As performance details are discussed, corrections given and fine points clarified, these are added to the score. It is at this stage that a full-time notator, resident with a company, faces a problem. The main structure of the work is recorded. Should he go on to notate another ballet to get its main structure, or should he stay on to attend the remaining rehearsals during which polishing and clarification take place? In these rehearsals the underlying concepts, motivation and performance details are revealed. Is it more important to capture these than to spend the time working on a new ballet? In such final rehearsals comparatively little material is notated relative to the amount of time spent. Therefore, for practical reasons the notator usually moves on to a new work (other rehearsals taking place each day), deeming this a better use of his time. The company may thus decide to be satisfied with memory-aid scores despite the value to posterity in getting the meaning, quality and texture of the movements. It may be argued that performance details can be seen in the video recording which most companies now make, but dancers too often fall short of the choreographer's intentions and the desired 'colouring' and interpretation are often missing. How can one tell what on the screen is an integral part of the choreography and what the personal mannerisms or movement mistakes of the performer? Freelance notators, commissioned to work on one particular ballet, have the advantage in being able to concentrate on one score at a time and see it to full completion.

At some point during the rehearsals the gradual pulling together of the score takes place. The layout (fitting the material on each page) is planned, and the various parts copied in neatly for the first draft. This draft provides a working, memory-aid score. Addition of details of style and interpretation then takes place before the score is considered finished. In the next chapter we will look into the specific stages in shaping up a score.

FIFTEEN

Stages in shaping up a score

When is a dance score finished? What is meant by a completed score? These questions may seem strange but for the notator they are very important. To understand their importance let us follow the score beyond the process described in Chapter 14.

The rehearsal period is over, the notator has written and copied out neatly all the sections of the ballet. In one sense the score is finished; everything is written down, and the notator breathes a sigh of relief and may even take a few much needed days off. Then comes the testing of the score. Testing may be done in several different ways.

First, the score is farmed out to a checker, an experienced reader who has no intimate knowledge of the ballet. This lack of knowledge of a particular work is important, for if you already know what is likely to occur, you may read into the notation indications which are not there, or overlook ones which should not be there. The checker reads through the score, 'dancing' it in his mind's eye, reading every part, seeing that what is stated in the movement description tallies with the floor plans and the music mark-up. Just as typographical errors occur in any newspaper, magazine or book, so there is enormous margin for error also in all the symbols that are needed to record a whole ballet. There may be omissions: When does the torso come up again? When does the head go back to its normal situation? An extra floor plan may be needed to make clearer the change of a group formation. And so on. The choreographer may have stipulated that a section should only be indicated in general terms, but were these general terms enough to give the right idea to the next reader? Perhaps more detail is required. Even the most experienced notator needs this kind of checking. Remember that notating movement is more akin to translating from one language to another than simply to writing down the words you are reading now. If the choreographer has tried to invent new, different movements, there will be no standard 'spelling' of known steps to fall back on. Does the translation 'hold together', does it convey a meaningful, logical movement message? The checker has altogether a very helpful role to play in making comments and criticisms on the score at this stage.

The second trial of the score is the very necessary 'proof of the pudding' through revival of the work solely from the score, preferably by someone with no previous knowledge of the work. At this time the reconstructor will find out what does not work, where clearer description is needed, where reorganization of the layout, of placement of floor plans, etc. may speed the reader's exploration and understanding of the score. As a rule the recon-structor makes a point of personally learning the material ahead of time so that sequences can be demonstrated swiftly at rehearsal, thus avoiding the waste of precious time in puzzling out information from a score while the dancers wait around. Ideally a notator trainee will be on hand who can follow the score and at any moment answer any question that might arise and remind the reconstructor of any detail overlooked.

The third trial of the score which may occur during the last stages of the second, is when the choreographer comes to see the results of the work taught from the score. This is a most valuable moment, since stylistic details can then be checked, and anything which looks wrong to the choreographer can be put right, and the score given his seal of approval. But here comes the snag! Knowingly or not, the choreographer may have new ideas about what he wants, and so in many places what the notator recorded quite accurately is suddenly 'wrong.' Material performed by different dancers often takes on a different 'look' and, to the choreographer's eye, needs modifying. In making such changes choreographers are often quite unaware of a depar-ture from the original version. The notator is informed of these 'wayward' sections and, with a sigh, goes back to the drawing board. Obviously choreographers must have the right to change and improve their works, but at times such changes appear to be only a whim, not an improvement. When scores are commissioned at a set fee, this extra work for the notator may not include extra pay. Nowadays most notators are on a full yearly salary, so that changes in a score are part of their regular work.

The fourth trial of a score comes at the time the neat ink copy is made, when every symbol is again scrutinized and further questions may surface. Then before printing, a final check will be made by a proof-reader. This process may seem like a lot of work, yet, except for the reconstruction of the dance, it is no more than that required to produce a book or a music score; each undergoes similar stages before publication. The difficulty for dance is that the time span from start to finish may cover several years through no fault of the notator. It is a question of opportunity, access to the material and availability of checkers, a performing company and the choreographer. There is also the matter of good communication and cooperation on the part of the choreographer. Obviously the most desirable arrangement would be for the choreographer to write his own ballets. A few less well-known choreographers are already capable of doing so. The next possibility is for a choreographer to have a personal notator, a choreographic secret-ary, who knows his style and ideas so well that an understanding of the choreographer's intention is automatically reflected in each score. But few choreographers can afford the luxury of such a choreographic scribe. Communication can be aided when a choreographer can verbalize the 'dance language', feeding the notator the information he needs: Ruth Cur-rier, for example, does not write but can read the scores of her works.

To a notator who is proud of the scores on which he has worked so hard, a most discouraging fact of life is the extent to which the score produced may, in certain circumstances, not be of practical value. If a notated work is kept in the repertory or revived after a few years without at any time reference being made to the notated score, within a short time considerable changes may take place. These changes may be the result of replacements among the dancers, and/or of direction by a ballet master not cognisant of every detail of the ballet. The version performed and the one written may, in time, vary too much for useful reference to the score at rehearsals. To give an idea of how easily changes may occur, consider the case of the dance sequences in the Broadway musical *Kiss Me Kate*! During the six weeks that I was in England assisting in putting on the London production from the notated dance score, despite eight performances a week by the New York company, four distinct changes had crept into the dance. These were mainly the result of rehearsing a replacement and of the captain wanting 'to clean things up'. At the next brush-up rehearsal following my return these differences surfaced. Fortunately there was a chorus of 'Let's do what the book says!', thus eliminating the usual time-consuming arguments about who passed in front of whom, on which count a certain action occurred, and so on.

It is an interesting psychological fact that when a dancer has learned a movement detail or sequence and it has 'settled into the bones', there is a great reluctance to change. If the score is not referred to constantly and corrections made, there will be a resistance to altering movements to conform to the score. Absence of a score allows freedom to digress, to change and to fiddle with the choreography often without the choreographer's knowledge. The only consoling thought to the notator whose score is not put to practical use is that, one day, when there is no one on hand who remembers anything of the work, the score is there as the means of resurrection – the work is not lost! A valid version exists.

To return now to our original question: 'When is a score finished?' One can see why the answer is not obvious. After stage one – the original notating – there exists a score through which the structure of the work can be revived as adequately as it would be by any ballet master or former dancer who had danced it. For ease of reading obviously the subsequent stages in perfection of the score are desirable. To have to wait until a score reaches stage three, the reproduction stage, seems a discouraging prospect to the notator, who loves to see a work reach completion and to feel that it is launched and off his hands.

To return to what is meant by a 'complete score'; in recent years the Dance Notation Bureau has established the idea that a 'complete score' means inclusion of all information needed to produce the work, not just the choreography itself. Included are the costume designs and swatches of material if possible; information concerning the sets; the sheet music and, where possible, a tape of an orchestral performance; lighting plots; background material on the date of first performance and the original cast; the date, company and cast at the time of notating; historical background of the work; verbal description of the style of the piece and of the characterizations of the leading roles – in short, everything which will help in future revivals. The need for all this supporting material arose from the many reconstructions done each year for companies all over the United States by dance directors not personally familiar with a work or the style of the choreographer.

At one time the Dance Notation Bureau was criticized for the number of scores left incomplete. What such critics did not realize was that work had stopped because of lack of access to the material. If a work is no longer rehearsed or performed, and no film exists, how can the score be completed? I must insert here for the record the problems early freelance notators faced in the days before the advent of video and film. Scores could not be completed because rehearsal schedules were changed without the notator being notified, or because different sections of the work were being rehearsed at the same time and the notator could only cover one. Weeks might be spent in trying to track down missing sections or vital details. Only a few pieces of information might be captured during a rehearsal – for the notator a frustrating waste of time. Having a notator on hand was so new that it was unthinkable to interrupt a rehearsal for his benefit. With the dancers at his disposal, questions could have been answered in a few minutes. The notator had to wait around, hoping that this or that dancer would be free to clear up some missing information. Cooperative dancers often could not tell when they would be free; other dancers would make appointments and then not keep them. Some good performers could not describe what they were doing, they could not count or could not remember sequences without the music and other performers on hand. Other dancers were crystal clear and wonderfully helpful. Maria Tallchief comes to mind and the session when she explained her timing of an adagio passage, stating "The walking around is ad lib. but I have to hit the arabesque on the high F sharp." She had the gift of perfect pitch as well as total awareness of every movement.

Some choreographers work in a fluid way leaving the movements in a roughly sketched state for some time – a disconcerting situation for both dancers and notator. In some instances a ballet is composed before it is set to music with the result that changes in timing as well as in movement will subsequently need to be made in the score. In the case of reconstructions, work on a score may be held up until differences of opinion have been resolved on what the movements should be. When a balletmaster forgets a sequence, that section may have to remain unfinished until he has been able to consult the choreographer or other knowledgeable sources.

The task of recording a ballet is today tremendously facilitated thanks to modern technology, to far greater cooperation on the part of company members, directors and dancers, and in some instances, to notators being attached to particular companies on a full-time salary basis.

As the decades go by and dance notation becomes more and more accepted as part of the whole dance scene, the trail-blazing and frustrations of the early pioneers in trying to create a dance literature will all have been worth while.

SIXTEEN

Public acceptance of notation

Some systems of dance notation had their day and are no longer 'alive.' In this century, despite the Stepanov system's usefulness in the reconstruction of full-length classical ballets, there was no rush to study the system and put it to daily use. Why? Without question its lack of use lay not in the nature of the notation system itself, but in man's natural resistance to change, a reluctance to depart from the habitual modus vivendi. 'But it has always been done this way' could be the byword of the ballet world. Outsiders, particularly musicians, see how practical and logical would be the full use of a system of movement notation. Dancers, however, are by nature physical people who took up the art because of an urge to move rather than to think. 'Feel, don't think. Don't analyse. Don't ask questions, just experience the movement.' Such admonitions have been given to generations of students by many ballet teachers. In commercial styles of dance, in tap, acrobatics and jazz, emphasis has been on the doing, not on any deep investigation into what actually occurs in the movements. On the other hand, modern dance developments in this century have sprung from people concerned with the roots of movement and with movement ideas. These new concerns have resulted in movement exploration, in discussion and verbalization of what happens in movement. Thus it is that modern dance has contributed to the development of the more highly evolved systems of notation, while the ballet world has gravitated to systems geared specifically to the ballet 'language'. Setting aside any replacement of notation by modern tech-nology, let us look at how notation has fared in its acceptance by the general public, the world concerned with movement and dance.

To cite my own experience, I stumbled on notation at an early age, met a few fellow enthusiasts and co-founded the Dance Notation Bureau in New York in 1940. It was into a notationless dance scene that the Dance Notation Bureau was born. The idea of bothering with notation was laughed at, scorned – it was ridiculous! Now, in 1984, there is no question but that notation is acknowledged as a serious subject and a much needed tool. But despite this major change in attitude, notation is still used by only a handful of people in dance and movement fields. Let us look into the reasons why and follow the stages in progression from 1940 to the present day. As human nature does not change, it may be of interest to delve further back and note some attitudes from the past which have their counterpart today.

Comments by the uninitiated

As we know, Noverre had no use for notation.[1] There were others. Francis Peacock, a dance teacher in Aberdeen, in his 1805 book, criticises the neglect of 'Choreography' (Feuillet's system), regretting that the art of writing down dance characters was discontinued without the substitution of a better contrivance.[2] He quotes from the famous dance master Gallini, who, having no use for (or knowledge of) notation, made the following statement: 'It may, indeed, be easily allowed that the track, or figure of a dance, may be determined by written or engraved lines, but those lines will necessarily appear so perplexing, so intricate, so difficult, if not impossible, to seize, in the various relations, that they are only fit to disgust and discourage, without the possibility of their conveying a satisfactory or retainable instruction. Then it is, that the article on Choreography, in the French Encyclopaedia, is universally exploded as unintelligible and useless, though nothing more than an elementary indication of the art, and an explanation, much as it is, of some of the technical terms of it.' Peacock comments: 'These observations respecting Choreography appear to me so arbitrary, and the difficulties pointed out so much exaggerated, that I must beg leave to say, I cannot acquiesce in them.'[3]

Gallini passed judgment, it appears, on the basic explanations given in the Encyclopaedia. Present-day researchers and students can attest that the Feuillet system in itself is not difficult and does not take long to master. The difficulty lies in what the notation did *not* include, if one is striving for a faithful revival of the dance style of the period.

Petipa puts forward a point of view echoed even today. In 1892 he wrote:

I am a great admirer of all fine things, but not at all of skeletons, which have no place in the choreographic art. It is possible to find balletmasters who have the patience to revive previously produced dances with the help of the method of Messrs. Thoinot Arbeau, Feuillet, Pecours, St-Léon, Zorn, Stepanov and others. . . ., but I consider it extremely difficult to show in one and the same measure, position of the arms, head, pelvis, upper part of the hips, movements of the knees, torso, turns of the body, flexion and extension of the shoulders, hands, wrists, and so forth.

The talented balletmaster, reviving earlier ballets, will compose dances in conformity with his own fancy, his talent and the tastes of the public of his own time, and will not come to lose his time and effort copying what was done by others long before. We note that in *La Fille mal gardée* Mr Taglioni changed all the previous dances, and Mr Hertel composed new music, and so too do I, without exception, every time I revive an old ballet. And then, each dancer of course performs these dances depending on her manner and capabilities.[4]

This attitude reinforces the argument for notation, and *La Fille mal gardée* is very much a case in point. Paul Taglioni produced an entirely new version of this ballet in Berlin in 1864 with a completely new score. Twenty years later Petipa used this music to rechoreograph the ballet in St Petersburg, possibly still retaining elements of Dauberval's original narrative action. Dauberval's choreography, however, was replaced, forgotten and lost forever. Had it been notated, a gem from the past would have been preserved.[5]

A school of thought which advocates the desirability of constant change must consider the great loss if the heritage from the past is not kept alive by being secured in notated form. Dance would be choreographically shallow-rooted and audiences would see only works currently in vogue. The recording of ballets does not preclude experimentation, innovation, transient styles and ideas, when these are wanted.

Closer to our own time, in 1939, Lincoln Kirstein, now director of the New York City Ballet, wrote:

> The invention of systems to preserve dance steps have, since the early 18th century, shared a startling similarity. All the books contain interesting prefatory remarks on the structure of dancing. The graphs presented vary in fullness from the mere bird's eye scratch-track of Feuillet to the more musical and inclusive stenochoreography of Saint-Léon and Stepanov, but all are logically conceived and invitingly rendered, each equipped with provocative diagrams calculated to fascinate the speculative processes of a chess champion. And from a practical point of view, for work in determining the essential nature of old dances with any objective authority, they are equally useless. The systems, each of which may hold some slight improvement over its predecessor, are so difficult to decipher, even to initial mastery of their alphabet, that when a student approaches the problem of putting the letters together, or finally fitting the phrases to music, he feels triumphant if he can decipher even a single short solo enchaînement. An analysis of style is not attempted, and the problem of combining solo variations with a corps de ballet to provide a chart of an entire ballet movement reduces the complexity of the problem to the apoplectic. . . .[6]

It is interesting to note that students with far lesser mental powers than Mr Kirstein have mastered Zorn notation, Stepanov, and others, and have produced interesting and valuable research based on these systems. Children grasp Labanotation rapidly. Coping with group formations and relationships produced no apoplectic results when 11–13 year olds, the Junior Dansnotators, read and learned the first movement of Balanchine's *Symphony in C* from the Labanotation score. This classroom experience vastly increased their understanding, appreciation and enjoyment of the work.

Inventors' comments on other systems

Such examples of specific adverse criticism of notation by individuals who have no experience with any system of notation are not unusual. But what of inventors of systems of notation commenting on systems other than their own? Many inventors include some historical background in their books and present a brief outline of some of the other systems. Often specific weaknesses are cited to illustrate the impracticality of other systems. In these comments the writers reveal a lack of understanding of, let alone experience in, the system in question. In connection with the Laban system, for example, a common lack of understanding involves a fact which a student learns within the first lesson: the movement interpretation of a long symbol which, let us say, extends over four beats of music. When I first met Leonide Massine in 1957 and we discussed the Stepanov and Laban systems, he took the length of the symbol to mean the length of time a position is held, instead of the length of time taken to move to the stated point in space.[7] Pierre Conté made exactly the same mistake in criticizing the Laban system at our meeting in 1956.[8] It is not enough to read the opening chapters explaining a system, one must actually use the system, read and write passages and have these checked. Walter Paul Misslitz was at least honest in stating plainly that the Laban system did not appeal to him, hence his desire to evolve another way – a system based on stick figures. This question of personal appeal cannot be overlooked. For whatever reason, people do react favourably or unfavourably to numbers, to stick figures, to oddly shaped symbols, etc., perhaps just a 'gut' reaction, but enough to make them throw down one book and pick up another.

Despite lack of sufficient knowledge of them, at least these inventors did inform their readers of the existence of other systems. Other present day inventors are not so informative, however; their textbooks are written as though no other systems exist and the system being presented has alone accomplished all that is needed in the field.

The dance profession – teachers, dancers

It is a rare teacher who, already established with a flourishing school, will find, nay *make*, the time to study a system of notation and put it to practical use. Such a teacher must have sufficient vision to foresee the advantages which such an investment of time and energy will bring. Most teachers and dancers just do not have time. But time is not the only factor, particularly with teachers. There is a natural resistance to changing their way of functioning. Introduction of notation does not basically change the physical dance class, but introduction of books, references to notated dances, building up a library – all the aspects which are part and parcel of literate dance, seem just that 'extra' which is too much to undertake.

There is another factor related to the resistance to change: the psychological block at having to 'go back to school' and start at square one in a subject so closely related to their main subject. This reluctance may stem from a fear of appearing stupid, of not knowing something which one ought to know. If, however, new information about movement is revealed – perhaps a new look at an old idea, or an aid in teaching a specific point – the experience can be very enriching and rewarding. Each dance discipline has inherited a particular 'language' and a way of looking at movement. Changes in terminology, though clearly an improvement, may not be welcome or understood and analysis of movement may be resisted for fear that it will 'kill' a feeling for dance. A different way of looking at and relating to movement may not be welcome. For example, a sensitive ballet teacher, who had been a lovely dancer in her time, was observing a series of Language of Dance classes held for a group of young teacher-trainees. Notation symbols were being used as visual aids for the teaching of young children. The movements included various rhythms, different forms of galops and skips, variations in direction, dynamics, etc. At the conclusion of the course, the visiting teacher commented: 'This has all been great fun, but I don't see what it has to do with dance!'

The dance profession – choreographers

Choreographers are so accustomed to working without notation, be it in rehearsing an older work or in creating a new one, that it has been difficult for them to adjust to the idea of having an amanuensis on hand, a choreographic secretary who is at their beck and call to serve all their choreographic needs. There have been many amusing, sad, and aggravating experiences as a result of the arrival of this strange new creature, a dance notator.

Choreographers vary enormously in their way of working, ranging from Martha Graham who would send everyone including the clock out of the room while she was giving 'birth' to new movement ideas to George Balanchine who did not mind who was sitting watching. Having arranged for a notator to attend rehearsals, what happened then? The pioneer notators were duly instructed that they must in no way interrupt the rehearsal. Els Grelinger, one of the first Labanotators trained, tells of being ushered on her first day with the Graham company into a corner of the studio where she could neither see clearly what was happening nor hear the verbal instructions and comments through which she could gain an insight into the intentions and movement motivations of the choreographer.

Choreographers and ballet-masters have not understood the degree to which a notator needs to be 'put in the picture'. This expression is exactly right for such circumstances; there is so much information which the notator needs to know, starting with such simple things as the names of the dancers, the parts they are playing (if it is a story ballet), use of props which may not yet have materialized, and so on. As notator for the New York City Ballet, I was accorded great courtesy and helpfulness by Balanchine outside of rehearsal, but in the studio he would completely forget I was there, standing in front of me so that I could not see, and inventing new material for forgotten sequences, oblivious of the fact that I was sitting there, score open, with the missing information in hand. How, diplomatically, could I remind him of this fact? Balanchine usually welcomed the reminder, but such was not the case with all choreographers. It was not unusual for a choreographer to set material one day and then the next day yell at the dancers 'What *are* you doing? I never showed you that!' The period of creativity can be fraught with emotional intensity, and to have on hand in written form proof of what had, in fact, been choreographed the previous day appeared to limit the choreographer's accustomed freedom to change his mind, hence the emergence of a negative attitude toward the notation. Later on choreographers became used to their notator-secretaries and would casually ask 'Just what was it I set for this part last week?'

An awkward situation could emerge from a simple misunderstanding. While I was notating for the Graham company, one day, during Graham's absence, the dancers took the usual five minute break after a period of hard

137

work. Stuart Hodes, then in the company, lit a cigarette and came over to see what I had been doing. He was sitting beside me asking questions when Graham swept in. She took one look at the scene and angrily accused me of interrupting the rehearsal. There was no question of any explanation. I was the scullery maid who had overstepped the mark.

The degree to which dancers themselves did not understand the notating process was illustrated during one modern dance rehearsal when, after I had notated the various step patterns, turns, etc. for two hours, the director said 'O.K. Now let's see it full out!' At this point a transformation took place, jumps appeared, rolling on the floor, all manner of movements not in the least resembling what I had written. The dancers had been 'marking' the sequences to save energy. I was destroyed and could do no more work that day. Ballet does not pose quite the same problem as there is a hand 'language' for marking certain steps – for example a certain twiddle of the finger represents a pirouette being marked and not performed. Many steps can be recognized even when done at minimum level, but modern dance explores the new and unusual, and such guessing is impossible.

In the notation of *Beau Danube*, the Street Dancer's first variation occurs in a slightly different form in the Finale. With my head buried writing quick notes, I did not hear Massine instruct the pianist and dancers to switch to the later section. Seeing the material slightly changed, I assumed that it was still the earlier scene and that I had been in error, or that Massine had changed his mind, so out came the eraser. Much time was wasted before I sorted it out. One word from Massine, the pianist, or someone else to check that I knew what was happening would have helped tremendously.

The minor ordeals notators suffered in the early days were teething troubles that were to be expected. Gradually choreographers found out how useful the notator could be to them, that they had on hand a willing servant, that every change they might wish to make would be made. The idea that the notation would 'imprison' them, would cut off their option to make changes, gradually disappeared. In some cases unused movement ideas were collected for possible future reference. In the early years of the Dance Notation Bureau members had opportunities to record works by Doris Humphrey, doing so gratis in the belief that whenever the opportunity arose such great choreography should be captured. Humphrey gave permission, at first, without enthusiasm; appreciation came later. Looking back over the years one can see that the process of education was – and still is – slow. To take a simple example. Doris Humphrey's *Variations and Conclusions* from *New Dance* begins with the group running around in a circle. It doesn't matter which foot they start with as long as all are the same. At the time the work was notated the right foot was used. A year later she retaught the dance and began with the left foot. Someone spotted this discrepancy and mentioned it. The verdict came without hesitation – the notation was wrong! In all such instances it was always the notation which was at fault. But gradually this picture changed. Humphrey would ask the notator for details she had forgotten. Shortly before her death she made a statement which made all our work worth while. On being handed the score of the latest of her works to have been recorded, she said: 'Now my dances are no longer legend, they are history.'

Notation eventually gained so much in status that Antony Tudor, for example, would not start a rehearsal without the notator Muriel Topaz being present, and if he had to be late, would instruct her to take the rehearsal, cleaning up details according to the score. Gradually practical use began to be made of scores and the work of the notator appreciated and enjoyed.

When *Kiss Me Kate!*, the first Broadway show to be notated, was produced in London early in 1951, choreographer Hanya Holm was able to sit back while I as her assistant taught the dancers their parts in record time from the notated score, no time being wasted in trying to remember what happened, how one dancer got from point A to point B, etc. A rehearsal of the Furies in Balanchine's *Orpheus* was expedited some years later through the dance score, particularly through distributing copies of the floor plans which any dancer can read at once. The ballet mistress on hand, Vida Brown, was delighted. Another typical instance of use of notation for the New York City Ballet occurred when Yvonne Mounsey had suddenly to learn the part of the chief Bacchante at very short notice. In the hallway of the New York City Center theatre I rehearsed her from the score just before the ballet began – there was no one else around who knew the part.

There are many similar stories to be told by the many Benesh notators who have worked with leading ballet companies and choreographers. In a moment of graciousness Rudolf Benesh acknowledged to me how much the acceptance which his system received was owed to the pioneer work done by myself and the other members of the Dance Notation Bureau.

Recording of examination syllabuses

For examinations in music or drama the material to be performed by the candidate is printed and distributed. The candidate is thus examined on how the particular material is performed. Dance examination syllabi are taught through personal demonstration to hundreds of teachers who learn the sequences and receive word notes. It is inevitable that before long there exists a variety of different 'correct' versions. Word descriptions, as history has taught us, allow far too much leeway. It is particularly difficult for overseas teachers and candidates to know what is wanted, since they cannot easily come to the fountainhead for personal instruction and correction.

Two main areas of difficulty exist in connection with dance examinations. A student preparing for an examination may seek final 'polishing' and correction of details by taking coaching from an authority. An unfortunate psychological as well as physical adjustment must take place when the student discovers during such coaching sessions that what was previously learned as correct performance is now pronounced wrong. The situation is compounded when the examiner finds further fault, indicating in the report that yet another version is considered correct. Practical use of dance notation in connection with examination syllabuses is the obvious answer. What is to be performed for an examination must be universally established in black and white. But who is to decide which version is to be selected as the correct one? The existence of personal preferences among the authorities delays such decision making. Candidates are reassured that no one will ever be failed on such minor differences, yet exam reports reveal such failures. The avoidance of selecting one version as the standard for examination purposes, to be recorded and published, is based on a lack of understanding of the use of notation. The authorities ask: 'Will not such specific pinning down of movement cause an undesirable rigidity? The children or students must have leeway, 'breathing space' within which to express themselves in performing the movement sequences.' What needs to be understood is that the notated version should be the standard version from which minor departures may take place to suit the line, build or personality of the student. In a moment of enthusiasm while performing, the dancer might exaggerate a movement in one way or another, yet the movement may be stylistically correct and artistically acceptable. It is up to the examiner to discern between actual changes in the basic material and variations resulting from the act of dancing. As notation comes more into use, dance examinations will follow more the lines of music and drama exams in which there is much leeway for personal interpretation even when the score or script is followed faithfully.

One further development is needed in use of notation in connection with dance syllabuses. When students can read the notated material but the teacher cannot, there may come the awkward moment when the students are aware that the teacher is drifting away from what was established in the notation. It is only human that slight changes will take place, and usually without the teacher being aware of them. Over the years such 'drift' can increase to a degree which could cause real concern. Is the notation now 'wrong'? Is the teacher 'wrong?' If the students mention the discrepancies, how will the teacher react? Notation imposes a discipline common in drama and music, but not yet in dance, and some teachers feel it entails an undesirable restriction. Of course when examinations are not at issue, dance teachers can take far greater freedom in tailoring dance material to suit the needs of their students.

Public impression of notators at work

When is a notation system to be blamed for an error, and when the notator or the person using it? It is often difficult for an outsider to know the difference between the potential of a system and the skill of its user. Someone is seen reading a score, painfully picking out a few movements, or a notator is seen at a rehearsal struggling to write down a sequence. If such struggling to read or write were observed in relation to ordinary books, or to a music score, the observer would know that the individual concerned had not had enough training or experience for the task. But when dance notation is concerned, lack of fluency is blamed on the system being used. The work of an enthusiastic beginner student of one system is compared with that of a graduate of a two year full-time training course in another. Again, in the comparison, it is the system that is given the credit or discredit, not the situation or the individuals.

A further stumbling block to the general public's assessment of the relative merits of different notation systems lies in the salesmanship ability (or lack of it) on the part of persons publicizing and promoting a system. To cite an example, an experienced user of one particular system is by nature a modest perfectionist. When interviewed by a journalist about the system, this notator made statements indicating that progress was being made but much work still remained to be done particularly in relation to viewing and analysing movement. Such statements are realistic but not good propaganda. Grandiose claims make good publicity and statements made in this field are not easy to prove. At the time one system was launched, it was announced as being complete, perfect, and capable of recording every kind of movement in fine detail. In fact, during the subsequent years much modification, additions and improvements in that system have taken place and practitioners of it know that all is not yet solved. A 1975 interview with leading exponents of the Benesh, Laban and Eshkol-Wachmann systems revealed far more about the personalities of the individuals and their promotional abilities than concrete facts concerning the systems. To cite an example, in answer to a question concerning the possibility of having only one system of notation in the future, two quite different kinds of answers were given. The one: 'One universal system will inevitably be accepted and used as already exists in the professional dance world.'* The other: 'I suppose it might be simpler if there were one system . . . but I don't know whether this will come to be. Each system seems to have developed for a particular reason and many look at movement from different points of view. These points of view should be taken into consideration as we study movement in all its forms. A danger is always to become too narrow in our thinking.'[9] Reticence, modesty, reluctance to make any claims which have not personally been experienced give the impression that the system in question is undeveloped, still feeling its way, possibly unsuccessful in practice, whereas in fact that system stands up as well as any other in how it functions and what it has achieved.

Such very different approaches to promotion of notation 'wares' make it difficult for the general public to know what to believe. Comparison between systems is not easy. Who wants to undertake such a study? And how deeply must one delve, how much experience must one have in the use of various systems to be in a position to judge their relative merits? Each year sees more people becoming bi-lingual, that is, familiar with more than one system. Tri-lingual people are appearing, and there are a very few who are conversant with more than three systems. The study of notation is comparable to the study of languages. If it is too late to establish one universal movement language (as would be highly desirable), then, when the incentive is there and the effort rewarding, learning to read, if not also to write, another notation system is not hard and can be taken in one's stride.

For an evaluation of the relative merits of different contemporary 'live' systems, ask those who are tri- or multi-lingual. When an individual praises

---

*More than one system is employed in the professional dance world.

one particular system to the skies and condemns another to the garbage heap, ask with whom the speaker studied each system, for how long, and which scores he has read or written. It is most probable that the speaker has never studied any system but has some personal reason for partisanship.

Changes in general attitude

Was it because he did not take the subject seriously that Philip Richardson, editor of the *Dancing Times*, was prompted to conclude a report on a demonstration of the Laban system, given by Albrecht Knust in the early 1930s, with the suggestion that a competition should be held to find a British system of dance notation?[10] He seemed not to be concerned with the merits of the Laban system but with the fact that it was foreign and that a native grown system would be preferable. Let us hope the world is now small enough so that we no longer care about the nationality of the man who builds a better mousetrap!

Many people in the early days refused to believe in or accept a notation system until there was proof that it was capable of recording everything, every detail. When indeed the Laban system had developed to that high stage of comprehensibility, it was then dismissed as being too complicated! We were not alone in this experience. The Russian historian, Yuri Bakhrushin, told of a meeting with Srbui Lissitzian at which they discussed her system of movement notation. He wrote: 'I remember how I sat with her at the school, drinking tea and discussing her book. I asked her could she note down how I am drinking tea at the moment. She answered that she is able to write it down with all the details and most exactly. Well, said I, then this system is no good for us. We don't need such details.'[11] At that time the Russians considered film the only way to 'fix' dance. However, by 1980 Russia was giving serious consideration to the need to preserve dance through notation and to arranging conferences with leading exponents of the different systems.

And so the dance world, with surprising reluctance, is coming to see the value of notation. The former attitude of scorn mellowed over the years to the point where dance people acknowledged the value of notation, though individuals still declared that it was 'not for them'. This attitude in turn gradually changed to admission that they 'ought to learn it, but are too old or haven't time'. Later more and more individuals began talk of definite plans to study, and a few actually to say 'when can I start?' With each passing year the notating of more works, the publication of more books, and the gradual increase in the number of people who are literate in dance and excited about the advantages and potential of dance notation, have all led to a change in the general attitude toward notation.

SEVENTEEN

Revivals – the dance director

Just as notating movement is too often thought of as the equivalent of writing a grocery list, so bringing a ballet back to life from the notated score is often thought of as comparable to a stenographer reading back to the boss the wording of a letter just dictated. To get a clearer idea of what the notation process should be, let us turn back to Noverre who, in his *Letters on Dancing*, wrote: 'Dancing is possessed of all the advantages of a beautiful language, yet it is not sufficient to know the language alone. But when a man of genius arranges the letters to form words and connects the words to form sentences it will cease to be dumb; it will speak with both strength and energy.'[1] Noverre had no use for notation and thus could not have foreseen the development of what we mean by 'The Language of Dance'. Notation is merely a means of capturing on paper the expression, the sense, the purport of this language. Once captured these then have to be transformed back into living dance, and this is where the dance director succeeds or fails. The dance director must bring the greatest command of the language to bear on the translation of symbols back into movement. If the choreography has been analysed correctly, recorded correctly, then, in Noverre's words, it will speak with both strength and energy.

Language in movement involves more than just dealing with the 'nouns' of static positions, or with copying a skeleton outline of a movement. Evolution of the process of using notation has advanced from an aide memoire to a rich means of communication. The movement and dance worlds are just beginning to discover that an intuitive understanding of and feeling for movement can actually be analysed and verbalized without being destroyed. Dance is not 'killed' by being notated. In the past few decades there has been a breakthrough to a richer, deeper understanding of what occurs in movement and its significance, and how this can be experienced, used, and above all communicated to others. Notation is one form of this communication. When the opportunity arises, a skilled notator can choose with great care how to express a movement on paper. This selection is comparable to that of a writer working and reworking a phrase of prose, thoughtfully selecting the right words to achieve a particular effect. In contrast, some writing has to take the form of brief, hurried notes. There are many degrees of complexity and many purposes, all of which exist also in the writing of movement. This chapter is concerned with the reverse process, the recreating of dance from the symbols on the page. But that process is vitally dependent on what has been written, the form and content of the notation.

The prime motive for recording dance has, up to now, been to preserve it, be it a short dance or a full ballet. Recording for educational and research purposes is a recent development, only just beginning to come into its own.

Centuries ago dances were recorded and published like sheet music, making the latest compositions of eminent dance masters available to the educated. These masters were at hand to instruct in the intricacies of how to perform the established vocabulary of steps. Today choreographic works are notated for future preservation, but also for immediate reconstruction. The advent of notators working with ballet companies has made many dance directors and choreographers aware of the advantages of having a score at hand, indeed, even of having the notator present as a choreographic secretary to read back sections where needed.

Reference to scores covers the gamut from an immediate reminder of what was choreographed yesterday to the dusting off of a score after ten years or more to revive a work already forgotten. How does the process work? Because reconstruction from notation is still so new, it can be beset with pitfalls.

State of the score

The state of the score is of utmost importance. Was the work accurately recorded? Did the notator understand the movement? Was the choreographer's intent faithfully captured, not just the framework of what the dancers made of it? Did the copyist of the score make any glaring errors which could affect the result? Was the score checked for movement sense? There is much latitude regarding the condition of a score. Let us assume that a good score has been produced. How does the work fare in the process of reproduction?

There are two factors to be considered: the work itself, the choreographic composition, comparable to the music score, and the process of teaching the movements to a company of dancers. Here direct comparison with an orchestra rehearsing a musical work breaks down. The first difference is obvious. Musicians can read music while most dancers cannot read dance. Musicians learn music with and through the written score; it is an integral part of their study and their subsequent work. They know how to handle notation; it is not a remote, colourless 'foreign language' to them. The percentage of dancers educated to be literate in dance is still so small we can take as a basic premise that most are not.

The other big difference between rehearsing a musical work and a dance work is that a musician can perform while reading a music score. The dancer has to commit everything to physical memory. In the process of learning a dance, a page of the score is often held in the hands; to be free of this limitation some fanciful gadgets have been designed such as a 'stand' hung from the neck and tied to the waist to support the score, thereby leaving both arms free to move (Fig. 17.1). The usual method is to mark through a phrase, often indicating the movement with the hands (much as a ballet teacher will 'hand dance' a ballet enchaînement), and then, leaving the paper, try the movement fully in the dance area.

144

Fig. 17.1

Since dancers don't read, someone must show them what to do. Who is this 'someone'? Is it the notator who wrote the score and is therefore familiar with the work? Is it someone who danced in the work and who is using the score as a memory aid? Is it a reader who does not know the work but who has access to a film or video to gain an immediate impression of a previous rendition of the work? Let us take the case where the reconstructor is none of these but is reviving the work 'cold', with no knowledge even of the choreographic style. Such a person is the dance equivalent of an orchestra conductor, but, as we have already seen, the responsibility is even greater, since most of the members of his 'orchestra' – the dance company – cannot read and movement is more complex than music. How does he proceed?

A professional level score should contain background information on the work. If the results of the revival are to come close to the choreographer's original concept, it is important for a dance director not familiar with the style and point of view of the choreographer, to undertake research. The day may come when a dance director will have established such a good artistic reputation that the public will be interested in his personal interpretation of a known work. This personal slant is accepted in music, and is quite common in the theatre where, for example, Shakespeare's plays are produced in very modern, off-beat ways without a word of the text having been changed. To some degree we see this personal influence in productions of the ballet classics. Here much liberty is taken with the mise-en-scène, and even with certain standard variations which may be modified or changed completely. But our concern is not with the much mutilated 'classics', but with a well-constructed, substantial choreographic piece which is not to be distorted, intentionally or otherwise.

Replica or re-creation?

Before examining the process, let us consider the first hurdle the reconstructor faces. Is the work to be as much as possible a replica of the work originally produced by the choreographer, looking just as it looked when first readied for the stage? Or is the dance director to be allowed the authority of the orchestra conductor in bringing something of his own style and taste to the work? For my own first efforts in reconstructing from notated scores, modesty dictated that I should show only what the movements were and should in no way interpret or colour them. At times this attitude was the right one, as the choreographer was on hand and only wanted a choreographic secretary; on the other hand it gave the impression that the consequent lack of interpretation and colour was the result of the notation and not of my modesty. Once the reconstructor has sole responsibility, it is another matter: a re-creative element must enter into the operation. It is interesting, incidentally, to observe how critics react to notation. A ballet may be revived poorly and the blame placed on the person who did the revival. But if it is known that notation was used, the notation is blamed, not the individual person and his artistic limitations. No one blames music notation because Verdi's Requiem is poorly rendered. The dance director is assuming an equivalent role to that of the orchestra conductor, striving to be faithful to the spirit of the work, while needing to make certain decisions based on his own artistic sense.

Thus the dance director arms himself with as much background information as possible before rehearsals start. Just as the orchestra conductor spends weeks getting to know and understand an unfamiliar work, so does the dance director. He will try out the dance sequences with the music until he has found a kinetic logic which fits the context.

The terms 'reconstruction' and 'revival' have been used in connection with mounting a dance work from a score. Perhaps the choice of term used is a minor matter, but 'reconstruction' seems to put the emphasis on the structure of the work; 'reproduced' suggests that some changes have been made, while the word 'revival' itself suggests the revitalization of the work, which is obviously the result desired – the work must 'come to life'.

And what are the choreographer's reactions when he sees the results of such revivals? Reactions have ranged from delight to horror. First, it must be realised that choreographers are not always happy with the results when they and their dance assistants personally teach a work to another company. Consider Balanchine's dissatisfaction over the performance by the Royal Danish Ballet of his ballet *Concerto Barocco* in 1954.[2] His choreography is bound to take on another 'look' when performed by a company with such a definite style as that of the Danes, in contrast to the unique style of his own New York City Ballet. In music such differences between orchestras in different countries are known, understood and expected.

It is not only the choreographer who wants a revived work to have the same look as the original performance, audiences harbour cherished memories of how a work was and therefore how it now should be. The interpretation and style of original cast members are still held lovingly in the viewer's mind's eye. But the training of dancers has changed, the world has changed, fashions and taste have changed, we are not seeing dance today with the same eyes. Even the most faithful revival will inevitably have a different 'look'. We cannot blame the dance director if there is a difference and certainly not blame the score.

From symbol to movement

Assuming that the style of movement is foreign to the dance director, how does he go about interpreting what is written? First, an overall glance at the score gives an idea of the density of movement, that is, movements of isolated parts, or clusters of many parts moving at once. This first glance tells much about the duration and rhythm of the movements, and in what parts of the body the movement is concentrated during certain passages. A glance at the floor plans gives immediate information about location on stage and travelling. Thus an overall impression is gained.

Coordination with the music is vital. A quick 'sight-reading' of the dance while listening to the music is an essential first step. The precise movements may not yet be known, but a sense of the relationship of dance to music is gained. This coordination is important also in that a real 'trap' for the unwary is practising a movement at too slow a tempo, only to find later that it must be danced four times as fast. Nothing changes the feeling and impact of a movement more than changing its speed.

Now for the movement itself. The patterns which the dance notation symbols make on the page clearly indicate the movement phrases, these may be quite short, or of several measures in length. Reading a dance score is comparable to reading prose in that one does not read letters (symbols), but words (movement units) which are read as a whole, and, like language, usually read in groups rather than singly. Whatever the size of the first movement phrase or fragment of a phrase, it must be practised until a kinetic sense is established and the original movement is 'recaptured'. Once a phrase is understood physically the next phrase is tackled and the two joined. Then a third, and a fourth, and so on until a whole section is completed. It is important to find in the movement sentence the existing equivalent of commas, semicolons, and full stops. At the end of each phrase one must find the kernel of the next. Such a link usually exists and provides an energy flow which connects and 'conducts' movement sense from the one phrase to the next. However, a complete break may occur, a totally new movement idea arising unrelated to the previous one. If dynamic markings are included in the dance score, these will help in the translation from symbol to action, otherwise it is up to the reader to respond to the music and find appropriate dynamic qualities.

With the movement now revived, one has to go back and check each symbol to be sure that some guesswork did not enter the picture. Did some physical preferences influence the result? Each symbol must be searched for the truth it holds.

With the material resurrected, the dance director is ready to work with the dancers. What needs to be conveyed concurrently with the movement is the concept – the reason, the idea, the motivation – in short, what it is all about. The dancers' interest must be captured and their imaginations aroused to get the best results from their physical and artistic abilities.

Once the dance director has the material at his finger tips, the process of working with the dancers begins.

This preliminary work is crucial, for dancers receive initial impressions concerning movement phrases that are often hard to modify later on. The approach to presenting the work is important. There is no one 'right' way, but there are many wrong ways. The dancers should know what the piece is about and listen to the music. The story, mood, setting, whatever information can be imparted verbally should be presented briefly. Performers like to know the characters they are representing and the theme, situation or story, and this information helps them to approach the movements more intelligently. (Incidentally, strange as it seems there are choreographers who do not give this kind of information to the dancers.) It is wise to start with movement phrases which are technically difficult so that the dancers will have ample time to master them. This thematic material usually establishes the style of the piece for the dancers.

The dance director must have artistic sense and a point of view on the work he is reviving. There are many fine dancer/notator/rehearsers who lack only artistic integrity to be a fine dance director. The dance director need not have been a great dancer, but he must be able to evoke the desired movement from the dancers. There are other means than personal demonstration. Doris Humphrey choreographed some of her finest works despite crippling arthritis. Massine, Nijinska and others recreated their great works long after they personally could dance the steps. It is the ability to communicate with dancers and convey imagery that produces the movement. The dance director needs to know how to handle people, how to touch the wellsprings of the dancers he is working with.

Adaptation of material

When a choreographer remounts a ballet, he frequently makes changes. These may be made because he believes the work needs improving, or because the dancers either cannot master the movements or look wrong performing them. The dance director working from a score does not have this same basic right to change the choreography, but should he make adjustments so that the dancers look better in what they are doing? So that the movement retains the same impact, the same message, even though its shape or timing has been slightly altered? This is a very important point. An artistic performance *must* result; the work is a theatre piece and must be theatrically valid. Dancers can achieve a valid performance of the notated material if they sincerely strive for it. Too many principal dancers are accustomed to having material tailored to their personal style. They are not prepared to undertake the concentrated work involved in adhering to the 'script'. Musicians and singers will work for hours to master difficult passages. This is rare amongst dancers. Time is a factor, but mainly the mastering of difficult passages is not demanded of them. To what extent should dancers' limitations be accommodated? Dancers have to master the art of 'playing' the instrument they were born with; there is no 'Stradivarius body' for sale at any price. Therefore some consideration must be given to a dancer's physical limitations. In this respect comparison with music cannot be total. Most dance directors insist on adhering to the 'script' until the eleventh hour when minor adaptations of material may be made to satisfy the artistic demands.

Such adaption is for the moment only; the next revival will again be based on the score, going back to the original, rather than treating the adapted material as the prime source.

The work and the performance of the work

It is still difficult for many people to distinguish between a choreographic work and its performance. In the case of, let us say, *Les Sylphides*, the work is so well known that it is the performance which receives attention. With a new piece of choreography, in the absence of a written score to study, there is no way of separating the work from the performance. Only when a work becomes well known and has been seen performed by other companies can the separation be made.

Most choreographers feel that no one else can teach their works; only they should be in charge of the rehearsals, only they can bring the movement to life; only they can make the movement 'sing' and restore the 'poetry'. But the increasing use of notation is changing this picture, and instances have occurred of choreographers accepting another interpretation of their choreography as a valid expression of the piece. The day may come, as it has, for example, in reading poetry, when the choreographer recognizes another's 'reading' as being superior to his own.

A classic, a fine composition, a sound piece of choreographical structure will stand on its own feet and survive despite different interpretations. It is the works which are constructed on a particular dancer to show that individual to advantage that are more likely to lose value and meaning when performed by others.

As Ray Cook observes: 'It is of interest to note that for centuries musicologists and scholars of drama, literature and art have been analysing the classics to discover what their creators meant. We can safely assume that more has been found than was consciously included. This discovery and rediscovery in terms of a generation's values is what has kept the classics alive and interesting to us.'[3] His advice to dance directors is: 'Do not stop and look only at what the choreographer did, look all around his world. You are directing for people living now. Look at the past with eyes of the present, interpreting it for our world. You will bring these dances to life by bringing to them a contemporary point of view, a contemporary point of view based on the "original manuscript", not a copy – of a copy – of a copy. . . .'[4]

EIGHTEEN

Movement notation as a career

With the establishment of dance notation as a serious study, we see a younger generation some of whom have chosen a career in this field. Retired dancers or those sustaining chronic injuries have turned to notation to continue to be active in the field they love. Many Benesh graduates from the Institute of Choreology in London have found jobs as notators with ballet companies around the world. Labanotators trained in New York at the Dance Notation Bureau serve similar functions with ballet and modern dance companies. What are the job opportunities, the rewards, and the pitfalls of a career in notation?

Though some distinct differences exist we can turn to the field of music to make a comparison and gain perspective. What are the job possibilities in connection with music notation? The specialist in music notation is a member of a rare breed, which falls into three categories:

(*a*) those specializing in the historical development of music notation, and hence capable of transcribing obscure old manuscripts into standard music notation;

(*b*) those conversant with all the fine details in the use of standard music notation and hence employed by music publishing houses to correct and proofread scores for publication;

(*c*) those concerned with development of new methods of music notation to serve contemporary musical compositions and the development of future modes and styles.

Concentration on music notation for its own sake is comparatively rare since use of notation is an integral part of music study and the two are not separated. It is true that a few 'fine' musicians exist who cannot read a note of music, but these are mostly singers and jazz musicians who have succeeded in the music world through help from others or by nature of exceptional talent. There are instances of fine instrumentalists being refused jobs in orchestras because of their 'illiteracy', but such instances are rare; most musicians are of necessity literate, having learned to read the intricacies of music notation while learning to play. In contrast widespread integrated use of notation in teaching specific forms of movement is, generally speaking, still in the future.

Nicolai Sergeyev was the first professional dance notator in this century. From the scores recorded in Stepanov notation, which were largely his responsibility he reconstructed the great classical repertoire of the Petipa era for companies in western Europe. In these later years he did no more writing, but in addition to conducting rehearsals with the aid of the scores, he often gave daily ballet classes.

The first person to make a lifelong career in notation was Albrecht Knust. A student of Laban's in the 1920s, Knust became fascinated by the emerging notation ideas and so, when Laban's interest in the script was diverted to the exploration of new movement and theoretical fields, Knust picked up the threads, making further development of the system his life's work. His chief interest in dance was in movement choirs, large group dances for laymen. Knust taught Kinetography Laban (Labanotation), notated ballets, and wrote textbooks, his magnum opus being his eight-volume encyclopaedia on the subject.

Few Labanotation specialists have made notation their sole career. Stemming from modern dance backgrounds, the earlier generations were interested in movement and in notation as its tool. All pursued careers as performers and dance teachers while working with notation, enjoying the balance between physical activity and the more cerebral demands of notation. Many notators have not found it easy to be full-time scribes, not because of the system of notation used, but because of the fact that they became notators as a result of their love of movement; and for some the need to move, to dance, to teach, remains strong. The hours spent recording, copying, drafting, etc. need to be balanced by time spent reconstructing ballets, reviving movement sequences from the notation, thus involving the recreative excitement of the rehearsal situation. For the ex-dancer and the natural movement lover a mixed diet is not only desirable but often psychologically necessary. Other notators have less need for such physical activity.

The movement (dance) notator

What kind of person makes a good notator? Obviously an eye for movement and the ability to analyse and make quick decisions is essential. But the same person must also undertake the painstaking task of filling in detail later, checking the work, and preparing it for the final copy – the less glamorous side of the job, done at a desk and requiring immense patience and concentration. The rewards of this labour come when the score is put to use and proves to be first class.

What of non-dancers, non-movement specialists training to be notators? Such study is quite possible, and has indeed been done to a limited extent, but it is a longer undertaking because of the need to learn about movement, to understand the processes of movement in order to write them down. Dancers, gymnasts, etc. have spent considerable time observing movement and physically mastering specific patterns, and are therefore way ahead of a beginner in movement studies. However, training in one particular movement discipline can mean a lopsided view of movement and hence limitations in understanding other forms. If a range of movement styles is to be notated, the notation student must take comprehensive courses in movement analysis and observation to fill in neglected areas and to counteract bias and limited thinking resulting from earlier movement specialization.

To date it is the Laban and Benesh systems which have produced professional notators employed full time by dance companies. Basically the job is the same whichever system is used. The first notator to be employed on a permanent basis was Faith Worth, working for the Royal Ballet in London. It was soon discovered that one person could not possibly cope with all the repertoire, and gradually others were added. As scores were written, even though still incomplete, use was made of them in sending the notator to mount the work for another company, the choreographer following later for the final 'polishing up' rehearsals.

As more works were mounted from scores, more choreographers and companies came to see the value of using notation and the many ways in which the notator could expedite the whole rehearsal process: acting as an assistant to the choreographer, taking over rehearsals, and eliminating the time-consuming arguments about what came next, thus saving much valuable rehearsal time. It is this last point which John Field, now director of London Festival Ballet, has so often stressed – sheer economics will demand that notation be used, and that all dancers learn to read it.

Professional notating jobs have included recording choreographic works for ballet and modern dance companies, and also recording Broadway shows. Many other possibilities exist. At the Royal Academy of Dancing in London, Bryce Cobain, originally a Labanotator, was sent to the Benesh Institute to become bi-lingual for his job as resident notator at the Academy. The recording and publication of the R.A.D. examination syllabuses in both systems is well under way.

Use of notation in the medical field has taken several forms, that most directly involving straight notation being the work done with Benesh Notation by Julia McGuinness in recording for clinical records the physical postures and movement patterns of the disabled before and after treatment. Her initial work which was chiefly in the field of cerebral palsy research, led her to devise an introductory syllabus in the notation and consequently to give training courses to therapists and clinicians around the U.K. In the U.S.A. Valerie Sutton moved from her original concentration on notating ballet to sign language for the deaf; this work resulted in publication of a quarterly newspaper, *The Sign Writer*.

These developments emerged from a dance background as did the work in the U.S.A. of Irmgard Bartenieff, founder of the Laban-Bartenieff Institute of Movement Studies. The significant differences in her approach lay in her concentration on movement understanding and awareness based on Effort-Shape concepts stemming from Laban. The success of her early hospital work with polio victims was founded on her ability, through her use of imagery, to inspire the patients to experience the spatial shapes and dynamic qualities in their movement 'exercises'. As the scope of her work increased, the training programme she established concentrated on application of the knowledge to many different fields – anthropology, physiotherapy, psychology, and movement analysis of many kinds, including many aspects of human behavioural sciences at all ages of human development. Notation is included in the training programme, its use initially being as an aid to clarification. The degree of subsequent use varies according to each individual need. Combining her Laban knowledge and medical experience, Bartenieff evolved a series of movement sequences originally called Correctives and later renamed Fundamentals, which incorporate her teachings and through which all movers – dancers, athletes, the handicapped – can gain improved coordination and efficiency in movement.

The notator as researcher

More and more research fellowships and grants are being given to projects which include the use of notation to record important dance material, particularly traditional (ethnic) dances in danger of getting lost, or to projects involving comparative research in investigating forms of movement.

As was mentioned earlier in connection with analysing a tennis stroke, it is only when movements are converted into symbols on paper that a direct, detailed comparison can be made. In his industrial work with F. E. Lawrence, Rudolf Laban employed this techique, recording at one stage, the actions of three workers performing the same task. In the resulting notations it was possible to see where the movements varied and hence why one person was the most efficient and another the least.

It might be thought that slow motion movies and other technical devices developed to analyse movement would suffice for such research. Universities and research centres have equipment with which to measure frame by frame the changes in angle of a limb, such analysis being recorded as a graph on paper or fed into a computer. Eventually a recording on paper, a printout, is needed to make comparisons between different performances. In many cases such painstaking measurements may be necessary, in others a good movement notation would serve the purpose far better and far more quickly. For example, the timing and height of lifting the knee can be recorded rapidly on paper with movement notation; there is no need to involve computers and other expensive technology when pencil and paper can be taken anywhere. Because there are so many aims and purposes in the recording of movement, more than one method of analysis is obviously required. What is important is that those involved in the field know what other means exist and are not using a tractor where a bicycle will do.

Through the detailed recordings of ballet techniques such as those of Bournonville and Cecchetti one can pinpoint similarities and differences, achieving a tangible study of style, until now thought so elusive. Once the recording work is done, analysis and evaluation can take place. Wonderful projects lie ahead in the way of theses and dissertations based on such comparative research.

Translation into a contemporary notation of dances of the past makes an important part of our dance heritage more accessible to present-day students. Direct translations of such dances provides a framework; further research is needed to flesh out the 'bones' with specific performance details not given in the original notations.

Examples are Arbeau's *Orchesography* carefully annotated by Julia Sutton with Labanotation transcriptions by Mireille Backer, and Ingrid Brainard's selection of Renaissance dances published with historical background and the dances presented in Labanotation. Wendy Hilton's *Dance of Court & Theatre*, which contains much Labanotated material as well as valuable information on the Feuillet system, will spread understanding of the style of the Baroque period and provide an opportunity for personal classroom experience to add to the enrichment gained by seeing performances by professionals who have made Baroque dance their speciality.

Augmentation of teaching skills

Whatever the field of movement study, a teacher has more to offer the student when notation is used as an integral part of the learning process. Acquiring a sound understanding of movement as well as specific physical skills is facilitated through the visual aid of notation, through a sound analysis of movement and logical terminology, and through access to and use of recorded materials. In dance such materials may be technique exercises, short dances of many kinds, excerpts from the classics (modern or ballet), and full choreographic works. The teacher who has facility with notation and has a library of notated materials has much more to offer students. Access is thus possible to dance materials otherwise unavailable. Students will have some idea of the wealth of dance material even if there is not an opportunity to study each piece. Browsing in a music library gives music students some idea of the extent of music literature: names of composers and titles of works can become familiar to them. There is pleasure in leafing through written music, getting a general idea of what a piece is about. This same possibility is open to dance students as they become literate and have access to libraries of notated materials.

Teachers who use notation functionally have the satisfaction of knowing that they are offering their students an avenue to greater information on the subject of their studies. They know they are making use of contemporary developments and are combining current methods with the heritage from the past.

Further details on the benefits brought to teaching by practical use of notation are discussed in Chapter 19.

Production of scores, books

With few exceptions every music publishing house is staffed by musicians, that is, by people who studied music but did not become performers or teachers. For every stage in the preparation of a music score for publication, specialists are needed who know the correct orthography of music notation. And so it is in publication of dance. Each score or textbook needs to be checked, edited, and certainly proof read before it goes to the printer. To produce the final ink draft the autographer requires a special skill in penship, or, as in the case of Labanotation, use may be made of the IBM Selectric typewriter with the Labanotation element. Typographical errors creep into notation, as they do in music, books and newspapers. Proof reading requires a special eye; it is a gift that not all have. Editing, checking, autography and proof reading are skills each of which provides a different challenge and enjoyment. As more and more books and scores are published jobs will arise for people with these various skills.

154

NINETEEN

Use of notation in academic study

Until recently movement study of any kind was undertaken without incorporating movement notation. Books were not introduced into dance technique classes. Books about dance, books of photographs, stories of the ballets, biographies of famous dancers, surveys of the historical development of dance and books describing dance technique in words and figure drawings were looked at outside of dance class by students who happened to have a thirst for knowledge, or whose teachers encouraged or insisted on such additional education.

If this lack of interest and involvement with the literature of dance seems strange to a non-dance reader, it must be remembered that students study dance because they are in love with moving; they are physically oriented beings concerned entirely with the physical activity of dance, with mastering technique and gaining performance experience. It is only in recent years that dance materials, recorded technique and choreography have become available in notated form, the form in which this material can most readily be combined with the mastering of dance technique and dance style. It is also comparatively recent that emphasis has been based on an intellectual approach to dance in dance training. The 'Don't think, just do!' attitude is being phased out. Educational use of notated materials is now growing and many forward-looking educationalists see it as essential to any cognitive study of dance. How can notation contribute to physical education, to gymnastics, to dance, to all fields in which serious movement study and research are undertaken?

The Language of Dance

The Language of Dance approach to movement study, spearheaded by the Language of Dance Centre, features the written language of movement (movement notation) because it provides a means through which to explore the nature of dance. Knowledge of the elements of which all movement is comprised provides a sound basis for investigating and experiencing the many possible combinations and permutations. The process can be compared to a kitchen store-house in which are kept all the basic ingredients used in cooking. By understanding the nature and properties of each of these ingredients and how each functions in relation to other ingredients, how each may be affected by temperature and time, the would-be chef learns to produce the combined forms which result in a soufflé or a bouillabaisse. By recognizing and understanding the basic ingredients of movement, students can master the particular mixture demanded by their chosen style of dance as well as learn to observe and understand what ingredients produce the dances of different cultures.

The traditional holistic approach in teaching ballet, national and ethnic dances presents each of the combined forms (e.g. a glissade, an attitude grecque) as an entity, a finished product comparable to an instant cake mix. The vocabulary of a particular dance form may be learned physically with comparative ease, but too often it is later discovered that certain essential ingredients were never understood. If teachers have difficulty in explaining a movement it may be lack of appropriate terminology or of the ability verbally to analyse exactly what should happen in a movement pattern. Choreographers are often similarly hampered in getting across a particular movement idea. A mutual language is needed for universal movement communication. Just as seeing the words in written form helps in the understanding and mastering of a foreign language, so representation on paper of the movement ideas – the movement 'letters', 'words', 'phrases' and 'sentences' – captures and clarifies the facts, the essential ingredients. The time for this educational process to take place is, of course, not when the dancer is already trained, but in the early stages when each movement is first explored and concepts and physical coordinations mastered.

The teaching process in dance must still be based predominantly on a person-to-person transmission, the student observing and copying while listening to the verbal explanations. But immediate reference to the same material in notated form both clarifies and reinforces the understanding. Integrated use of notation during training clarifies the whole process by illustrating in an objective form the movement aspects under consideration.

It has been a common experience that, on reading through the notation of dance material just learned, students discover that though they had grasped the general pattern they had missed one or more particular points – perhaps the focus or the concept of the movement. What an untrained eye sees or does not see in movement can vary to a remarkable degree. What one person considers important another may not have observed at all. Nothing captures the dance structure as clearly as its transcription into symbols on paper. Here movement content and intent can be clearly stated. When written in detail in a sophisticated notation system, the manner of performance, the 'attack', the kinetic message can all be clearly captured to guide the performer. Though much notated material is at present at a memory-aid level, the level of description will rise and fluency develop as notation becomes an everyday tool.

Training the eye

In art appreciation and in training the artist emphasis is placed on developing the eye to see and perceive. The eye must learn to discriminate between what is of prime importance and what are the secondary, supporting features. The main shapes and relationships must be recognized and significant details appreciated for the part which they play in establishing balance, interest and particular effects. Movement requires a similar discipline in observing and evaluating what is taking place. The eye must be trained to know what to look for; a frame of reference is needed. A good system of movement notation provides codification of movement elements – an essential step in understanding the structure of any series of movements.

The purpose for which movement observation and evaluation is required will dictate the choice of parameters. A highly developed movement notation system can serve each specific need.

Comparative research

In the study of movement techniques such as swimming, golf or tennis, film often plays a major role. But even with the device of slow motion, comparison between two or more performances may be difficult unless each is carefully notated and the results can be placed side by side, thus revealing exactly where the differences lie.

The basic question in any research is – what does one need to find out? The answer to this question determines how the movement will be notated. Just as ten people looking at a movement sequence may look for and see different aspects, so the notation can focus on specific factors. A total recording in notation of everything about a movement sequence can be made but it is a time-consuming job, and one which is not undertaken unless it is needed. Usually the recording is geared to a specific purpose and extraneous information is omitted. In an acrobatic stunt it might be enough to state the overall action. For ballet a memory-aid outline may suffice. In the medical field the purpose might be to record the range of motion in a joint, while for ergonomics the energy pattern might be paramount. In drama the focus may be on the manner in which a gesture relates to another person.

Research in the field of movement studies is only just emerging. The advent of slow-motion movies revealed much that was previously inaccessible. Facts became known which aided the understanding of body mechanics. Other more sophisticated forms of visual recording have provided greater detail, and use of computers has facilitated storage of information and comparison of results. Printouts take the form of mathematical equations, of use to scientists but not readily applicable to the student, teacher, or general researcher concerned with movement. A research tool needs to be based on the common language of movement, specifically on its written form.

The written form of music has made possible rewarding investigations into music compositions; indeed it has made possible the whole field of musicology. What book about music does not contain illustrations in music notation of the points being made? Subtle differences in development of a motif and of harmonic progression are revealed through notated examples. Such pinpointing of facts which comprise the structure and style of a sequence in music is now taking place in dance.

The existence of libraries of notated dance techniques and notated choreographic works provides a tremendous potential for dance research.

This wealth of material and information concerning the art of dance can now be part of the total study of the dances of mankind and of dance as an art form. Reconstruction of dance scores may occur for the physical experience or for an evaluation of the content.

Research may take many forms and may range from in-depth investigation of a small selection of material to a wider survey of related works. An exploration of how much change had taken place in the Fairy Variations from the Prologue of *Sleeping Beauty* since they were recorded in Stepanov notation in the first decade of this century was undertaken by two students at The College of the Royal Academy of Dancing. The project included learning the Stepanov system, transcribing the dances from the scores in the Sergeyev collection into Labanotation, notating the variations as currently taught and comparing the results with the already published scores of the Sadler's Wells version of circa 1950. Research into Doris Humphrey's choreographic use of music has been the subject of a Ph.D. thesis by Stephanie Jordan, senior lecturer/head of dance at Crewe and Alsager College. This study made use of all available notated Humphrey scores as well as some films.

Classroom reconstruction provides the opportunity for personal knowledge of material not otherwise accessible. Research may centre on modes of dance training, some of which, like classical ballet, have roots extending back for centuries. On what are these techniques based? What does each 'school' stress, what range of movement does it encompass, how are its exercises structured? How do Asian techniques in dance training compare with western disciplines? Specific differences exist which can be studied through the notated form. A tremendous amount of material awaits the dedicated researcher. For example, to what extent has the personality or personal physique of the originator of a technique, for example, that of Martha Graham, affected the resulting vocabulary of movements and training program?

The number of Congress on Research in Dance (C.O.R.D.) research papers which include notation examples has noticeably increased over the years. Serious monographs now include notation in a way comparable to the use of music notation in any book or article on music style, structure or composition. Many academic theses now include notation to illustrate the arguments under discussion. Because the relevant material has been notated it was possible to discuss in detail fine points in the Bournonville style, as in my article in *Dance Chronicle*.[1]

Choreographic study

In the past many people have felt that dance exists only at the moment of performance. Only when a ballet is performed on stage with full costume and lighting does the choreography exist. The gradual accumulation of notated dance scores has provided the opportunity for people to experience the fact that a choreographic work exists in two forms, as does music – the recorded structure of a work (its written score), and the performance of that work (the bringing to life of the basic structure through the personal interpretation of a performing artist). This dual existence of a work has long been familiar in the field of music; now it is being recognized in dance.

Study of performance and comparison between particular interpretations of a work must take place by observing stage presentations or performances captured on film or video. Study of the work itself is best based on the notated form. If only a memory-aid score exists then only the fundamental facts captured can be studied – basic structure, use of rhythms, group formations, etc. If stylistic details have been included then a deeper, more three-dimensional study can be undertaken.

In the U.K., where dance has only comparatively recently been accepted as a subject in higher education, the focus is not on dance as a performing art but on its cultural and historical aspects. The consensus has been that for an academic discipline the inclusion of notation is essential. Whereas in the U.S.A. emphasis still is on the study of scores for performance, in the U.K. study of scores features the classroom physical experience of the material as a necessary part of understanding and evaluating the work as a whole and of comparison of its structure and content with other similar or dissimilar works.

Research into the content and structure of choreography is in its infancy. The works of a particular choreographer such as Humphrey or Balanchine may be studied through the scores, evaluation being made of the use of thematic material, modes of repetition, rhythm as it relates to the accompanying music, use of stage area and group formations. Or comparative research may focus on how a particular story, such as *The Prodigal Son*, or piece of music, such as *L'Après-midi d'un Faune*, or national dance material was used by different choreographers.

Notation as a teaching tool

As a teaching tool notation has four significant roles to play in dance education:

1. It sharpens the eye for movement observation and develops understanding of the structure of movements being learned. A system based on universal movement analysis also provides deeper investigation and awareness.
2. Movement notation may serve as a visual aid in understanding the organized structure of time (beats, measures, etc.) and of rhythms.
3. It serves as a memory aid from one class to the next.
4. It provides access to materials otherwise unattainable.

As an example of access to materials, courses on dance history can now include actual dances from different eras. Thanks to dance notation of past centuries as well as recent efforts to capture knowledge already swiftly fading away, enough examples exist to enrich dance history courses previously illustrated only through inconography. Such teaching has been spearheaded by educators such as Varina Verdin at East Sussex College of Higher Education (formerly Chelsea College).

Because the teaching of dance technique and of dances has traditionally been a purely physical activity without a blackboard or chart in the room, it is difficult for dancers to visualize how notation could be used without interrupting the flow of a movement class and causing the dancers to stand around and get cold. Many have the idea that notation would obviously be taught in a room with desks, blackboard, etc. Such equipment might be needed for a theory examination, but otherwise it is unnecessary. Before going into how notation can be incorporated into a dance class, let us consider the need for special classes focused on the mastering of technique in which each exercise is carefully taken apart, and the spatial pattern, use of the body, and the involvement of various muscles (the anatomical facts) are discussed, discovered in oneself and observed in others. Such classes are a much needed back-up to the usual continuous activity class. In such thought-provoking classes there is time for questions and discussions and for notation to play its part.

As was mentioned before, no one should learn to dance from a book, but when movement study includes specific exercises, composed sequences and excerpts from major works, as is so often the case in dance training, then having access to the material in written form can clarify important points which are often missed in the movement class. Availability of the material in notated form for study outside of class is a tremendous advantage to a student. It is a benefit enjoyed in other fields of study — why not in movement?

Reference at the end of a class to the notated form of a movement sequence just learned often reveals differences between the teacher or choreographer's intention and the student's understanding. Through reviewing the carefully notated material, the teacher can point out important technical and expressive details, particularly in relation to timing. One modern dance teacher became convinced of the value of dance notation through comparing her son's study of music with her daughter's study of dance. The son brought his music home to practise, but the daughter could not practise because she could not remember what the movements should be. Through notation dance students can take home the dance they are learning and, memories refreshed, can save class time by not having to go over half-forgotten material each week.

The educational use of notation should not start in college; notation has proved to be of particular value in teaching children. Introduction of the basic symbols at the time movement is first explored (usually at about the four or five-year level) clarifies differences and develops the basis of dance literacy without interfering with the usual physical activity of the dance class. Such a basic introduction comes before structured dance techniques such as ballet become the focus of the dance class. Children are introduced to the raw material of dance: the main directions, parts of the body, time values, parts of the room, basic forms of relating to one another, and so on — all of these being applied to creative exploration of dance. At the time each type of movement is explored, experienced physically and explained verbally, the notation symbol is also introduced, thus providing an additional visual aid to understanding and memorizing.

Apart from the general benefits which all teachers have experienced in using this visual aid, introduction of these symbols helps significantly in overcoming selfconsciousness. Children become so engrossed in interpreting the symbols, in focusing on something outside themselves, that they cease to feel exposed. This is particularly true of boys who initially tend to suffer from embarrassment. To them using symbols poses a challenge: it becomes a game, a secret code. Cut-out Labanotation symbols which can be arranged on the floor make it easy for young children to make up their own movement sequences and to discover the delight of improving on their first ideas by switching the symbols around. By dancing the patterns arranged by their neighbours, the children begin to develop a sense of which movements feel good, which sequences are interesting and which not. These are the early beginnings of choreography, an enjoyment of dance which includes creative thinking and evaluating in addition to physical activity.

By the time the children have advanced to mastering structured forms and concentrating on a specific technique, they already know a great deal about movement in general, the basic workings of notation, and how movements look in notated form. Rose Lorenz of Des Moines, Iowa, found that children mastered assemblés and sissonnes much more quickly from reading the symbols; leaving the ground from one foot or two and the appropriate landings were visually so obvious.

When personal demonstration accompanied by various forms of verbal explanation fails to get the movement idea across, notation symbols provide an additional visual aid by means of which the information can be imparted. Many instances of such use have occurred at the Philadelphia Dance Academy, directed by Nadia Chilkovsky Nahumck. Having mastered the notation herself, she made it an integral part of all teaching in the school, requiring every teacher (ballet and modern dance) to be fluent in it. In the dance studio the upper part of the walls was painted a pleasant green which served as a blackboard. A wooden ledge along each wall allowed chalk to be kept at handy intervals around the room. In trying to teach a temps-levé chassé one day, the ballet teacher, Michael Lopuzanski, could not get the children, aged nine or so, to understand the correct rhythm. Suddenly he remembered they all knew notation, he grabbed a piece of chalk and wrote what was wanted, stressing that the hop should come just before the bar line, to be followed by the sliding step on the strong beat, the count of 1. The result was miraculous. Composition classes in the school included writing down the pieces as well as dancing them. By the time the students were ready for the performing company they were able to read the parts handed out to them of any new choreography to be performed.

Notation has also been used as a tool in teaching deaf children. For example, an interesting experiment took place in Holland at the Institute for Deaf Children in Sint Michielsgestel where I was invited by the dance teacher, who, having heard of Labanotation, was interested in seeing whether it might be used as an aid in teaching the children. After observing how he handled the various age groups, I tried my hand, achieving purely through mime and the natural visuality of the symbols results which astonished and delighted everyone. The director of the school thought notation could have an important part to play in the teaching of dance to the deaf: moving as a result of reading the symbols, the children were creating the movements from within themselves – a sharp contrast to the superficial experience of watching and then copying the teacher. In learning by mimicking they go through the motions without thinking, moving in an almost a robot-like way. By initiating the movements through the reading of symbols they become personally involved. Other teachers of deaf children have included notation with similarly rewarding results. In Australia Margaret Abbie Denton has experimented with using notation as an aid to helping clumsy children find a different kind of awareness of themselves and of space.

The important fact to remember when incorporating notation into any teaching of dance is that it is *dance* that is being taught, not notation. Notation is dance in written form. For this reason Laban called his first book 'Schrifttanz' – 'Written dance', and not 'Dance script'.

TWENTY

Promises of modern technology

The process of notating has already been made easier through the availability of modern gadgetry. In the early days the material to be notated was only accessible through attending rehearsals and performances, or questioning the dancers.

Ray Cook was the first notator to use a small movie camera at a dress rehearsal to capture missing details. He also brought a cassette tape recorder to rehearsal and, as the music was being played, quietly called into the microphone key actions as they occurred. Thus, back at his desk, he could work out complicated musical cues without having to wait for run-through rehearsals or performances. The advent of video and its use by most dance companies has made the notator's task much easier. Many early scores could never be completed since the notator did not have access to the information. With company cooperation and use of video, scores need no longer be incomplete.

These devices have aided in recording the material, the choreography to be preserved. The next step in need of help is the drafting of the score. Before seeing what has already been accomplished and the technological promises for the future, let us review the steps required to capture a ballet on paper:

1. Quick notes taken as the rehearsal progresses, often rough, often needing changing.
2. First draft of the various parts into a score, correlated with the music.
3. Checking the material, making corrections, filling in gaps.
4. Layout for final score.
5. Neat ink copy (autography) of final score.

Each of these steps requires expertise. For some of them computer use has already been explored and for the last stage a typewriter element has been evolved for Labanotation.

Use of a typewriter

A clear, clean final score is not only an aesthetic pleasure to the eye, but makes reading easier. Ink copywork requires talent and training. The advent in 1973 of the Labanotation element ('golf ball') – developed by IBM in consultation with the Dance Notation Bureau for use in the Selectric Typewriter – has been a great step forward in producing final scores, particularly materials to be published (Fig. 20.1).

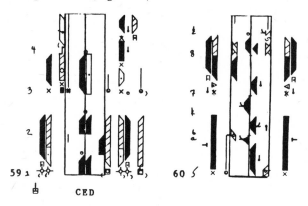

Fig. 20.1 Excerpt from Paul Taylor's ballet *Aureole* typed with the IBM element. (Courtesy Paul Taylor)

Trained typists work at considerable speed thus saving time; some details, however, are still added by hand. This technology has expedited step 5 above, but what of the other stages?

Use of computers

Dance-related use of computers falls under six main headings:
- (*a*) creative choreographic experimentation – assisting choreographers and others to visualize and experiment with body movements for creative purposes;
- (*b*) use of human movement language for computer animation – the actual composition (i.e. fixing) of dance sequences;
- (*c*) implementation of dance notation systems – facilitating the stages involved in the process of producing a finished score, i.e. the making of changes and corrections and the production of a final printout;
- (*d*) machines for use in teaching dance notation;
- (*e*) computer interpretation of dance notation – translation of existing notation scores into 'movies' of simple figures performing the dance sequences;
- (*f*) storage of movement information for comparative study.

(a) Computer versatility in creation of choreography

Choreographers have always preferred to work with live dancers, deriving inspiration from their reactions to ideas and from the atmosphere and stimulus of the rehearsal situation. Usually music is chosen in advance and movement phrases developed to relate to it. The degree to which choreographers plan ahead by jotting down notes varies, but it is very rare for anything but an outline to be recorded beforehand. The interplay between creativity of choreographers and dancers is time-consuming and several computer-orientated minds have considered possible ways in which choreographic ideas could be developed by providing other avenues of inspiration or means of experimentation and selection without requiring the dancers to be present.

The first use of a computer in connection with dance focused on its use for choreographic inspiration. In 1964 Jeanne Beaman and Paul Le Vasseur at the University of Pittsburgh fed twenty different time variations, twenty different spatial directions or patterns, and twenty different types of movements into a computer which was able in four minutes to print out seventy 'dances' in verbal form. This material fell into the aleatory type of composition with which Merce Cunningham had experimented some years before. But composition through drawing pieces of paper out of a bag or throwing dice is a much slower process.

The Pittsburgh material offered instructions such as: 'Three medium beats, half turn clockwise, arc backward,' or 'Six slow beats, jump, diagonally back.' Such material stretches the imagination. One has to find an inner reason, intent or impetus to produce what is stated. Minor actions may be included to give character and style, but they must not dominate and 'drown' the main instructions. The idea is to focus on the freedoms, not on the limitations of the instructions. Choice in use of dynamics was purposely left open to the interpreter to assist in creating dance movement from such unfamiliar material. The resulting dances can relate to existing music or can co-exist with unrelated music, or music may be composed especially for the purpose, producing a variety of interesting effects.[1]

Quite another idea was uppermost in the mind of A. Michael Noll working at the Bell Telephone Laboratories in New Jersey. In 1966 he considered the possibilities of a filmed version of a ballet as input to a computer which would convert the results into movement notation. The dancers wore lights and performed in a dimly lit room with cameras at different locations; the resulting films could be analysed by a computer and converted into motion patterns which could then be transferred into any desired dance notation. Noll realized this process was much too sophisticated for the programming potential at that time, so he concentrated on providing a digital computer with visual display through which choreographers could experiment with ideas free of the need to have a company of dancers on hand. The movements of a stick figure appearing on the display screen, as in Fig. 20.2 could be controlled by the choreographer and then stored for later recall.

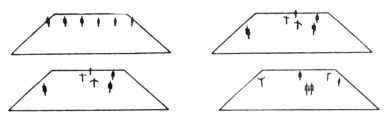

Fig. 20.2 Noll: experiments with computer choreography.
(*Dance Magazine*, January 1967)

Elements of chance and randomness could be used, producing new dance forms. Noll made a film to illustrate the basic possibilities. He discovered, as have all others, that body gestures are comparatively simple to handle, whereas ordinary walking is a complex action difficult to represent on the screen with a stick figure. The potential for choreographers trying out ideas in maninulating large groups on the screen seemed to him particularly advantageous.[2]

Who better to experiment with computer choreography than someone involved in the arts? Such a person is John Lansdown, an architect and member of the Computer Arts Society in London who, having observed computer experiments in composing music and poetry, saw possibilities for dance. In 1974 Lansdown turned to Benesh notation in the early phase of his experiments, but though satisfied with the first simple results, he realized the vocabulary of movement would have to be enhanced to match the achievements of a human choreographer in quality and scope. Like other experimenters he turned to direct representation of the human figure.

Several programs, often unrelated, have developed computerized body-modeling for vehicle crash simulation, sport, aerospace travel, cartoon animation and general ergonomic design. Three-dimensional representation of the human form on the two-dimensional display unit has been tackled in several ways. Lansdown settled on the two-dimensional outline figure, as in Fig. 20.3.

Fig. 20.3 Lansdown: computer use for creation of choreography.
(Courtesy John Lansdown)

The choreographic idea here was comparable to the establishment of 'key frames' in movie cartooning, another person being responsible for the 'inbetweening' necessary to link one frame to the next. In the case of dance, the computer chose the key frames from a vocabulary of traced drawings, and the dancer created the 'inbetweens'. The set instructions included location of the dancer on stage (shown by UL = upstage left, etc.), the direction faced at that point (shown by an arrow) and the number of beats before the next key frame should be achieved. Results of these experiments were performed by Another Dance Group. In some instances computer control included the lighting effects and camera angles. The filmed results provided effective interplay between colour and tone surrounding or highlighting a moving, off-focus figure.

Lansdown feels that what he was able to achieve is only a start, but it demonstrates how new ground can be broken. No matter how free, experimental and different a choreographer feels his avant-garde creation may be, inevitably it results from built-in human 'programming' and natural preferences. Only a computer can be totally objective in its choices.[3]

In our concern with the use of notation to capture for posterity great choreographic works and ideas, the results of total computer choreography can be captured on film in the same way that electronic music is captured on tape. It is a one-of-a-kind work to be viewed but not to be translated into symbols and recreated by others. Copies of the film may be made for distribution, but the work itself cannot be realized by another interpreter.

(b) Human movement language for computer animation

In 1970 an experiment was undertaken at the Biological Computer Laboratory, Department of Electrical Engineering at the University of Illinois, headed by Heinz Von Foerster, which involved application of the Eshkol-Wachmann movement notation system. The project which was jointly sponsored by the U.S. Army Research Office, the U.S. Air Force Office of Scientific Research and the Movement Society in Israel aimed at a unified system of descriptions, commands and execution of movements performed by a human body, by artificial limbs or automata, or by computer simulations. The basic principles of the notation having been established, the syntactic elements were then translated into equations of motion in a set of Cartesian coordinate systems each of which was associated with a movable part of the body. By a cascade of transforms, any desired (and executable) movement was then describable. A computer program was written which carried out these transformations with the result that any movement prescribed by a sequence of symbols in Eshkol-Wachmann notation could be represented by the appropriate trajectories which, in that program, were printed out with a CALCOMP plotter as projections into the three principal planes, the XY-plane, the YZ-plane and the ZX-plane. Numerous illustrations exemplified the rich possibilities of an algorithm which translates symbolic commands into effective movement. Two notational programs were developed, DANCER and STKMAN (Fig. 20.4) both basically position oriented.

Fig. 20.4 Foerster, University of Illinois: computer animation – STKMAN. (University of Illinois Library)

Concern with language design led Don Herbison-Evans of the Basser Department of Computer Science at the University of Sydney to consider movement notation among the many different forms of 'language'. The need for a realistic, basic movement analysis soon became apparent. To describe the placement of the specific parts of the body and subsequent changes in position, he turned to the skills of a Benesh trained notator. In 1979 he reported:

> The resulting process, termed Numeric Utility Displaying Ellipsoid Solids (NUDES), is a computer system that attempts to combine the generality of natural language with the temporal control of the animation chart and the precision of numerical language. In converting a choreographic sequence into body images, the Benesh score was used to provide the sequences, the notation being transformed by the operator into verbal commands which are keyed with a computer terminal. The results are then transferred to film. Advances over earlier attempts include the use of solid ellipsoids (like elongated balloons) which give a better appreciation of the three-dimensional disposition of the figure [Fig. 20.5], which can undergo regular locomotion (walking, running, jumping, etc.) when so commanded. Future plans include making the use of NUDES more facile for dancers having no computer experience.[4]

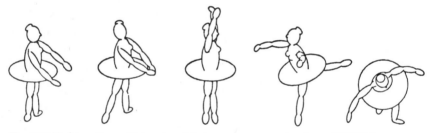

Fig. 20.5 Herbison-Evans, University of Sydney: computer animation – NUDES 3 output. (Courtesy D. Herbison-Evans)

(c) Implementation of dance notation systems

At the University of Waterloo, Canada, Gordon J. Savage of the Department of Systems Design and Jillian M. Officer of the Dance Department carried out in 1977 an exploration based on the use of interactive computer graphics as a tool for both learning and interpreting dance notation. Both Labanotation and Massine (Stepanov) methods were used. The aim of the project was:

  (i) To improve eye-estimation of the location of body parts while learning to write notation.
  (ii) To provide a visual simulation of a notated score, valuable as a record of a work of art in dance and also as a fast method of settling copyright claims.

In their words:

> The operation of a computer graphics model of a dancer was outlined and two methods of dancer-machine interaction, for purposes of describing a dance to the computer and obtaining the resultant simulation, were

described. The first method of interaction was based on the Massine method of notation, where the dancer describes a dance to the computer in the language of dance by means of a system of menus and a ten-key function box. (A 'menu' comprises a list of logically arranged items, choices or options for the computer user. This may be either of a 'command' nature, whereby branching in the program is initiated, or a 'data' nature, whereby body position or timing information is supplied to the computer. It is from the 'menu' that the body part is selected, the movement type, degree and time duration of each action.) Because of the lack of suitable interactive devices, it was decided to use the language of dance, which is inherent in the Massine dance notation method, rather than the symbols themselves, as a means of describing key body positions to the computer. The second method of interaction was based on the Labanotation method where the dancer describes the dance to the computer by selecting the actual Laban symbols from a menu using a pointer, such as an acoustic pen, and a digitizing tablet. With such replacement of the typewriter-like key-board by a tablet, the notator retains the customary 'feel' of working with pencil and paper.

The project enamated from the need to find a practical application for a computer graphics model of a man. Nordin (1974) perceived that this model could serve as a useful tool for dancers. However, it was apparent that a suitable method of interacting with the computer was imperative if dancers were to be stimulated by the concept. It was clear that dancers could not be expected to become knowledgeable about the computer in order to use it effectively. In other words, a communication problem existed. The problem was overcome because the highly organized nature of notation systems was amenable to the methods of interactive computer graphics. This meant that dancers could communicate with the computer in their own language.

The report concludes:

The results to date have been encouraging, primarily because the system has been accepted by both students of dance and professional dancers. Students of notation have found the interactive computer graphics approach to be a useful tutor; while professional dancers have found the methods of interaction easy to learn and use. At present the system does not handle motional type of commands (walking, jumping, etc.).[5]

Each of these experiments provides a success at a basic level of movement description. Each recognizes that much more detail needs to be added to spell out in notation or figure simulation the intricate movements of which the body is capable.

The most intensive program on use of movement notation with a computer has taken place at the Department of Computer and Information Science, the Moore School of Electrical Engineering at the University of Pennsylvania, where work which started in 1975 has continued to the present time of writing.

Presenting in 1979 the results of research done in this whole area, Norman I. Badler and Stephen W. Smoliar wrote:

In seeking a digital representation of human movement, established movement notation systems provide a wealth of well structured information. One such system, Labanotation, has led to the design of a 'machine language' based on a set of primitive movement concepts. Programs in this language can be interpreted by a simulator to produce an animated display of human movement. A computer may be provided with such programs through a straightforward compilation of the symbols of Labanotation, through data provided by visual input, or through natural language. Thus, this 'machine language' provides a highly flexible approach to movement representation. Components of the movement representation system are being constructed by the authors, based on the Labanotation abstractions.[6]

Several processes have been programmed including:

(i) a graphic editing system for Labanotation (including floor plans);
(ii) Most of the simulator which interprets the primitive movement concepts;
(iii) a display system for the human figure.

Labanotation was chosen for its basically applicable movement analysis. Working in cooperation with computer specialists Badler and Smoliar, Maxine Brown designed and implemented the first version of the Labanotation editor. Lynne Weber, an advanced professional Labanotator, contributed to the project as a whole – especially the abstraction of 'primitive movement concepts' from Labanotation. Vicki Hirsch contributed to the development of the floor plan part of the editor. A procedure was established of writing notated movement sequences directly onto the display unit, providing the following instructions: number of staves required per page, number of beats per measure, direction, level, duration and placement on the staff (both in the appropriate body-part column and at the moment in the time sequence). The potential use of a computer so programmed was obvious in removing much of the drudgery connected with the production of a dance score.

As for the future, results produced indicate the possibility of an interactive graphic text editor based on the notation system being used in the rehearsal room, the notator seated at a terminal programming data entry during initial rehearsals. Quite apart from the notator's skill in analysing movement, in making quick decisions concerning what is happening and how it should be described, and in employing a terminal, successful use of such an editor would depend very much on how the choreographer chooses to work. According to mood or inspiration a choreographer may switch suddenly from one section to another; not all movement is presented clearly or chronologically. For some time to come it may be quicker for the notator to continue as at present, i.e. to take a pad of paper, make notes, then, when a change in sequence occurs, grab another pad and possibly come back to the first a few moments later. Coordinating the pages into a ring binder with identification and dividers for easy location follows as soon as possible. Such split-second switching may not be so easy with a computer terminal where specific instructions have to be given to recall a particular section. Should the choreographer suddenly switch from one part to another to fill in more details, shuffling pages or pads may be quicker. However, if the movement staves can be swiftly named, numbered, or otherwise 'tagged' the computer could be faster.

But the above comments refer to the old days when notating was a catch-as-catch-can procedure. A company that has invested in the hardware of computer terminals, etc., will have discovered the advantages of full cooperation with the notator in the financial need to save time as well as in the production of a first class score.

With such studio use of computers still lying a few years ahead, what more immediate benefits does a computer provide? Skill in drawing the notation symbols such as in the Laban system is not needed; symbols automatically appear neatly drawn on the screen and on the print-out. A recurring movement theme 'written' and stored in the computer can be inserted into the score at the appropriate places. Corrections made on thematic material can be automatically applied to each instance where this material appears. Similarly, discrepancies in the writing of the same material may be questioned by the computer. Much routine checking can be automatic, for example cancellations of previous physical placements so often overlooked by the notator.

Use of a typewriter-like keyboard has been replaced by a tablet on which the notator writes with a sensitized pen, thus retaining some of the customary 'feel' of working with pencil and paper.

Representing the moving body through images on the display unit was also undertaken as an extension of the program at the Moore School of Engineering. The work of others in this area had demonstrated the limitations of stick figure representation; parallel overlapping planes produced certain limitations; polygon models produced unnatural results, such as deformity. The failure of surface modelling techniques led to use of spheres, as in the Bubble Man, (Fig. 20.6 (*a*)) and a later, more sophisticated model in which each sphere projects into a circle or shaded disk which gives a three-dimensional look and solves the problem of overlapping of parts of the body (i.e. by indicating which is in front) (*b*).

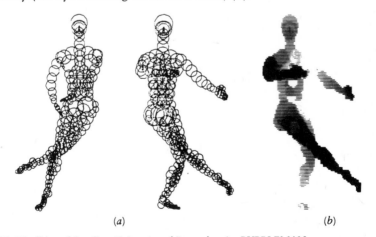

(*a*)   (*b*)

Fig. 20.6 Badler and Smoliar, University of Pennsylvania: BUBBLEMAN.
(Courtesy Norman Badler)

In contrast to the 'key frame' position approach, goal-directed movement descriptions were explored, e.g. contact, support, surround, etc.

Developments at the University of Iowa have paralleled in many respects the work achieved at the University of Pennsylvania. Through the cooperation of the Computer Assisted Instructional Laboratory of the WEEG Computing Center and the University of Iowa Dance Program, Dave Sealey and Judith Allen developed, in 1979, a computer package to aid in the efficiency of recording and editing movement in Labanotation, with the following specific goals:

(i) to enable the notator to record and edit movement in Labanotation more quickly than by hand;

(ii) to enable the user of this program to work effectively on the computer without training in computer programming, technology or terminology;

(iii) to provide a printed copy of movement stored in computer files.

The equipment makes use of comparatively small, portable hardware and of floppy discs, on which the score is stored and from which printouts can be made for immediate classroom or rehearsal use.[7]

Recent research has provided a way in which to search the computer for particular patterns of movement occurring in a dance score, these being analysed also in relation to material appearing immediately before and after. The second version of their work, Notate II, provides a much expanded notation package which includes coding to store scores, and the ability for material to be run on many different computers. Research is continuing to develop a method of putting Labanotation onto a micro-computer.[8]

(d) Computer use in teaching dance and notation
The Allen-Sealey team at the University of Iowa have also embarked on a program of computer aided teaching, for recognition of ballet steps, mastering ballet terminology, and for initial programmed learning of Labanotation.

(e) Computer interpretation of dance notation
At Simon Fraser University in Canada, Zella Wolofsky, a dancer, developed a computer system for the interpretation of selected Labanotation commands: this involved producing animated movies on a computer graphics terminal. Wolofsky's work culminated in her M.Sc. thesis in 1974 and since then Thomas W. Calvert, John Chapman and Aftab Patla in the Kinesiology and Computing Science Departments have substantially expanded the original work and have developed it in a number of new directions.

The goals of the work going on at Simon Fraser at the time of writing include:

(i) To complete the development of the original system for interpretation of Labanotation. While any standard Labanotation command can be interpreted, the input normally requires that each command be manually translated into an alphanumeric code. The input editor developed at the University of Pennsylvania is being considered for use as a 'front end'. The system output is normally a stick figure but this is now enhanced to either the Herbison-Evans 'Sausage Woman' (Fig. 20.5) for a vector graphics display or the Pennsylvania 'Bubble Man' (Fig. 20.6) for a raster graphics display. A variety of short films have been made to illustrate the capabilities of this system.

(ii) To utilize the computer interpretation system to assist in the characterization of movement abnormalities. A restricted subject of Labanotation commands is used to characterize abnormal patterns of locomotion, and the resulting animated figures are viewed on the computer graphics terminal. In addition, instrumentation in the form of goniometers which measure the angular movements of the hip, knee and ankle joints, is used to feed movement patterns directly into the computer. The physiotherapist or physician can enhance the animated movement produced from the instrumentation by adding notation to characterize his own visual analysis.

(iii) To develop an inexpensive, self-contained computer graphics system for use in dance studios, rehabilitation clinics, etc. By making use of new and inexpensive computer technology it has been possible to design and build a prototype self-contained system for less than $10,000. This is currently being evaluated.

(iv) To develop instrumentation which will provide inputs which the computer can automatically translate into notation. Preliminary results from goniometers on the lower limbs are quite promising. Any instrumentation which is to capture the free and uninhibited movements of a dancer must result in minimal impediments. A proposal for a body stocking with strain gauges built into the fabric is being studied.[9]

(f) Storage of movement information for comparative study

Comparative study and research in movement has only begun to develop in recent years; at the time of writing we are on the threshold of computer use for such investigation. Storage and retrieval of a range of information will be greatly facilitated through the computer and hence encourage in-depth study in many fields.

Many of the projects described in this chapter may have made significant advances by the time this book is published. The increase in use of notation as a teaching tool, as a source of information and as a record of choreographic works and movement knowledge for future reference, will all demand practical use of modern technology. Developments may be so swift in miniaturization of equipment and in mass production, thus putting computers financially within reach of every school and college, that the promises of the present may be the facts of the very near future. Every aid to general dissemination of knowledge concerning movement, and particularly dance, is welcomed by those who feel that dance is to be experienced intelligently and culturally as well as physically.

TWENTY-ONE

Comparisons of notation systems

Information on systems of movement notation has been relatively unavailable. Through the reprinting of historical dance books, notably by Dance Books, Dance Horizons and Gregg International, more information on the old systems is now becoming readily available. The largest collection of information on the subject is at the Language of Dance Centre in London. This collection has been assembled over a period of several decades under my direction and with the help of dance historians, libraries and fellow enthusiasts in many countries. Information on current, active systems such as the three most established and widely used, the Benesh, Eshkol-Wachmann and Laban, can be obtained from the appropriate centres, as listed in Appendix E.

The desire to know how systems compare and what advantages one may have over another has led to some investigations, perhaps the best known of these to date being *An Enquiry into Systems of Dance Notation* by Gordon Curl. Soon to be published is the report on the three-year in-depth study by William C. Reynolds of the Benesh, Eshkol-Wachmann and Laban systems, undertaken at Anstey College, now part of Birmingham Polytechnic, England.

Comparison of systems of notation as discussed in this chapter means direct representation of how a specific action is written in each system; it is neither a survey of systems down the ages, nor a first general introduction to how each system works. Such presentation rarely provides direct comparisons, and conclusions drawn, if any, must inevitably be superficial.

The Curl enquiry

In 1966, as part of his work for a Masters degree at Leicester University, Gordon Curl sent twenty questions to Rudolf Benesh, Valerie Preston-Dunlop and myself. The answers were published in 1967 exactly as received; no actual research was undertaken. The results have little value for a number of reasons. Though the questions are the same for both systems of notation, the answers are too diverse to provide any direct comparison. To make an analogy, if, when asked to describe New York, one person speaks of the tall buildings and another refers to the food in the restaurants, the answers are not comparable. One learns something about the thinking of the person giving the answer, but information for a one-to-one direct comparison is absent.

Curl selected an excerpt from Balanchine's ballet *Serenade* which he published in both Benesh and Labanotation. This excerpt would appear to provide a direct comparison, but a close examination of the two notations reveals that the Benesh version provides much less information. To cite one example, the outward facing of the palms (an unusual and important stylistic detail) when the arms open sideward at the end of a series of enchaîné turns is missing in the Benesh version. As I was at the rehearsal when this material was taught and notated in both Benesh and Labanotation I know this detail was demonstrated. With such differences an exact comparison cannot be made.

The Curl study also included a modern dance passage described in words from which the sequence was notated in each system. Unfortunately the word descriptions were often interpreted differently by each system of notation; thus different movements were produced. For example, for the starting position, the wording stated: 'the arms downwards and in front of the body and bent so that the angle at the elbow is 90°.' Fig. 21.1 illustrates the position written in Benesh notation (seen from side view), while Fig. 21.2 depicts (from front view) the Labanotation interpretation. In Benesh terminology 'the arms downwards' refers to the upper arm. 'In front of the body' refers to the forearms. The 90° angle at the elbow is achieved by flexing at the elbow. In Labanotation the basic direction for a limb, whether bent or not, is the line between the extremity and the base, i.e. between hand and shoulder for the arm. Thus the arms would still be down. 'In front of the body' refers to the relation of the fingertips to the centre line of the torso: thus the resulting position was a rather bent balletic *bras bas* (5th *en bas*). This example illustrates how different interpretation of words easily renders a true comparison impossible. Had Curl studied each system he would have been able to control the material and to make sure that both the verbal and notated answers were directly comparable.

Fig. 21.1   Fig. 21.2

The Anstey project

The three-year research project carried out at Birmingham Polytechnic and funded by the Radcliffe Trust focused on a close study of the Benesh, Eshkol-Wachmann and Laban systems. Two major books have resulted. The first is a comprehensive coverage of theory and factual bases for notation system design and use. This coverage included several experimental procedures for evaluating systems. One of these resulted in the second book, which is a large scale parallel presentation of Benesh, Eshkol-Wachmann and Laban systems. In this procedure a video tape of basic actions of the body was prepared (for example, raising the arm, rotating the lower arm, bending the trunk, simple steps). The tape included about 400 movements which were presented in random order for the notators of each system to record. The resulting notations were then read back by another notator, and the movements thus produced recorded on video. In each system some mistakes were made naturally, both in writing and reading back. At times the reader, in performance, actually corrected the writer's error.

For publication the sets of notated examples are arranged on each page along with a description of the action in basic terminology (i.e. wording carefully selected to avoid favouring any one school of movement analysis.) This book has been checked and approved by experts in each system and, as a result, is the most exact and thorough comparison available. The Benesh and Laban systems kept to the established standard notation for each item; Eshkol-Wachmann introduced simplifications and signs not yet published.

Some of the points which came out during the investigation are revealing of differences in attitude toward the activity of notating and toward the systems themselves. Of the total number of points of comparison developed in this research, the following are the major ones, some of which put to rest longstanding controversies about notation.

Here is Reynold's brief summary on the project:

(1) In all three systems the number of cases in which no error occurred was very high. This fact demonstrates that notation systems can be remarkably efficient and accurate, and puts to rest the often-heard assertion that observation based on notation is not adequate for recording movement.

(2) Writing errors were more common than reading errors, indicating that the perception and cognition of movement itself is more difficult than the reading and performance from notation. This fact is also reflected in timing scores, in which writing took considerably longer than reading.

Inadvertently this is strong evidence for the practical value of notation over film. Movement can be reproduced from notation in half the time of reproduction from film, with half the number of errors.

(3) Human errors made by the users of a system were far more common than errors caused by the system design itself. Given greater checking and control among users, errors can be reduced to a very low level.

(4) Eshkol-Wachmann and Laban systems were nearly equal in amount of error tolerated. However, recording in the Eshkol-Wachmann system was very much slower, taking more than twice the time of the Laban system, primarily due to a general attitude which does not favour speed in application.

(5) The Benesh system allowed many more errors than the other two. Most of these are errors in accuracy, and many are caused unavoidably by the system design itself. This weakness prevents the Benesh

system from being widely applicable to fields requiring great accuracy. It remains best suited for artistic applications in which such accuracy is neither necessary nor desired.

(6) In practice the Benesh and Laban systems required about the same amount of time to record. In spite of its simpler appearance the Benesh system does not achieve a significantly higher practical capability than the Laban system.

(7) In sum, the Laban system is more practical than the Eshkol-Wachmann system and more accurate than the Benesh.

(8) Overall time to produce notation from observation is far greater than running time of the original movement. Thus all claims for producing notation within the time of the original event are seriously fallacious.

(9) The amount of time spent actually copying notation is very much less than that spent observing and making decisions as to what to write. Therefore, it is much more important to design a system which facilitates clear thinking than one which offers rapid copying. Pressure for a shorthand movement notation is misplaced; reduction in the graphics cannot shortcut the thinking time required in notation use.

(10) The major factors affecting overall notation speed are the degree of organization in the movement and the degrees of the notator's familiarity with that organization. A high degree of familiarity can reduce notation time to $\frac{1}{3}$ that of unfamiliar movement. Thus, high speed in notation, a common requirement in professional application, is achievable not by shorthand graphics but by high personal familiarity of the notator with the structure of events notated. The professional success of the Benesh system has been achieved by a concentration on ballet (which is highly structured in nature), by selection of notators with professional experience in ballet, and by placement of notators in full-time positions within dance companies. This approach has not been followed by the other systems.

(11) Speed of copying. One of the tests undertaken which yielded unexpected results was that of speed of copying. Test cards were prepared with simple notation materials in each of the three systems and the notator was given a blank card with the staff for the system being tested. As each test card was produced the notator was to copy it as rapidly as possible. An unexpected result was that the Benesh system proved slower than the Laban system in spite of having fewer marks. The reason for this time difference is the need for careful placement of the indications on the Benesh staff. The slightest displacement will change the meaning of an indication. Thus extra time must be spent in accurate drawing. In the Laban system the seemingly cumbersome block symbols can be scribbled rapidly and, even if untidy, can still be clearly recognizable. The Eshkol-Wachmann system was very much slower than the other two, possibly because the need for speed has not been experienced. Ordinary language written longhand was twice again as slow. In

the Laban system the copying test was given a second time using totally blank cards to see whether the absence of the staff and graph squares would make a difference. Despite the notator's having to draw in a centre line and mark off the beats, the result was, surprisingly, significantly faster than the previous Laban test.

(12) Understood elements. The application to isolated, mechanical movements proved at times a problem for all systems, especially, however, for the Benesh system because it functions normally within a known style of dance, a particular 'language' (ballet, modern dance, etc.). If one does not know which 'language' is being represented, one does not always know exactly how to interpret the symbols on the page. The redundancy avoidance which Benesh stressed so much has resulted in the omission of much information, and thus the system only works satisfactorily when one knows the kind of movement which is being represented.

The basis for the above conclusions is revealed in the full account of Reynold's research conducted during and after the project.

The Eshkol-Wachmann and Laban comparisons

In 1960 Eshkol and Wachmann published a supplement to their 1958 textbook specifically for students of Labanotation, its 22 pages being devoted to illustrating in their system examples taken from the 1954 Labanotation textbook. A more substantial study, *Movement Notations, A Comparative Study of Labanotation (Kinetography Laban) and Eshkol-Wachmann Movement Notation*, was published in 1979 by the Movement Notation Society, Israel. Part Two appeared in 1982. Such direct comparison is indeed most useful; unfortunately, however, a number of mistakes have occurred in the Labanotation examples which could easily have been eliminated had the materials been submitted to an authority on the Laban system for checking prior to publication. What Eshkol has not clearly stated in either book is that she purposely did not confer with any Labanotation specialists, preferring to work in isolation so that the Labanotation presentation would be her own understanding of the system derived from available text books. In the 1979 book she laments that

'we found it impossible to obtain any written material (literature) in Labanotation, as exists in music, science, poetry, mathematics, etc. The only available publications in bookshops contain again and again the same 'basics' and 'fundamentals' of the system, but not its application and use – scores.'

This statement reveals that she avoided contacting any centre using Labanoation from which lists of published works and available scores can be obtained. It also accounts for the mistakes in her presentation of Labanotation.

Ideally comparison between systems and evaluations of the results should be made by individuals who have achieved professional level proficiency in all systems under consideration. Such a time-consuming task is unlikely to be undertaken unless financially supported by an impartial educational institution. Whatever the results of such a study, many people will still be attracted to one or other movement notation system according to personal preference, their field of movement involvement and their need for simplicity or complexity. How a particular system functions in a particular field or situation will be revealed only through practical use. Like water, each system will eventually find its own level and hence its own practitioners and applications. Only time will tell whether different systems can or should be combined to make one universal system. A universal written language of dance may be highly desirable, but local needs may dictate local 'tongues'.

TWENTY-TWO

Rights and copyright

Before the advent of notation, film and video tape, the question of rights and copyright seldom came up, or certainly was seldom squarely faced. Without notation or other means with which to secure a choreographic work and thereby prove its ownership, dance had always been wide open to plagiarism. People felt free to copy steps and sequences and use them as their own. Indeed whole sections, even ballets, were reproduced by individuals who had danced in them, with no credits or royalties going to the original choreographer. Nothing had existed which made people aware that a choreographer's work was not common property. Now, when a score bears a copyright notice on the front page, the reader is aware that this property cannot be treated as his own and that restrictions exist which must be honoured.

Copyright law varies in different countries. Most European countries adhere to the Berne Convention. Within the past decade changes have occurred in the U.S.A. law which not only bring it more in line with the Berne Convention but which also vitally affect dance. Before investigating specific details, let us look at some historical examples concerning choreographic rights.

Historical examples

The first attempt to establish copyright in choreography of which we have specific details occurred in 1862 when Marie Petipa wanted to perform at her benefit in Paris a *Pas* originally arranged by Jules Perrot in St Petersburg for his ballet *Gazelda*. Perrot refused consent, but Marie Petipa went ahead notwithstanding, performing a very thinly disguised version. Perrot, his complaints to the Director of the Paris Opéra ignored, took recourse to litigation. During the court case the question arose: 'How is it in fact to be established that a *Pas* danced in St Petersburg is the same as a *Pas* danced in Paris? . . . Unfortunately Perrot does not write (his works) down.' A declaration made by Saint-Léon attesting that the two dances were the same strengthened Perrot's case. It is of interest to us that the defence put up the argument that 'it is the artiste herself who is everything, it is her grace, her strength, her expression, all the play of her body and features that make up the success.' This is the age-old confusion between the performance and the material being performed. The court found for Perrot, holding that although the *Pas* was based on certain well-known national dances, their combination could nevertheless constitute a composition in which copyright might exist. Perrot was awarded 300 francs damages, only a small proportion of the amount he claimed.[1]

An early court case in the U.S.A. was that of Fuller v. Bemis, 1892. Loie Fuller had originated the idea of manipulating yards of flowing silk under variegated lights. Explicit descriptions of her composition *The Serpentine Dance* had been registered with the Copyright Office, but when she brought infringement action against Minnie Bemis for performing this dance, the court ruled against Fuller. According to law only a dance work with narrative or dramatic content was protected under the Copyright Act.

For years this case was cited whenever the question of dance copyright arose. No category for choreography existed, it had to be registered under 'Dramatico-Musical Compositions', another indication of the low esteem in which dance was held. A ballet had to be described in words and pictures, it had to tell a story, convey a dramatic concept or idea, develop a character; it had to express a theme or emotion by means of specific dance movement and physical actions. If the copy submitted for registration was merely a diagrammatic representation of dance movements and actions (for example, recorded in Labanotation), it had to be accompanied by a verbal description of the production as a whole, explaining the plot, characters, themes, or emotions expressed by the choreography. Dance as pure design, movement for its own sake, was not acceptable.[2]

The first Labanotated score in the U.S.A. registered for copyright was Hanya Holm's choreography for *Kiss Me Kate!* in 1952. Balanchine's ballet *Symphony in C* submitted earlier was rejected at first because it had no story line. A 'story' incorporating thematic ideas and emotions was then outlined for the four movements and the work was accepted. Similarly, the scores of *Symphonie Concertante* and *Bourrée Fantasque* were given 'synopses' and successfully registered for copyright.

The first court case involving dance notation in Europe occurred in Essen in 1951. The 'Green Table' scene from Kurt Jooss's famous ballet of that name had been copied in the film *Sensation in San Remo* made by Jungen Filmunion. The court ruled that choreography and pantomime are protected when the action is laid down in writing or by some other means. Because the actions and dance movements had been written down in careful detail (I had recorded the ballet in 1938), *The Green Table* enjoyed the same copyright protection as literature and music. Through the dance score Jooss was able to prove the many instances where identical movements had occurred in addition to the obvious similarity of the table, the costumes and masks.[3]

General rights in movement and notation

What dance material can be copyrighted? Obviously the vocabulary of dance – the familiar steps in ballet, modern jazz and national dance, as well as what are considered 'new' movements is public domain. It is the unique combination of a selection of all this material which can be protected when fixed, i.e. recorded in tangible form. As in music, a sequence of identical movements beyond a certain length can be established as plagiarism if irrefutable proof exists.

The question of rights first comes up as soon as any notes are taken. A student jots down a memory aid of classroom technique. The technique class has been paid for. Has the student the right to those notes? Can the student later teach from those notes? Can the student publish those notes? Up to the question of publication, the answer is yes. If the teacher has already copyrighted the sequences, then the student has no rights to publish. If the teacher's name is being used in a publication, permission must be sought and ownership of the material established. It is possible that the student may publish without giving credit: a few changes in the material and the source may not be immediately recognizable. The act of teaching is one of giving, and payment is made for what is given; in that respect the teacher has 'sold' the material in the process. Much of what is taught in dance technique classes is common property, but if the material is very specialized and has been worked out by the teacher, then it is up to the teacher to record it in writing and register it for copyright, publish it and benefit from the sales. Students will not then have to write notes which so often are incorrect, but can purchase the correctly recorded material and thereby enrich their understanding and hence mastery of the technique.

In the case of a dance composition, a choreographic work, the work itself remains the property of the choreographer, while the notated score of it is the property of the person or company who paid for it. If it was not paid for, the score belongs to the notator. He should, however, neither publish the score nor reconstruct the work without the choreographer's permission, but may use the score for his own personal needs. If he plans classroom teaching of a full score or a major section of it, the choreographer's agreement should be sought.

Materials from bygone days and folk materials are in the public domain, there is no specific ownership and hence everyone is free to use them. This is true also of music and often one is forced to use public domain music when royalty fees are too high for the available budget. Classical ballets such as *Swan Lake* and *Sleeping Beauty* are all in the public domain now and one has only to learn the dances from a reliable teacher to perform them as much as one pleases. But though the dance movements of a ballet like *Swan Lake* are in the public domain, the dance notation score of the ballet is the property of the person who wrote it. Since there are different versions of the classics and notators may vary in their way of 'seeing' and hence recording the work, scores of the same ballet may vary enough to be considered different scores and hence have independent copyright registration.

Common law copyright

Two types of copyright protection are available: common law and statutory. For common law protection a work must constitute an original creation and must be recorded in tangible form. The creator must identify ownership by placing the copyright notice on the title page, or the page immediately following. Notice of copyright consists of either the word 'Copyright', the abbreviation of 'Copr.' or the universally accepted symbol

©, followed by the year and the name of the copyright proprietor. The simple form for owner John Smith would be © 1981 by John Smith. The wording 'all rights reserved' may be added. Such copyright statement should be put even on pencil copies of scores. When the work of a choreographer is written down the copyright is in the name of the choreographer and the date is the year of creation, unless the dance was sufficiently reworked to constitute another version, in which case the year of notating is used.

Statutory copyright

Common law copyright protection ends with general publication of the work. General publication includes disclosure, exhibition, or distribution of the work to the general public. This may be by sale, by rental, or merely by the handing out of copies. In music and drama, performance of the work does not constitute publication but the sale of scripts or sheet music does. Hence it follows that a performance of the dance does not constitute publication.

In the U.S.A. the author should deposit copies of a published work in the Copyright Office to apply for registration of his copyright claim, using the correct form and paying the required registration fee. Such official registration of the work establishes firmly the fact and date which may be crucial later in proving ownership should a court case arise. No lawsuit may be brought unless the work has been registered. Another method of proof of date is to mail the work to oneself in a sealed envelope, not to be opened until proof is needed. The postmarked date on the envelope establishes priority on any claim.

It is important to note the difference between the statements 'copyrighted' and 'registered for copyright.' Only a court case proves actual copyright, as we have seen in the case of Jooss' *The Green Table*. Because the dances for *Kiss Me Kate!* were notated and registered for copyright, reproducers of that Broadway musical have avoided plagiarism by using totally new choreography. In contrast, the dances from *Oklahoma* and other of Agnes de Mille's Broadway successes, which had not been notated, were reproduced, virtually intact, around the world by dancers who had performed in the shows, with de Mille receiving neither credit nor royalties for her creations. Since those days the picture has changed, but choreographers, particularly of commercially successful works, have been slow to see the advantages of notation and the copyright protection it brings.

As Jules Perrot said: 'It is a matter for regret that "choreography" (i.e. dance notation) has not kept abreast with the progress of the dancing. Creative ballet masters would not then be exposed to being robbed by infamous rascals.'[4]

The new 1978 U.S. Copyright law gives specific statutory recognition to choreography. It now comes under the heading of Performing Arts, and the 'fixing', i.e. recording in tangible form, can be through notation, pictorial or narrative description of the movements, or in the form of film, video tape, video disc, hologram or any similar method.

The method chosen for fixing choreography must be detailed enough to permit performance of the work from the score. If copyright registration is issued to a general textural description of the work which would not provide enough detail for performance of the work, protection might lie only in the verbal text itself. The same might be true of a motion picture too fragmented or unclear to permit full reconstruction; the film might be protected, but not the choreographic work. A clear, detailed notated score is the best means of fixing a dance.

The term of copyright in the U.S. has now been extended to conform to the Berne Copyright Union, which established the duration to be for the life of the creator plus 50 years.

There are no statutory requirements of registration for copyright in the United Kingdom. Copyright exists as a consequence of an act of original creation of a literary, dramatic, musical, or artistic work. A choreographic work comes within the definition of a dramatic work so long as it has been reduced to a written form.

It is obligatory to send a copy to the British Library and customary to send copies also to the other five National Libraries. Such organizations as there might be for registering works for copyright do not have a statutory basis. Registration with such an organization does not confer copyright, because this exists from the moment of creation, but a receipt of registration is useful evidence in the event of a dispute between two claimants that rests upon the priority of the creation of a particular work.

It is important to note that film, video tape, etc. are *not* accepted in the U.K. as a form of fixing the choreography.[5]

Fair use of published materials

Fair use of a copyrighted work for purposes such as teaching, scholarship or research is not an infringement of copyright. Interpretations of the law varies from country to country but in most countries a student may make a copy of a page for personal use. In the case of multiple copies for classroom use permission must be obtained from the copyright owner and such copies made can be used only within the classroom, not given away or sold. The law is concerned that allowance be made to facilitate education through the transmission of knowledge, but at the same time the author or copyright owner's property must be protected. In the case of consumable materials, e.g. workbooks, tests, answer sheets, etc. copying is prohibited. The laws of some countries cite specific limits regarding the number of pages of a book (percentage of the whole) which may be reproduced for research and educational purposes.

This brief presentation of the facts has attempted to put the reader in the picture. Full information on all copyright questions should be sought from the Copyright Office at the Library of Congress in Washington, or, in the U.K., from legal experts on the subject.

Notator's rights in a choreographic score

Because there often is more than one way of expressing a dance movement in notated form, the question arises as to whether the notator, in making the most appropriate choice of description, is not in fact functioning as a translator rather than as a mere stenographer. A translator who has transformed a literary work from one language into another has definite rights to the results of his work. This does not invalidate or minimize the rights of the original author; the translation is an entity in itself. To what extent does or can a similar situation exist in the notating of a choreographic work? There exist differences of opinion. The first Labanotated scores were what would now be called general, outline scores, for which knowledge of the style of dance was taken for granted. At that time the notator only felt that a service had been done, he had acted as a choreographic secretary. Now there are many instances in which great pains are taken to capture the precise movement feeling and intention of the choreographer, and many notators are individuals with both a greater sensitivity to movement and a more advanced knowledge of the system of notation. The process thus becomes far more an act of translation or transliteration, rather than a direct representation, as in typing a business letter already dictated.

Rights in the use of systems of notation

Publication of a system of movement notation provides copyright protection for the book itself, but how much does such publication include protection in the use of the system? The inventor wants the system to be used, but how far can he maintain control over its use by others? Two basic patterns have emerged in this century. All publications and further development in the Eshkol-Wachmann system are centered at The Movement Notation Society in Israel, headed by Noa Eshkol. Joan and Rudolf Benesh retained complete control of their system, even requiring students to sign agreements not to discuss the system or show the materials to outsiders. All publications are controlled by the Benesh Institute of Choreology, and all notated scores, even handwritten copies, must have the Benesh copyright notice on each page.

Laban never established a centre of control. The original copyright in his system underwent an extraordinary series of events as a result of World War II and Allied requisitioning of property – too long a tale to tell here. Laban reserved the rights to the basic meaning of the symbols, but laid restriction neither on the teaching of the system nor on publication of materials such as dance compositions in which the symbols were used without explanation of their meaning. Thus, legally, anyone can record and publish his own dance in Labanotation, but an unwritten code of ethics has been established through which all serious notators submit works for authoritative checking and proofreading, and notators and teachers adhere to the usages published in authoritative textbooks. Such lack of stringent legal controls has provided negligible disadvantages but at the same time given great encouragement to those studying it to spread the knowledge and use of Labanotation as a tool in their work. Specific qualifying examinations in Labanotation have been established in theory, teaching, notating and reconstructing.

Greater access through notation

The existence of a notated score of their work has given some choreographers the idea that even greater access for plagiarism exists than before. If the score is unpublished, it is up to the choreographer to see that it is in safe hands, that it is being carefully controlled. Centres such as the Dance Notation Bureau, the Language of Dance Centre, and the Institute of Choreology take great care that all choreographers' rights are protected and their wishes followed regarding use of the scores. If a work is published, the choreographer will receive royalties from the sale of each copy as well as performance royalties. It is common for dance works as well as for contemporary plays to require performance permission and payment of fees or royalties. Permission for performance may vary from one choreographer to another. Some, such as Fred Berk, have generously put no restrictions on performance of their works. Others are concerned that only companies with a high level of training and artistry should be given performance permission.

Now that ballets are being revived from notation, choreographers have not only copyright protection but also the advantage of the work being produced in several places at the same time, and of receiving royalties from these performances. The work most frequently revived from the score is Doris Humphrey's *Shakers*. The recorded artistic heritage she left is now enjoyed by hundreds of dancers and thousands of spectators because a few dedicated notators recognized the value of the pieces, won Humphrey's approval, and took the opportunity to notate. Today her works are the backbone of the classical American modern dance repertoire. Three of these works have been published, the first full choreographic scores of a major choreographer ever to be made availabe for all to purchase.

TWENTY-THREE

Evaluating a system

If you want to learn a system of movement notation, how do you go about deciding which is best? By the advertising – impressive advertisements must mean a successful system? By the look of the notation – if it looks like dance it must be best for dance? By word of mouth? Who is there who can give knowledgeable advice?

Studying just the three or four most active systems is an enormous undertaking, obviously you turn to the opinions of others. Are they already using one system or another and therefore already 'biased'? When you are in the market for a car, each salesman will of course say his product is the best. Turn to the man who has tried out and owned several makes and kinds of car. He will give you first-hand experience and base his advice on your particular needs. And so you should turn to a person who knows and has used several notation systems.

Where are the multi-lingual movement notation people? Such people are few because there is little interest in studying notation systems just for their own sake. A system is studied to be used as a functioning tool. What kind of person would have the incentive to study other systems, to know all the ins and outs of the problems met in recording movement and in reviving dance works recorded in those systems? Obviously it would have to be a practising notator, one who is determined to find out which indeed is the best tool, the best system for the purpose, and who therefore has investigated other systems. Is there somewhere a better mousetrap? Or in this case, a 'movement-trap'? If a person claims that a particular notation system is the best, then that person must know all about other available systems so that the claim is founded on fact.

But on the subject of movement notation the field seems wide open. People who have no personal knowledge of any system feel free to express unqualified opinions. 'The Stepanov system was abandoned because it was too complicated,' states a leading ballet critic. 'In the Laban system you have to learn 350 symbols' is another favourite. There is no truth in either statement, but these and other unfounded 'reasons' are given by those who prefer to dismiss the idea of serious study of any notation system.

Setting aside the opinions of others, you decide to see which system attracts you. If you are interested in dance then which system *looks* most like dance? You may immediately select a stick figure system and find that this is just what you need. Or you may have needs for which figure representation is too simplistic. Abstract representation, with its greater flexibility, is your choice.

Type of signs used

Is 'looking like dance' a necessity? Does written language look like the sounds which the letters represent? Despite the delightful *Just So Stories* the alphabet has no 'sense'; it has to be learned by rote, but we learn it young and so take it in our stride. Does music notation look like music? One has also to learn how to read music notation; then the visuality of it becomes apparent. Again, music notation is learned young and absorbed along with learning to play an instrument. Notation and the study of music are so closely linked that you do not think of them as separate entities; the symbols on paper represent the sounds. The block symbols of Labanotation don't look like flowing movement until the visuality of the flow of movement revealed through the symbols is understood. Not only is timing visual but so are the signs for direction and the symmetrical pattern which the symbols make on paper when representing symmetrical movement. Benesh notation appeals to the eye since it looks light and airy, as ballet dancing should be, but even trained ballet dancers have to learn to read it. There is no magic which causes the signs in any system to burst into movement before your eyes. Sufficient background training is essential to enable one to see the movement, even with a stick figure system.

The most directly representational system at the moment is that of Valerie Sutton, which uses a fully fledged figure looking like what it represents – a captured position in a movement sequence. To interpret the figure fully she provides extra movement symbols which must be learned. Even the simplest systems or those simplest in appearance require considerable spade work in regard to learning. The first three lessons are easy in any system; it is when you demand more than kindergarten level that real study begins.

If you are attracted to numbers and an impersonal, mathematical analysis of movement, you will be drawn to the Eshkol-Wachman system which satisfies many because of its clear basic logic. Not that it doesn't, like all systems, have its moments of illogicality, though they are admittedly few.

No in-depth study has yet been made in comparing signs used by the eighty-five or so systems of movement notation. For example, how does each one indicate the direction forward? Such an investigation is for a later book, but the following anecdote sheds some light on the question of choice of signs. In Jean-Jacques Rousseau's *Confessions* he describes his idea of indicating music notes by numbers, a simple, convenient system which would be applicable to all keys, time values, etc. The only serious objection made against his system was by Rameau, Rousseau relates:

He saw its weak side the moment I explained it to him. 'Your notation', he said, 'is excellent in so far as it determines the value of notes simply and clearly, accurately represents the intervals and always shows the original phrase and its doubling together, all things that common notation does not do. But it is bad in so far as it demands a mental process which cannot always keep up with the rapidity of the execution. The position of our notes,' he continued, 'springs to the eye without the assistance of the mind. If two notes, one very high and the other very low, are joined by a passage of intermediate notes, I can see at a glance the progress from one to the other down the scale. But in order to make sure of the passage in your notation I have to decipher all your numbers one after the other; a general glance will not do.' His objection seemed irrefutable, and I instantly admitted it; although it is simple and striking, it is one that only great experience of the art could have lighted on. It is not surprising that it did not occur to any of the Academicians. But it is strange that all these great scholars who know so many things are still not aware that nobody is capable of judging anything outside his own field.[1]

This last statement is particularly pertinent to dance notation. How many people who know nothing about it are willing to make profound and authoritative statements, particularly in condemning notation in general, or one or other system in particular?

Scope of table of contents and index

One good word of advice: much can be learned in a short time about a book (and this is true also of a notation system) by reading the table of contents and the index at the back. The index to a notation textbook will give you a good run-down on the kind of movements covered. If the textbook has a glossary of symbols this will also illustrate the range, and with a few minutes' reflection you can see whether there is a basic logic in the development of signs used for the different movement categories. If starting at the back of the book is like jumping in the deep end, remember that a good notation system is like a language, you can learn just a little for your everyday needs, and always embark on advanced study later. When there is the need there will be the incentive. In other words, you do not have to learn it all at once.

Criteria for a good system of movement notation

To serve the needs of teachers, choreographers and research workers in fields where movement is recorded and studied, the following points have been established as being requirements of a good system of notation.

(a) Universality
The system should cover every form of movement, not only all forms of dance, but also other physical activities, sport, gymnastics, physiotherapy, anthropology, industrial studies.

(b) Comprehensiveness
The system must be able to cover every aspect of movement to the degree of detail required for the purpose for which the recording is taking place.

(c) Movement analysis
The analysis of movement on which the system is based must be anatomi-

cally, scientifically and psychologically sound.

(d) Versatility in movement description
It must be possible to record movement in the way in which it is conceived. In addition to the fact of the action, there is the intent which may be of greater importance in capturing a truthful representation of the movement. Movements should not be distorted to fit a more convenient description.

(e) Flexibility in application
A whole range of level of description from the broadest to the most detailed indication must be possible.

The system must allow for statement of isolated information; details which are neither needed nor relevant should not have to be included because of the design of the system. Use of a part of the body, of space, time, etc. should, when needed, be indicated separately without requiring a full context. General statements as well as specific must be possible. Shorthand notes should be convertible into full notation when necessary.

(f) Logicality
The system should contain a logical development of symbols and rules. There should be an overall consistency in presentation of the concepts underlying the system and simplicity in general structure.

Related types of movements should have related signs. The same kind of action should be indicated by the same kind of signs, for example, rotary movements should be represented by the same basic sign. A logical relationship should exist among signs representing related aspects.

(g) Visuality
The system should be as visual as possible to facilitate learning and to allow for cursiveness in reading. Arrangements of signs should provide visual patterns through which movement patterns can be recognized, thus making sightreading possible. Deciphering, the slow piecing of the parts together, should be avoided for general usage of the system where speed may be important. Symmetrical movement should appear symmetrical on the page.

(h) Legibility
The signs should be discrete, providing a distinct difference between symbols. Placement on the paper should allow for easy location of information.

(i) Practicability
  (i) Economy. The staff and symbols should not be unnecessarily space-consuming. Maximum information should be given with as few symbols as possible.
  (ii) Clarity. Additional information which reinforces a main statement should be provided to avoid misinterpretation and to assist the reader.
  (iii) Penmanship. Drawing the movement indications should not require fine penmanship. A slip of the pencil should not produce a different

statement. The signs should allow for quick writing and still be legible.

(iv) Single meaning. One sign should not have several meanings.

(v) Conventions. Conventions should be used to provide a simple means for writing familiar but complex actions such as walking, jumping, etc.

(vi) Assumptions. For general practice it is desirable to assume certain knowledge on the part of the reader, thus avoiding inclusion of unnecessary detail.

(vii) Range of use. The system should be like a language in that in simple form, it can be understandable to a child and at the same time, through its detailed, logical development, can satisfy scientific needs.

(viii) Modern technology. The system should be capable of being computerized for statistical analysis of movement components and other applications as they develop.

(ix) Reduction. The notation should be capable of considerable reduction and still be legible, should printing limitations require it.

Requirements of a system of movement notation

In any investigation of a system of movement notation, the following specific points should be considered. This list of requirements has developed from the demands made on systems of notation by the fields in which they have been applied. It is often thought that those responsible for the development of a system of notation indulge in inventing complex ways of writing. The complexities come from the demands of movement. Movement is not simple, and if an assignment demands detail, then a specific description must be produced.

Description of movement – choice; comprehensiveness

Put simply, a system of movement notation must answer the questions: 'who?', 'what?', 'where?', 'when?', 'how?', and 'why?', at different levels of specificity. 'Who?' translates into the part or parts of the body involved in the action; 'What?' is the kind of action occurring; 'Where?' deals with directional matters, both in relation to gestures and to the performer's location on stage; 'When?' deals with timing, the moment an activity takes place and its duration; 'How?' involves the manner of performance, including dynamics, the level of energy used; 'Why?' deals with the intent of the action, its relationship to the environment, to other people, etc.

In a comprehensive system indication should be provided for the categories listed below.

(a) The body
Are indications for the following clear and logically developed?

191

(i) the body as a whole;

(ii) the main parts of the body (a limb, a section such as the torso, chest, etc.);

(iii) the secondary parts (lower arm, hand, etc.);

(iv) the specific parts (a surface, segment of finger, part of the face, etc.).

(b) Space (direction, level)

How are the following handled?

(i) indication of the main directions;

(ii) intermediate directions;

(iii) subtle minor directional variations;

(iv) reference to direction based on the body cross of axes;

(v) reference to direction based on the line of gravity;

(vi) reference to directions based on the constant room (stage) directions;

(vii) reference to the fixed points or areas on stage or in the performing area;

(viii) reference to directions based on a focal point;

(ix) reference to the Line of Dance (L.O.D. as in ballroom);

(x) reference to directions related to an established path.

(c) Basic actions

How are the following handled, in isolation or in combination?

(i) flexion, the difference forms (folding, contracting, etc.);

(ii) extension, the different forms (elongating, spreading, etc.);

(iii) rotation, the different forms for the body as a whole and within the body (turn, twist, etc.);

(iv) travelling, path in space, the different forms of progression for the body as a whole, for gestures;

(v) aim, destination of a path, arrival at a specific state;

(vi) motion, the nature of change, no destination stipulated.

(d) Weight, centre of gravity

Are the following covered satisfactorily?

(i) weight-bearing for parts of the body, shift of weight;

(ii) partial weight-bearing, leaning;

(iii) release of weight;

(iv) situation of centre of gravity in relation to point of support;

(v) equilibrium, balance; loss of balance, falling.

(e) Design

A design may be a shape made by the body itself or a tracing in the air by an extremity. Can the following be clearly indicated?

(i) the shape of the physical design;

(ii) shape of the air design, the trace form;

(iii) location of the air design (in relation to the body or the room);

(iv) size of the air design.

(f) Degree

How is the amount, the degree or distance of an action or displacement shown?

    (i) for a general indication;

    (ii) for a specific statement.

(g) Relationship to the environment

The 'outside world', the environment, may refer to a partner or other performers, props, costume, furniture, areas of the stage, stage sets, etc. How are the following degrees of involvement indicated?

    (i) awareness;

    (ii) visual contact, addressing (as in pointing, etc.);

    (iii) approaching (moving toward);

    (iv) retreating (moving away);

    (v) proximity (near, close to);

    (vi) contact, touch (timing of contact, momentary, prolongued);

    (vii) grasp, encircle, intertwine;

    (viii) carry, (lift, transport an object or person).

(h) Timing

Are the following clear and satisfactorily handled?

    (i) a general indication of duration (breath rhythms);

    (ii) continuity of motion, continuous flow;

    (iii) interrupted flow – very slight pause; marked breaks between actions;

    (iv) the duration of an action in relation to a basic pulse;

    (v) metric indications of all kinds;

    (vi) relation of actions to accompanying music;

    (vii) independent duration or phrasing for separate parts of the body in relation to each other;

    (viii) subtle variations in timing; accelerando, ritardando, within a phrase, within a movement;

    (ix) exact duration of an action in seconds, tenths of seconds, etc.

(i) Initiation of movement

How does an action occur? Can the following be shown?

    (i) the part leading, initiating (source of the movement);

    (ii) sequential movement, successions;

    (iii) guidance, a part of the body or surface guiding the movement;

    (iv) inclusion, a part of the body carried along, included in another action;

    (v) passive, resultant changes or displacements;

(j) Dynamics

The amount of energy used in an action colours the movement and changes its impact. How the energy changes, how it appears, disappears, remains constant in various actions and in different parts of the body, provide a wealth of 'colouring' to movement. Among the many possibilities to be

indicated are:
- (i) forceful or gentle;
- (ii) tense or relaxed;
- (iii) buoyant (uplifted) or heavy (giving in to gravity);
- (iv) combined forms, e.g. bounce, rebound;
- (v) stressed, emphasized actions or the reverse, unemphasized actions;
- (vi) actions with much expression, high intensity;
- (vii) actions with no expression, puppet-like;
- (viii) breathing, variations in manner of breathing;
- (ix) inner attitude toward the movement affecting the expression of the action.

(k) *Stage location*
- (i) Location of the performer on stage (performing area);
- (ii) entrance, exit;
- (iii) paths across the stage, floor plans;
- (iv) stage directions faced;
- (v) relation of actions to the audience, to stage areas.

(l) *Group indications*
Many different group arrangements and relationships exist. Can the following be shown?
- (i) performer's situation in relation to other dancers;
- (ii) passage in front of or behind other persons, objects, etc.;
- (iii) changes in group formations, opening, closing ranks;
- (iv) simple statement of group formations;
- (v) statement of number of people involved;
- (vi) indications of male, female or neutral (could be either);
- (vii) group circling, wheeling;
- (viii) choice of a leader, following the leader;
- (ix) canon form, in time or in space.

(m) *Interpretation specified*
The reader needs to know with what fidelity the indications should be followed. Can the following be indicated?
- (i) ad libitum, freedom in performance of the material;
- (ii) precise interpretation of what is written;
- (iii) freedom in timing;
- (iv) exactness in timing;
- (v) freedom in choice of part(s) of body involved;
- (vi) freedom in choice of direction (spatial pattern);
- (vii) freedom in choice of degree (e.g. turning, flexing, etc.).

(n) *Technical indications*
For writing scores, have the following been provided?
- (i) repeat signs, the type and number;
- (ii) 1st and 2nd (3rd, 4th, etc.) endings;
- (iii) 1st and 2nd beginnings;

(iv) analogy signs, use of forms of symmetry.

Practical considerations

Apart from a system's capacity to cover the many categories of movement components in recording movement what of the choice of signs used?

(*a*) *The signs*
  (i) Are the signs easy to read?
  (ii) Are the signs easy to draw?
  (iii) To what extent are the symbols visual, pictorial?
  (iv) Are signs which represent symmetrical directions or parts of the body symmetrical in design?
  (v) Is there economy in use of signs?
  (vi) Are the signs clearly differentiated?
  (vii) Is there a logical relationship among the signs, a visual hierarchy?
  (viii) Has multiple meanings for one sign been avoided?
  (ix) Do the signs lend themselves to being combined?
  (x) Can the signs be used by themselves or do they have meaning only when placed on the staff?
  (xi) Can the signs be reduced in size for publication and still be clear?
  (xii) Is use of language (English or other) part of the system, thus posing a language barrier?

(*b*) *The staff*
Most systems use a staff of some kind; in most instances this staff represents the body.
  (i) Is the staff space consuming? How many staves can be written on one page?
  (ii) If the staff represents the body, does it reflect the symmetricality of the body?
  (iii) Must the full staff always be written? Can isolated movements be expressed without it?

(*c*) *Rules*
Every system must have some rules.
  (i) Are these kept to a minimum?
  (ii) Are the rules logical?
  (iii) Do they have a movement basis or are they related to the design of the system?
  (iv) Are they easy to memorize?
  (v) Are the cancellation rules logical? Practical?

(*d*) *Conventions*
Every system should have certain conventions to allow for simple recording of complex actions.
  (i) Are the conventions logical?
  (ii) Are there too many? Too few?

(e) Purpose of the system
Most systems were devised with a special purpose in mind.
- (i) Does the system achieve what it sets out to do?
- (ii) Does it justify its particular approach?
- (iii) Is it limited to its initial purpose?

(f) Drafting the notation
Two stages in drafting the notation must be considered: the first handwritten notes and the final neat copy prepared for publication.
- (i) Can movement indications be swiftly jotted down and still be legible?
- (ii) Is preparation of the final draft for printing time-consuming?
- (iii) Does the final copy require special draftmanship?
- (iv) Are there rules for drafting based on the aesthetic look of the final draft?
- (v) Are mechanical devices available for producing the final copy?

(g) Modern technology
Modern technology is making tremendous changes in the way information can now be stored and retrieved.
- (i) Can the system be computerized?
- (ii) What practical tests have already taken place?
- (iii) Is it capable of use with teaching machines?

(h) Movement analysis
The development of any system results from the way movement is viewed, how it is analysed. Thus the following questions arise.
- (i) Is the movement analysis basically sound?
- (ii) Is it universally applicable to all forms of movement?
- (iii) Is it objective, impersonal? Does it avoid culture-bias, or is it based on one form of dance or type of movement?
- (iv) Is it anatomically sound?
- (v) Is it scientifically based?
- (vi) Is it broad enough in scope to serve all needs?
- (vii) Is the terminology used logical and universally applicable?

(i) Level of description
What level of detail is generally expected to be included in a movement score? People have very different ideas on this subject; some expect less detail, some expect more. The full range of progression from the most general statement to the most specific has probably only been experienced by those whose profession is movement notation. Obviously the choice of specificity rests with the purpose to which the notation will be put. The following possible levels exist:
- (i) general indication of movement type or idea (e.g. turning, approaching);
- (ii) an outline sketch of the action;
- (iii) general statement of the structure of the movement sequence;

(iv) specific indication of the movement structure;

(v) precise details given for the use of time, space, body, dynamics, etc. The system should allow for mixed descriptions, e.g. precision in dynamics combined with a general statement in use of the body, or precision in timing combined with a general statement concerning use of space, and so on. The more notation is used in exploring movement, in trying out movement ideas for compositional purposes, and as a tool in teaching dance or general movement research, the more flexibility will be needed in choice of level of description. No longer is movement notation used merely to enable us to remember the structure of a dance for later on.

Appendix A

Notes

Chapter 2

1. George Washington University, Department of Physical Education. Advanced Topical Studies, 1971.
2. Chief Examiners' Report on the first examinations of the University of London's 'O' Level Dance syllabus held in June, 1983, quoted through the assistance and kind permission of the University of London University Entrance and School Examinations Council.
3. Institute of Court Dances of the Renaissance and Baroque Periods, C.O.R.D. (Committee on Research in Dance) publication, New York, 1972, pp.1,46.

Chapter 7

1. Arbeau, *Orchesography*, Dover Publications, New York, 1967, p.118.
2. Discussion with Harald Lander, Paris, April 1956.

Chapter 8

1. Described in a letter from Lucy Venable, 20 March 1982.

Chapter 9

1. Discussion with Mrs Joseph Schillinger, New York, November 1957.

Chapter 10

1. Derra de Moroda, 'Chorégraphie', *The Book Collector*, The Collector Ltd, London, Winter 1967.
2. *The Tatler*, No. 88, London, 1 November 1709.
3. Noverre, *Letters on Dancing and Ballets*, trans. C. W. Beaumont, London, 1951, Letter 13.
4. Angiolini, *Lettere di Gasparo Angiolini a Monsieur Noverre sopra i Balli Pantomimi*, Batista Bianchi, Milano, 1773. Quoted by Juana de Laban, Dance Index, New York, April-May, 1946, p.112.

Chapter 11

1. Gorsky, *Two Essays on Stepanov Dance Notation*, trans. Wiley, C.O.R.D. Special Publication, New York, 1978, p.xi.
2. Karsavina, foreword to Marylin Wailes' book *Dance Type*, Milbank Press, London, 1928.
3. Karsavina, *Theatre Street*, Heinemann, London, 1930, p.86.
4. Discussion with Balanchine, New York, 1949.
5. Wiley, *Dances from Russia: An Introduction to the Sergejev Collection*, Harvard

Library Bulletin, January, 1976, p.95.

6. Interview with Bridget Kelly Espinosa, London, 11 November 1980.

7. Interview with Dame Ninette de Valois, London, 25 September 1980.

8. Ibid.

9. Interview with Harry Haythorne, London. c.1957.

10. Interviews with Leonide Massine, 1957 and 1973. 'Recognising the value of Labanotation as the most precise method of recording his ballets for posterity Mr Massine will endeavour to record as many of his ballets in Labanotation as possible.' Contract, A. H. Guest and L. Massine, 14 April 1973.

Chapter 12

1. Curriculum vitae of Conté, provided by Michelle Nadal, Association Ecriture du Mouvement, Paris.

2. Letter, Misslitz to Ann Hutchinson, October 5th, 1977.

3. Interview with Zadra, Rome. April 1956.

4. Interview with Ruskaja, Rome. April 1956.

5. Curl, *An Enquiry into Movement Notation*, (privately published), England, 1967, p.28.

6. Benesh, 'Birth of a Language', Theoria to Theory, Vol. II, London, 1978, pp.267,278.

7. Ibid, pp.269–270.

8. Ibid, pp. 264–265.

9. Benesh, *Reading Dance*, Souvenir Press, London, 1977, p.62.

10. Benesh, 'Birth of a Language', pp.270–271.

11. Joseph Schillinger, *The Mathematical Basis of the Arts*, Philosophical Library-New York, 1948.

Chapter 14

1. *Sutton Movement Shorthand: Notation Supplement*, The Movement Shorthand Society Press, California, 1975, p.20. Letter, Valerie Sutton to Ann Hutchinson, August 1979.

2. Letter, Monica Parker to Ann Hutchinson, 24 December 1980.

3. Letter, Muriel Topaz to Ann Hutchinson, 25 February 1981.

Chapter 16

1. Noverre, ibid Letter 13.

2. Francis Peacock, *Sketches relative to the History and Theory but more especially to the Practice of Dancing*, Aberdeen, 1805, p.116.

3. Ibid, p.113.

4. R. J. Wiley, *Two Essays on Stepanov Dance Notation*, pp.xii, xiii.

5. Ivor Guest (ed.), *La Fille Mal Gardée*, London, 1960, p.49.

6. Lincoln Kirstein, *Ballet Alphabet, A Primer for Laymen*, Kamin Publishers, New York, 1939. Excerpt from the entry entitled "Notation (stenochoreography or Dance-Script)".

7. Interview with Massine, Stockholm, May 1957.

8. Interview with Conté, Paris, 1956.

9. Seymour Kleinman, 'Movement Notation Systems: An Introduction', *Quest*, Monograph XXIII, 'The Language of Movement', Winter issue, January, 1975.

10. P. J. S. Richardson, *The Dancing Times*, September, 1930, p.544. The Sitter Out: 'Herr Knust told me that Laban's method of choregraphy – using the word in its strictest sense – has proved most efficient. I would like to suggest that the 'Imperial' or the 'Operatic Association' offer a substantial prize of, say, one

hundred pounds for the best system of choreography invented by an Englishman suitable for writing down ballets of the 'operatic' type.
11. Letter, Yuri Bakhrushin to Ivor Guest, 27 March 1963.

Chapter 17
1. Noverre, ibid Letter 2.
2. Interview with Una Kai, London, 1964.
3. Cook, *Dance Director*, p.19.
4. Ibid, p.67.

Chapter 19
1. Ann Hutchinson, 'The Bournonville Style', *Dance Chronicle*, Vol. 4, No. 2, 1981, pp.113–150.

Chapter 20
1. Interview with Jeanne Beaman, London, 1965.
2. A. Michael Noll, 'Choreography and Computers', *Dance Magazine*, January 1967, pp.43–45.
3. Interview with John Lansdown, London, 1981.
4. Correspondence, D. Herbison-Evans and Ann Hutchinson, 1975, 1981.
5. Correspondence, J. M. Officer and Ann Hutchinson, 1980.
6. Correspondence, S. W. Smoliar, N. I. Badler and Ann Hutchinson, 1980, 1981.
7. Demonstration by Dave Sealey, London, July, 1979.
8. Interview with Dave Sealey, August, 1982.
9. Correspondence, T. W. Calvert and Ann Hutchinson, 1981.

Chapter 22
1. Ivor Guest, *The Ballet of the Second Empire*, (2nd ed.), London, 1974, pp.170–171.
2. Interview with Thomas H. Fisher, U.S. Copyright Office, 1950 and subsequent correspondence with Richard S. MacCarteney, 1950–1952.
3. Letter from Anna Jooss Markard, 16 January 1981.
4. Ivor Guest, *Jules Perrot*, Dance Books, London, 1984, Chapter 19.
5. *Halsbury's Laws of England*, 4th ed., London, 1974, Vol. 9, para.840.

Chapter 23
1. Jean-Jacques Rousseau, *Confessions*, trans. J. M. Cohen, London, 1953, pp.268–9.

Appendix B

Movement notation systems – chronological order

Year	Name	Type of system	Country
Mid 15th C.	Cervera	Abstract (letter) (mss)	Spain
1588	Arbeau	Letter	France
1650	Playford	Words/floor plans	England
1671	Beauchamp (*see* Feuillet)	Track (unpublished)	France
1682	Menestrier	Floor plans (horse ballets)	France
1688	Lorin	Signs, figures, track, words	France
1700	Feuillet	Track	France
1720	Landrin	Words/floor plans	France
1751	Favier	Abstract/music	France
1762	De la Cuisse	Floor plans	France
1815	Despréaux	Letter	France
1831	Théleur	Abstract symbols	England
1832	Biosca	Floor plans	Spain
1852	Saint-Léon	Stick figure	France
1855	Bournonville	Words/signs (mss)	Denmark
1855	Klemm	Music notes	Germany
1859	Adice	Figure drawings	France
c.1880	Manzotti	Floor plans (mss)	Italy
1887	Zorn	Stick figure	Germany
1892	Stepanov	Music notes	Russia
1892	Poli	Letters/numbers	France
1892	Giraudet, A.	Letters/numbers	France
c.1910	Melik-Balasanov	Music notes	Russia
1911	Zoder	Words (folk)	Austria
c.1915–18	Nijinsky	Music notes (mss)	Russia
1919	Böhme	Stick figure	Germany
1919	Desmond	Stick figure	Germany
1926	Alexander	Letters/signs	U.S.A.
c.1926	Grimm-Reiter	Abstract symbols	Germany
1927	Peters	Diagrams/music	France
1927	Fischer-Klamt	Abstract symbols	Germany
1927	Kool	Stick figure/music/ plans	Germany

1928	Laban	Abstract symbols	Austria
1928	Parnac	Stick figure	France
1928	Morris	Abstract symbols	England
1928	Sotonin	Abstract symbols	Russia
1928	Wailes	Abstract/pictorial/music	England
1930	Humphrey	Stick figure	U.S.A.
1931	Conté	Music notes	France
1931	Meunier	Word abbrev./signs	France
1932	Chiesa	Music notes	Italy
1934	Cross	Letters/signs/ numbers (thesis)	U.S.A.
c.1935	Zadra	Abstract symbols	Italy
1939	Babitz	Visual (stick figure)	U.S.A.
1940	Korty	Figures/signs	Germany
1940	Ruskaja	Abstract symbols	Italy
1940	Lissitzian	Stick figure	Russia
c.1940	Schillinger	Abstract (ms)	U.S.A.
1942	Craighead	Stick figure (thesis)	U.S.A.
c.1945	Nikolais	Music notes (mss)	U.S.A.
1946	Bourgat	Abstract symbols	France
1946	Saunders	Words	U.S.A.
1949	Zganec	Music notes	Yugoslavia
c.1950	Kurath	Abstract symbols	U.S.A.
1950	Conev (Tsonev)	Words, abstract signs	Bulgaria
1951	Arndt	Stick figure	Germany
1951	Kahn	Abstract symbols	U.S.A.
1952	Birdwhistell	Abstract symbols	U.S.A.
1952	Raiz	Floor plans	U.S.A.
1954	Misslitz	Stick figure	Germany
1955	Loring/Canna	Abstract symbols	U.S.A.
1955	Katzrova	Abstract symbols	Bulgaria
1956	Benesh	Visual (abstracted stick figure	England
1956	Harrison	Pitman notation	Scotland
1956	Proca-Ciortea	Letters/abstract	Romania
1957	Jay	Stick figure (mss)	U.S.A.
1958	Eshkol/ Wachmann	Abstract numbers	Israel
1959	Fee	Abstract symbols (ms)	U.S.A.
1960	Paige (Arpegian)	Abstract symbols	U.S.A.
1964	McCraw	Music notes	U.S.A.
1965	Halprin	Floor plans	U.S.A.
1965	Agolli	Abstract/letter	Albania
1965	Suna	Abstract/figure	Latvia
1968	Blom	Letters/signs	Norway
1968	Schwalb-Brame	Abstract symbols	U.S.A.
1969	Vasilescu/ Tita	**Abstract/music**	Romania
1971	Haralampiev	Music notes	Bulgaria
1973	Bakka	Abstract symbols	Norway
1973	Pajttondziev	Music notes/abstract	Yugoslavia

1973	Judetz	Letters/signs	U.S.A.
1973	Sutton	Stick figure	U.S.A.
1974	Escudera	Abstract signs on music staff	Spain
1974	Fitz	Abstract symbols	U.S.A.
1978	Blair	Word abbreviations, simple signs	U.S.A.
1979	Jørgensen	Abstract symbols	Denmark
1981	Pavis	Abstract/floor plans	France

Movement notation systems – alphabetical order

For published systems this list gives the first book produced and the country of publication.

Name	*Title of book*	*Type of system*	*Type of dance*	*Date*	*Country*
Adice	*Théorie de la Gymnastique de la danse*	Figure drawings	Ballet	1859	France
Agolli	*Valle Popullore*	Abstract/letter	Folk dance	1965	Albania
Alexander	*Universal Danceograph System*	Letters/numbers	Ballroom	1926	U.S.A.
Arbeau	*Orchésographie*	Letter, verbal expl.	Social	1588	France
Arndt	*Tanz und Bewegungsschrift*	Stick figure	Folk	1951	Germany
Arpegian, *see Paige*					
Babitz	*Outline of a New Method of Dance Notation*	Abstract/stick	Dance	1939	U.S.A.
Bakka	*Norwegian Dance Notation*	Abstract/words	Folk	1973	Norway
Beauchamp, *see Feuillet system*					
Benesh	*An Introduction to Benesh Dance Notation*	Visual (abstracted figure)	Ballet emphasized	1956 1969	England
Biosca	*Arte de Danzar*	Floor plans	Contredanses	1832	Spain
Birdwhistell	*Introduction to Kinesics*	Abstract signs	Facial expressions	1952	U.S.A.
Blair	*Disco to Tango and Back*	Word abbreviations, Simple signs	Contemporary social dance	1978	U.S.A.
Blom	*Notasjonsproblemer i Folkedans Forskningen*	Letters, signs	Folk	1968	Norway
Böhme	*Rhythmographik*	Stick figure	Dance	1919	Germany
Bourgat	*Technique de la Danse*	Stick figure	Ballet	1946	France
Bournonville	*Études Chorégraphiques (& mss)*	Words, signs	Ballet	1855	Denmark
Cervera	(Manuscripts)	Letter/signs	Basse danse	Mid-15th c.	Spain
Chiesa	*Motografia (Ritmografia)*	Music	Movement	1932	Italy
Conev (Tsonev)	*Horos and Ruchenitsas*	Words, abstract signs	Folk	1950	Bulgaria
Conté	*Chorégraphie Écriture*	Music notes	Ballet	1931	France
Craighead	*A System of Notation for the Modern Dance*	Stick figure	Modern dance	1942	U.S.A.
Cross	*A System of Notation for Recording Dance in Kinesiological Terms*	Misc.	Kinesiological	1934	U.S.A.
De La Cuisse	*Le Répertoire des Bals*	Floor plans, signs	Contredanses	1762	France
Desmond	*Rhythmographik . . . (Tanznotenschrift)*	Stick figure	Movement	1919	Germany
Despréaux	*Danse-Écrite ou Terpsi-coro-graphie*	Letter	Ballet	1815	France
Escudera	*Notation for Spanish Dance (unpublished)*	Abstract, signs, music staff	Folk dance	1974	Spain
Eshkol/ Wachmann	*Movement Notation*	Abstract	Abstract movement	1958	Israel
Favier	*Mêlés de la Musique et de Danse*	Abstract on music staff (Feuillet based)	Baroque	1751	France
Fee	*The Anatomical Notation (ms)*	Abstract	Modern dance	1959	U.S.A.
Feuillet (Beauchamp)	*Choréographie, ou l'art de décrire la danse*	Track	Baroque dance	1700	France
Fischer-Klamt	*Tanzschrift*	Abstract	Modern	1927	Germany
Fitz	*Stepnotes*	Music staff/abstract	folk dance	1974	U.S.A.

Giraudet, A.	*Mimique: Physionomie et Gestes*	Lines, letters, numbers	Mime, facial expression	1892	France
Grimm-Reiter	*Tanzkurzschrift*	Abstract signs	Modern	ca.1926	Germany
Halprin	*Motation*	Abstract	Motion through space	1965	U.S.A.
Haralampiev	*Pravo Trakiisko Horo*	Music notes	Folk dance	1971	Bulgaria
Harrison	*Pitmanotation*	Shorthand	Ballet	1956	England
Humphrey		Stick figure	Modern	1930	U.S.A.
Jay	*J-Notation*	Stick figure	Dance (ethnic, etc.)	1957	U.S.A.
Jørgensen	*Ska' Vi Danse*	Abstract	Folk dance	1979	Denmark
Judetz	*Judetz Folk Dance Notation*	Letter and signs	Folk dance	1973	U.S.A.
Kahn	*Kahnotation. The K Symbols for Writing Tap Dancing*	Abstract	Tap	1951	U.S.A.
Katzarova	*Bulgarian Folk Dance*	Abstract	Folk	1955	Bulgaria
Klemm	*Katechismus der Tanzkunst* (later: *Handbuch der Tanzkunst*)	Music note	Ballet	1855,	Germany
Kool	*Tanzschrift*	Mixture	General movement	1927	Germany
Korty	*Tanzschrift*	Abstract	Ballet	1940	Germany
Kurath		Abstract	Anthropology	ca.1950	U.S.A.
Laban, R. von	*Schrifttanz*	Abstract	Movement	1928,	Germany
Landrin	*Pot-pourri des contredanses anciennes*	Words, floor plans	Contredanses	1720,	France
Lissitzian	*Notation of Movement*	Stick figure	Folk	1940	Russia
Lorin	*Livre de la Contredanse du Roy (ms)*	Signs, figures, track, words	Contredanse	1688	France
Loring/Canna	*Kineseography*	Abstract	Dance	1955	U.S.A.
McCraw	*Scoreography*	Music notes	Basic movement	1964	U.S.A.
Manzotti	*Excelsior, Amor* (MSS)	Floor plans (elaborate)	Production Ballets	c.1880	Italy
Melik-Balasanov	*Grammatika*	Music notes	Ballroom	ca.1910	Russia
Menestrier	*Des Ballets Anciens et Modernes selon les règles du Théâtre*	Floor plans	Horse ballets	1682	France
Meunier	*Stenochorégraphie*	Word abbrev., signs	Ballet	1931	France
Misslitz	*Tanzfigurenschrift*	Stick figures	Ballet	1954	Germany
Morris	*The Notation of Movement*	Abstract	General	1928	England
Nijinsky		Music	Movement, Ballet	1915–18	Russian
Nikolais	*Choroscript* (mss)	Music	Modern	c.1945	U.S.A.
Paige	*Arpegian Ballroom Dance Notation*	Abstract	Ballroom	1960	U.S.A.
Pajtondziev	*Makedonski Narodni ora*	Music notes	Folk	1973	Yugoslavia
Parnac	*Notations des Danses*	Stick figures	General movement	1928	France
Pavis	*Reflections sur la notation et la mise en scène théâtrale*	Abstract, floor plans	Stage movement	1981	France
Peters	*La Dansographie*	Music, abstract	Ballroom	1927	France
Playford	*The English Dancing Master*	Words/floor plans	Country dances	1650	England
Poli	*The Recording of Gestures*	Letters, numbers	Movement in general	1892	
Popescu-Judetz, *see* Judetz					
Proca-Ciortea	*Romanotation*	Letters/abstract	Folk	1956	Rumania
Raisz	*Recording of English Dances with Symbols*	Floor plans	Folk dance	1952	U.S.A.
Ruskaja	*Metoda Grafico della Danza*	Abstract	General, ballet	1940	Italy
Saint-Léon	*La Sténochorégraphie*	Stick figure	Ballet	1852	France
Saunders	*Danscore and Skatiscore*	Words	Dance, skating	1946	U.S.A.
Schillinger		Abstract	Movement	c.1940	U.S.A.
Schwalb-Brame	*M S Method*	Abstract/stick	Folk dance	1968	U.S.A.
Sotonin	*Sisteme Notnoi Zapisi*	Abstract signs	Folk dance	1928	Russia
Stepanov	*L'Alphabet des Mouvements du Corps Humain*	Music	general, ballet	1892	France
Suna	*Dejas Notacija* (Dance Notation)	Stick figure	Modern, folk	1965	Latvia
Sutton	*Sutton Movement Shorthand*	Stick figure	Ballet, etc.	1973	U.S.A.
Théleur	*Letters on Dancing*	Abstract	Social	1831	England
Tsonev, *see* Conev					
Valishev	*Motography*	Visual	Sport	1972	Russia
Vasilescu/Tita	*Folclor Coregrafic Romànesc*	Abstract/music	Folk	1969	Rumania
Wailes	*Dancetype*	Abstract/pictorial	General	1928	England
Zadra	*Manual of Method Zadra*	Abstract	Exercises	c.1935	U.S.A.
Zganev	*Narodni Plesovi Hrvatske* (*see* Ivancan in Bibliography)	Music notes	Folk dance	1949	Yugoslavia
Zoder	*Wie Seichnet Man Volkstänze Auf?*	Words	Folk	1911	Austria
Zorn	*Grammatik der Tanzkunst*	Stick figure	Ballet	1887	Germany

Appendix C

Bibliography

Where is the dividing line between what is 'a system of dance notation' and what is not? Words are a form of notation, but they are not a system. Figure drawings are a form of recording movement, but in most cases they are not a system; the figure must be modified and signs added to qualify as a system. Footprints are a primitive method of recording steps; a few such 'systems' are included in this bibliography but, for the most part, ballroom notations using footprints are not included.

Some books listed here do not include 'symbol' notation but are of related interest in providing background information regarding dance steps or on the development of the history of movement notation and analysis.

Only one example of a publication of dances is included for each system in which much notated material has been published, for example the many Recüeils de Danse published in the Feuillet system or the series of books published in the Laban and Eshkol systems. However, all books in which a system is explained are listed. ,

There are separate lists of articles on copyright and use of computers.

Where possible the location of rare books has been given. This is not a complete listing, but reflects where I found them. Recent reprints of old books are listed. The following abbreviations have been used:

B.L. – British Library (formerly the British Museum), London.
B.N. – Bibliothèque Nationale, Paris.
B.Op. – Bibliothèque de l'Opéra, Paris.
D.d.M. – The Derra de Moroda Archives, University of Salzburg, Austria.
Gregg – Gregg International Publications.
H.T.C. – Harvard Theatre Collection, Cambridge, Mass., U.S.A.
L.A.M.G. – Laban Art of Movement Guild (magazine).
L.C. – Library of Congress, Washington, D.C.
L.N. – Leslie-Niles collection, now at the Würtemburgische Landesbibliothek, Stuttgart, Konrad-Adenauer-Strasse 8, West Germany.
L.O.D.C. – Language of Dance Centre, 17 Holland Park, London W11 3TD, England.
N.Y.P.L. – New York Public Library, Library of the Performing Arts, Dance Collection, 111 Amsterdam Avenue, New York, N.Y.

Abbie, M. (*see also* Denton), 'Physical treatment for clumsy children', *Physiotherapy*, London, 10 July 1978.
Addison, J., 'From my own apartment', *The Tatler*, London, 31 October 1709.
Adice, L., *Théorie de la Gymnastique de la Danse*, Chaix, Paris, 1859, (B.Op.).
'Des signes conventionels et capricieux', (mss), Paris, 1873, (B.Op.).
Agolli, N., *Valle Popullore*, Institute Folklorit Tiranë, 1965. Booklet on Albanian folk dance (based on Proca-Ciortea notation).

Ahroni, Y., 'Analytical study of the anatomical notation system', MS thesis on the Fee system, University of Wisconsin, 1968.

Albert, *L'Art de Danser à la Ville et à la Cour*, pub. by the editor, Paris, 1834 (L.N.).

Alexander, N., *Universal Danceograph System*, Danceograph Normal Schools, U.S.A., 1926, (L.N.).

Andrews, C.B., 'A comparative study of video tape and Labanotation as learning tools for modern dance', George Washington University, Physical Education Advanced Topical Studies, 9 July 1971.

Anon, 'Benesh shorthand', *The Dancing Times*, London, January 1958.

Anon, 'Choreographic notation is adapted to study cerebral palsy victims', *Medical Tribune*, London, January 1968. (Benesh system).

Anon, *L'Art et instruction de bien dancer*, c.1488; facsimile printed Royal College of Physicians of London, 1936.

Anon, Mss, in the Cervera Municipal Archives, Catalonia, mid-15th C.

Arbeau, T., *Orchésographie*, Langres, 1588.

Orchesography, ed. Julia Sutton, Dover Publications, New York, 1967.

Archbutt, S., 'Choreology in education and dance', *Laban Art of Movement Guild Magazine*, England, November 1967. (Laban system).

Arena, A., *Ad Suous Compagnones*, Lyons, 1529 (B.L., H.T.C.).

Leges Dansandi, Avignon, 1529 (B.L.).

Arndt, W., *Tanz und Bewegungsschrift*, Dresdner Verlag, Dresden, 1951.

Babitz, S., *Dance Writing*, Babitz, Los Angeles, 1939. (L.O.D.C.)

'Dance notation at U.C.L.A.', *Dance Observer*, New York, December 1940.

'Write your dances', *American Dancer*, New York, November 1939, February 1940, September 1940.

Baciu, G., Ghiur, G., *Dansuri populare din tara lăpusului si tara chioarului*, Baia Mare, Rumania, 1973 (2 vols.) (Vasilescu system).

Bakka, E., *Norwegian Dance Notation*, Norway, 1973.

Baron, A., *Lettres à Sophie sur la Danse*, Dondey-Dupré, Paris, 1825, (R.A.D.).

Beaumont, C.W., *A Miscellany for Dancers*, Beaumont, London, 1934.

A Bibliography of Dancing, Holland Press, London, 1963.

Bedford, P., 'Laban or Benesh', *The Dancing Times*, London, November 1955.

Benesh, J. & R., *An Introduction to Benesh Dance Notation*, A. & C. Black, London, 1956.

Reading Dance: The Birth of Choreology, Souvenir Press, London, 1977.

Benesh, R., 'Birth of a language', *Theoria to Theory*, Vol. II, London, 1978.

Benesh, R. and McGuinness, J., 'Benesh movement notation and medicine', *Physiotherapy*, Vol. 60, London, June 1974.

Bense, J., *Danses à Claquettes*, Editions Danse et Rythme, Paris, 1947.

Bickham, G., *An Easy Introduction to Dancing*. T. Cooper, London, 1738.

Biosca, A., *Arte de Danzar*, Lib. de Sauri y Comp., Barcelona, 1832.

Birdwhistell, R. L., *Introduction to Kinesics: an annotation system for analysis of body motion and gesture*, Washington, D.C., Foreign Service Institute, 1952.

Kinesics and context, Allen Lane, The Penguin Press, London, 1971.

Blair, S., *Disco to Tango and Back*, Blair, Downey, California, 1978.

Blasis, C., *Traité Élémentaire*, Paris, 1820 (B.L.; L.C.).

The Code of Terpsichore, E. Bull, London, 1830 (L.C.; D.d.M.).

Blom, J.P., 'Notasjonsproblemer i Folkdans Forskningen', Norway, 1968–9.

Blum, H., 'A primer for dance notation' M.Sc., thesis, Wellesley College, Mass., U.S.A., 1945. (Laban system).

Bourgat, M., *Technique de la Danse*, Presses Universitaires de France, Paris, 1954.

Bournonville, A., *Etudes Choréographiques*, Imprimerie de Thiele, Copenhagen, 1861 (B.Op.).

Brock, N., 'Notation for the dance', *Music Teachers' National Association*, Pittsburgh, U.S.A., 28 December 1941.

'The history of dance notation', Parts 1–3 in *Dance Observer*, New York, November 1941, January 1942, March 1942.

Buelens, R., '*Inventaire des systems d'Écriture du mouvement*', thesis, Louvain University, Brussels, 1980.

Cabreira, J. T., *Arte de Dancar à Franceza*, Lisbon, 1760, (Gulbenkian Foundation, 1970).

Carducci, A., *Balleto À Cavallo*, Il Mondo, Florence, 1661.

Caroso, F., *Il Ballarino*, Appresso Francesco Ziletti, Venice, 1581, (B.L., D.d.M.).

Nobiltà di Dame, Presso il Muschio, Venice, 1600 (D.d.M.).

Carreras y Candi, F., *Folklore y Costumbras de Espana*, A. Martin, Barcelona, 1931 (L.C.).

Causley, M., *An Introduction to Benesh Movement Notation*, Max Parrish, London, 1968.

'A language for movement – Benesh notation', *L.A.M.G. Magazine*, England, June 1968.

Cervera, *see* Anon.

Challet-Haas, J., *Manuel Élémentaire de Cinétographie*, Centre National d'Écriture du Mouvement, Paris, 1963. (Laban system).

Charpentier, A. W., *Chorégraphie: Handschrift des XVII Jahrhunderts*.

Chiesa, A., *Ritmografia*, Edizione Fuori Commercio, Milan, 1932.

'Motografia' *Perseo*, Milan 15 March, 15 April, 1 July, 1934; 1 January, 1935.

Chilkovsky, N., 'Labanotation for ethno-musicologists', *L.A.M.G. Magazine*, England, November 1958.

Introduction to Dance Literacy, International Library of African Music, Transvaal, S.Africa, 1978. (Laban system).

Christout, M. F., 'La documentation technique de ballet. Principaux systèmes de notation chorégraphiques', *Bolletino del Museo Biblioteca dell'attori*, Genova, 5–7 April, 1970.

Clarke, M., 'Folk dance and Benesh notation', *English Dance and Song*, Spring 1977, Vol. XXXIX. No. 1.

Clement, C., *Principes de Corégraphie (sic)*, Denis, Paris, 1771, (B.L.; N.Y.P.L.; D.d.M.).

Closson, E., *Le Manuscrit dit des Basses Danses*, Société des Bibliophiles et Iconophiles de Belgique, Brussels 1912.

Conev, B., *Horos and Ruchenitsas*, Sofia, 1950.

Conté, P.,*Le Guide Chorégraphique* (periodical) L'Art et Mouvement, pub. by author, Paris, 1933–6.

Ecriture, pub. by author, Paris, 1955.

Technique Générale et Écriture, pub. by author, Paris, 1957.

Danses Anciennes de Cour et de Théâtre en France, Dessain et Tobra, Paris, 1974.

Cook, R., *The Dance Director*, pub. by author, New York, 1977.

'Labanotation in zoology', *Action! Recording!*, Language of Dance Centre, London, January 1976.

Coote, R., *Ballroom Dancing without a Master*, Kent. London, 1869.

Copland(e), R., *The Maner of Dauncynge of Base Daunces*, translated from the French by R. Coplande, London, 1521. (Reprint, Pear Tree, Sussex, England, 1937.)

Cornazano, A., '*Il libro dell'arte del danzare*', ms Bib. Vatican, Italy, 1465.

Corso, R., *Dialogo del ballo di M. Rinaldo Corso*, Sigismondo Bordogna, Venice, c. 1555.

Coton, A. V., *The New Ballet*, Dobson. London, 1946.

'Some thoughts on dance notation', *The Dancing Times*, London, February 1968.

'Notation: a summing up', *The Dancing Times*, London, September 1968.

Craighead, J., '*A system of notation for the modern dance*', M.A. thesis, University of Louisiana, U.S.A., 1942.

Cross, G., '*A system of notation for recording dance*', M.A. thesis, Claremont College, California, U.S.A., 1934.

Curl, G., *An Enquiry into Movement Notation*, pub. by author, Eastbourne, England, 1967.

Czompo, A.I., 'Dance: an illiterate art?', *Journal of Health, Physical Education and Recreation*, U.S.A., 2 August, 1973.

de Laban, *see* Laban.

De la Cuisse, *Le Répertoire des Bals*, Cailleau, Castagnery, Paris, 1762.

Denton, M. Abbie, 'Laban notation and its application to treatment of clumsy children', *Developmental Medicine and Child Neurology*, 1978, Vol. 20, Spastics International Medical Publications, London.

Derra de Moroda, F., 'Chorégraphie', *The Book Collector*, London, Vol. 16, No. 4, Winter 1967.

'Die Tanzschrift des 18. Jahrhunderts', in *Maske und Kothurn*, 13 Jahrgang, Heft 1, pp.21–29, Graz, Wien, 1967.

'The dance notation of the 18th century: Lorin-Beauchamp-Feuillet', for the International Federation for Theatre Research Congress, Copenhagen, September 1971.

Die Tanzliteratur des Achtzehnten Jahrhunderts, pub. by author, Salzburg 1972.

'La Sténochorégraphie', *The Dancing Times*, London, December 1931.

Desmond, O., *Rhythmographik* (Tanznotenschrift), Breitkopf & Härtel, Leipzig, 1919.

Despréaux, J. E., 'Terpsichorography', Danse-Écrite ou Terpsi=coro=graphie, (ms, B.Op.) Paris, 1815.

Diderot and D'Alembert, 'Chorégraphie', *Encyclopédie Méthodique*, Paris, 1786.

Dolmetsch, M., *Dances of England and France from 1450–1600*, Routledge & Paul, London, 1949.

Dances of Spain and Italy from 1400–1600, Routledge & Paul, London, 1954.

Domenico da Piacenza, 'De arte saltandi et choreas ducendi', (ms, Bibliothèque Nationale, Paris,) c. 1445.

Dufort, G., *Trattato del Ballo Nobile*, Felice Mosca, Naples, 1728, (L.C., D.d.M.), (Reprint: Gregg 1972).

Dufort, P., 'A study of dance notation', MA thesis, University of Michigan, U.S.A., 1963.

Dupré, L. (the elder), *Methode très facile*, pub. by author, Le Mans, 1757.

Dyke, J., 'Dance notation: a comparative analysis and evaluation of various systems, MS thesis, Wellesley College, U.S.A., 1939.

Ebreo, G., 'De practica seu arte tripudii vulgare opusculum', (ms, B.N.), Milan, 1463.

   Trattato dell'arte del ballo, late 15th C. (reprint Francesco Zambrini, Bologna 1873).

Ellis, H. M., 'The Dances of J. B. Lully', Ph.D. dissertation, Stanford University, U.S.A., 1967.

Engelhardt, G., *Grammatik der Tanzkunst* (revised version of Zorn's book), Eduard Bloch, Berlin, 1920.

Eshkol, N., *Exercises in Movement Notation*, Jerusalem Academy of Music, Jerusalem, 1963.

   Moving, Writing, Reading, The Movement Notation Society, Israel, 1973.

Eshkol, N. and Nul, R., *Classical Ballet*, Israel Music Institute, Tel Aviv, 1968. (Note: All Eshkol-Wachmann system books on dance and movement contain basic explanations. As examples of applied use of the system, they are not all listed here.)

Eshkol, N. and Wachmann, A., *Movement Notation*, Weidenfeld & Nicholson, London, 1958

   Movement Notation. Supplement No. 1 for Students of Labanotation, N. Eshkol, A. Wachmann, Tel Aviv, 1960.

Essex, J., *For the Further Improvement of Dancing*, I. Walsh and P. Randall, London, 1710. (Reprint: Dance Horizons 1970.)

   The Dancing Master (translation of Rameau's book), pub. by Essex, London, 1728, 1731.

Favier, Mr, *Mêlés de la Musique et de Danse*, Paris, 1751–2.

Fee, F. M., *Fee-Notation, An Introduction*, pub. by author, Florida, 1980 (1959).

Feldstein (*sic*). C. J., *Die Kunzt nach der Choregraphie*, Schrödersche Buchhandlung, Braunschweig, 1767.

Feldtenstein, C. J. Von, *Erweiterung der Kunst nach der Chorographie zu tanzen*, Braunschweig, 1772, 1775 (D.d.M., N.Y.P.L.).

Ferriol y Boxeraus, B. D., *Reglas Utiles para los aficionados a danzar*, Capoa: Joseph Testore, Malaga, 1745 (N.Y.P.L.; B.L.; D.d.M.).

Feuillet, R. A., *Chorégraphie, ou l'art de décrire la danse*, pub. by author, Paris, 1700, (reprint George Olms, Hildesheim, N.Y. 1979).

   Recueil de Dances composées par M. Pecour, pub. by author, (an example of many published dances), Paris, 1700.

Feuillet, R. A., et Dezais, *Chorégraphie ou l'art de décrire la danse*, pub. by Dezais. Paris, 1713.

Fischer-Klamt, G., 'Dancing extraordinary, a new system of dance notation', *The Dancing Times*, London, December 1927.

   'Neue Wege der Choreographie', *Der Tanz*, Jahrg. 2, Heft 8, Juni. Berlin, 1929.

Fitz, J., *Stepnotes*, pub. by author, Berkeley, U.S.A., 1974.

Fletcher, I. K., *Bibliographical Descriptions of Forty Rare Books Relating to the Art of Dancing*, London, 1954.

Giraudet, A., *Mimique, Physionomie et Gestes*, Ancienne Maison Quantin, Paris, 1892 (N.Y.P.L.; B.L.; D.d.M.)

Goodman, N., *Languages of Art*, Oxford University Press, London, 1968.

Gorsky, A., *Table of Signs & Choreography* (original in Russian), St Petersburg, 1899.

   Two Essays on Stepanov Dance Notation, translation of Gorsky's book by R. J. Wiley, C.O.R.D., New York, 1978.

Grauert, R., 'Choroscript' (Nikolais System), *Journal of Health, Physical Education and Recreation*, Washington D.C., May-June, 1959.

Grimm-Reiter, H., 'Tanzkurzschrift', notes by Helen Priest (L.O.D.C.), Germany, c. 1926.

de la Gueriniere, M., *École de Cavalerie*, par la Compagnie, Paris, 1769.

Guilcher, J-M., *La Tradition Populaire de Danse en Basse-Bretagne*, Mouton-Paris-La Haye, 1963.

'André Lorin et l'invention de l'écriture chorégraphique', *Revue d'Histoire du Théâtre*, Paris, October-December 1969.

Guillemin, C. J., *Chorégraphie ou L'Art de décrire La Danse*, pub. by author, Paris, 1784.

Hall, F., 'An alphabet of movement', *New Scientist*, October 1965; reprinted in *Music in Britain*, April 1966.

Halprin, L., 'Motation', *P/A*, California, July 1965.

Haralampiev, K. & Djenev, K., *Universolen tancopis* (*Universal Dance Notation*), Nauka i Izkustvo (Science and Art), Sofia, Bulgaria, 1971.

Heiser, R. A., *The Analytical Method of Dancing*, pub. by author, Cleveland, Ohio, U.S.A., 1923.

Hilton, W., *Dance of Court & Theater*, Princeton Book Company, U.S.A., 1981. (Feuillet, Laban systems).

Holden, R., *A Dance Notation System Developed in Romania*, booklet pub. by R. Holden, Cincinnati, Ohio, 1950; Folkraft Press, Newark, N.J., 1962. (Proca-Ciortea system).

Humphrey, D., System, examples of in *Doris Humphrey: An Artist First*, by S. J. Cohen, (pp.236–8), Wesleyan University Press, Conn. U.S.A., 1972.

Hutchinson, A., *Labanotation*, New Directions, New York, 1954; revised and expanded edition, Theatre Arts Books, New York, 1970.

'The dance scribe in action', *Center Magazine*, New York, 1950.

'Labanotation a tool for the exploration and understanding of movement', *Physical Education*, 18,144, London, 1956.

'Neils Bjørn Larsen on Notation', *The Dance Notation Record*, New York, Vol. VIII, No. 4, Winter, 1957.

'The preservation of the dance score through notation', *The Dance Has Many Faces*, ed. W. Sorell, The World Publishing Company, New York, 1951, 1966.

'A survey of systems of dance notation', *L.A.M.G. Magazine*, England, Part 1, November 1966; Part 2, May 1967.

'Experiences of Dance Notation', *The Dancing Times*, March, 1968.

'Notation: a means of communication in movement and dance; *Anthology of Impulse*, San Francisco, 1969.

'Perspectives on the dance notation situation', *Dance Scope*, New York, Fall 1970.

'Dance for deaf children', *The Dancing Times*, London, March 1971 (pp. 308–9).

'Choreography and dance notation', *Encyclopaedia Britannica*, U.S.A., 1974.

Ivancan, I., *Narodni Plesovi Hrvatske*, Zagreb, 1964. (use of Laban and Zganec systems.).

Jay, L., *Jay Notation* (ms., L.C., L.O.D.C.), New York, 1957.

Jolizza, W. K. von, *Die Schule des Tanzes*, A. Hartleben, Vienna & Leipzig, 1907.

Jørgensen, C., *Ska' Vi Danse*, Wilhelm Hansen, Copenhagen. 1977, 1979.

Juana, 'J-(JAY) notation', *Journal of Health, Physical Education and Recreation*, Washington, November 1958.
Judetz, *see* Popescu-Judetz.

Kahn, S. D., *Kahnotation*, pub. by author, San Francisco, 1951 (1977, 1979).
Katsarova, R., *Bulgarian Folk Dances*, The Science and Art State Publishing House, Sofia, Bulgaria, 1955, 1958.
Klemm, B., *Katechismus (Handbuch) der Tanzkunst*, J. J. Weber, Leipzig, 1855, 1882, 1887, 1894, 1910.
Knust, A., *Handbuch der Kinetographie Laban* (8 vols), Das Tanzarchiv, Hamburg, 1950.
  Abriss der Kinetographie Laban, Das Tanzarchiv, Hamburg, 1956.
  Handbook of Kinetography Laban, Das Tanzarchiv, Hamburg, 1958.
  Dictionary of Kinetography Laban (2 vols), Macdonald & Evans, England, 1979.
Kool, J., *Tanzschrift*, Duvignau-Canet, Bordeaux, 1927.
Korty, S., *Tanzschrift*, B. Schott's Söhne, Mainz, 1940.
Kurath, G. P., 'A new method of choreographic notation', *American Anthropologist*, U.S.A., Vol. 52, No. 1, January-March 1950.

Laban, J. de, 'Introduction to dance notation', *Dance Index*, New York, April-May 1946.
  'Movement notation: its significance to the folklorist', *Journal of American Folklore*, New York, January 1954.
Laban, R.,* *Principles of Dance and Movement Notation*, Macdonald & Evans, London, 1956, 1975.
Laban, R. von., *Choreographie*, Eugen Diederichs, Jena, 1926.
  Schrifttanz: Kinetographie Methodik, Universal Edition, Vienna, 1928.
  Script Dancing – La Danse Écrite, Universal Edition, Vienna, 1930.
Laban, R.* and Lawrence, F.C., *Effort*, Macdonald & Evans, London, 1947.
Laderman, E., 'An experiment in cooperation: meet a composer who writes the dance score too', *Dance Magazine*, New York, March 1957.
Landrin, M., *Recueil des Contredanses*, pub. by author, Paris, c. 1770 (B.Op.).
Lange, C. C., *Anfangsgründe der Tanzkunst*, pub. by author, Erlangen, 1751, Leipzig, 1765. (Feuillet system).
Lange, R., *Podrecznik Kinetografii* Polskie Wydawnictwo Muzyczne, Krakow, Poland, 1975. (Laban system).
  'Principles underlying the universality of Laban's movement notation', *L.A.M.G. Magazine*, England, May 1977.
Layson, J., '*A critical evaluation of systems of movement notation*', dissertation, University of Manchester, England, 1967.
Leslie, S., *A Bibliography of the Dance Collection of Doris Niles and Serge Leslie* (3 Vols), C. W. Beaumont, London, 1966, 1968.
Lissitzian, S., *Notation of Movement*, Iskusstvo, Moscow & Leningrad, 1940.
Lorin, A., '*Livre de la contredance du Roy*', (ms) B.N., Paris, 1688.
Loring, E. and Canna, D.J., *Kineseography*, The Academy Press, Hollywood, U.S.A., 1955.
Love, Paul, 'Write down your dance', *Dance Magazine*, New York, June 1937.

*Laban dropped the 'von' when he came to England.

McCraw, C., *Scoreography*, printed by Edwards Bros., Ann Arbor, Mich., U.S.A., 1964.

McGuinness, J., 'Benesh movement notation – an introduction to recording clinical data', series in *Physiotherapy*, London, August 1980, Vol. 66, No. 8; September 1980, Vol. 66, No. 9; November 1980, Vol. 66, No. 11; December 1980, Vol. 66, No. 12; February 1981, Vol. 67, No. 2.

McGuinness-Scott, J., *'Movement study and Benesh Movement Notation'*, Oxford University Press, London, 1983.

Magny, M., *Principes de Chorégraphie*, Duchesne, Paris, 1765. (Feuillet system).

Magri, G., *Trattato Teorico-practico di Ballo*, Presso Vincenzo Orsino, Naples, 1779.

Magriel, P., *A Bibliography of Dancing*, H. W. Wilson Company, New York, 1936, 1966.

A Bibliography of Dancing, Fourth Cumulated Supplement, 1936–1940, H. W. Wilson Company, New York, 1941.

Malpied, N., *Élémens de Chorégraphie*, L'Editeur Mtre. de Danse et Guersan, Paris, 1762. (Feuillet system).

Traité sur l'Art de la Danse, Bouin, Paris, c. 1770.

Manzotti, L., 'Floor plans for Excelsior & Amor', (mss) La Scala, Milan, 1880s.

Martin, J., 'The dance script', *New York Times*, New York, 21 December, 1947.

'They score a dance as others do music', *New York Times Magazine*, New York, July 1950. (Laban system).

'May I write the next dance?', *Theatre Arts*, 36, 18, New York, 1952.

Mason, E. C., 'Margaret Morris on dance notation', *Dance & Dancers*, London, July, 1956.

'Dance lecture: Nijinsky system of notation', *Dance & Dancers*, London, August 1956.

'Ann Hutchinson on contemporary approaches to recording movement', *Dance & Dancers*, London, April 1957.

Menestrier, C. F., *Des Ballets Anciens et Modernes selon des règles du Théâtre*, René Guignard, Paris, 1682 (L.C., B.Op.).

Meunier, A., *La Danse Classique (École Française), Figures Sténochorégraphie-Dictionnaire*, Firmin-Didot, Paris, 1931.

Michel, A., 'The oldest dance notation', *Dance Observer*, New York, November 1937. (Cervera manuscripts).

Earliest Dance Manuals, reprinted from Medievalia et Humanistica, III, Boulder, Colorado, 1945.

Mingúet, P., *Arte de Danzar à la Francesa*, pub. by author, Madrid, 1750, 1758 (D.d.M., Bod.).

El noble arte de Danzar à la Francesa y Espanola, pub. by author, Madrid, c. 1764 (D.d.M.).

Misslitz, W.P., *Tanzfigurenschrift*, pub. by author, Dreieichenhain, Germany, 1954.

Ballettlehre, pub. by author, Dreieichenhain, Germany, 1960.

Gymnastiklehre, pub. by author, Dreieichenhain, Germany, 1960.

Morrice, N., 'Advantages of Benesh notation to a choreographer', *Ballet Today*, London, January/February 1967.

Morris, M., *The Notation of Movement*, Kegan Paul, Trench, Trubner, London, 1928.

Danscript, MMM Movement Therapy, Glasgow, 1980.

Morse, B., 'Dance notation and Aboriginal culture', *Hemisphere*, Australia, 1968. (on Benesh notation).

Muliukova, Z. M., *Movement Notation Textbook*, (original in Russian), Academy of Sciences of the U.S.S.R. (Ibrahimov Institute) Kazan, 1971.

Negri, C., *Nuove Inventioni di Balli*, Girolamo Bordone, Milan, 1602, 1604.
Nijinsky, V., 'Afternoon of a faun', (ms. British Library, 1915).
 Classroom exercises, 'Sarabande', (ms., Bib. de l'Opera), Paris, c. 1915.
Nikolais, A., 'Choroscript' (ms), New York, 1945.
 'A new method of dance notation', *Theatre Arts Magazine*, New York, February 1948.
 'Status of notation Choroscript', by Glen Tetley in *Dance Observer*, New York, Vol. 15, No. 9. November 1948.
Noverre, J. G., *Letters on Dancing and Ballet* (original: Stuttgart & Lyon, 1760) (trans. Beaumont), London, 1930, 1951.

Paige. J. A., *Apegian Ballroom Dance Notations*, pub. by author, Miami, Florida, 1960.
Pajtondziev, G., *Les Danses Populaires Macédoniennes*, L'Institut de Folklore, Skopje, 1973.
Parnac, V., 'Notations de danses', *La Revue Musicale*, Paris, March 1928.
Pasch (I.H.P.), J., *I.H.P. Maître de Danse oder Tanz Meister*, Gotthilff Lehmann, Leipzig & Gluckstadt, 1705.
Pavis, P., 'Reflections sur la notation et la mise en scène théâtrale', *Revue d'Histoire du Théâtre*, Paris, October-December 1981.
Pemberton, E., *An Essay for the Further Improvement of Dancing*, J. Walsh, London, 1711, (reprint: Gregg, 1970). (Feuillet system).
Perin et La Hante, *Chorégraphie nouvelle*, pub. by author, Paris, 1762.
Peters, A. (pseud.) Prof., *La Dansographie*, Editions 'Dansons', Paris, 1923.
Petersen, T. F., *Praktische Einleitung in die Chorégraphie oder Tanz*, König, Hamburg, 1768; Serringhausen, Schleswig, 1791. (Feuillet system).
Playford, J., *The English Dancing Master*, (18 editions), London, 1650–1728.
Poli, G., *The Recording of Gestures*, 1892.
Pollenz, P., 'The comparative study of dance', *The American Anthropologist*, U.S.A., 51, 1949.
Popescu-Judetz, G., *Judetz Folk Dance Notation*, Duquesne University, Pittsburgh, U.S.A., 1973.
Preston, V., 'The birth of Labanotation', *L.A.M.G. Magazine*, England, December 1954.
 An Introduction to Kinetography Laban, London, 1963, 1966.
Preston-Dunlop, V., *Readers in Kinetography Laban, Series A*, Macdonald & Evans, London, 1966.
 Readers in Kinetography Laban, Series B, Macdonald & Evans, London, 1967.
 Practical Kinetography Laban, Macdonald & Evans, London, 1969.
 'Dance literacy', (article in *Dancing and Dance Theory*, edited by V.P.-D.), London, 1979.
Proca-Ciotea, V.,*Hoe schrijve we onze dansen op Romanotatie*, Dutch booklet on Romanotation, pub. by N.E.V.O., Holland, (English translation, Holland, 1956).
 Notierung-System für Volkstanz, German explanations and some dances, Germany, 1956.
 'Despre notaria dansului popular Romanesc', *Revista Di Folclor*, Bucharest, Vol. II, tome 1 & 2, 1957.
 15 Roemeense Volksdansen in Romanotatie, Netherlands Volksdansvereniging, Holland, 1957.

Raisz, E., 'Recording of English dances with symbols', *The Country Dancer*, New York, Vol. 8, No. 4, Winter 1952.

Rameau, P., *Le Maître à Danser*, pub. by the author, Paris, 1725.
  The Dancing Master, translated and pub. by Essex. London, 1728.
  The Dancing Master, translated and pub. by Beaumont, London, 1931, (reprint: Dance Horizons, New York, 1970; Gregg, 1972).
  Abbregé de la nouvelle méthode dans l'art d'écrire ou de tracer toutes sortes de danses de ville, pub. by the author, Paris, 1725.

Ravnikar, B., *Kinelografija* Založila Zveza kulturnih organizacij Slovenije, Ljublyana, Yugoslavia, 1980. (Laban system).

Reynolds, W. C., 'Braille: Labanotation for the blind', *Action! Recording!*, London, No. 4, October 1976.

Roller, F. A., *Systematisches Lehrbuch der bildenden Tanzkunst*, Bernh, Fr. Voigt, Weimar, 1843.

Rousseau, J. J., *The Confessions*, Paris, 1781, (reprint: Penguin Books, England, 1953. Book Seven, pp.268–9).

Ruskaja, J., 'Metodo grafico della danza', *Accademia Nazionale di Danza*, Rome, Italy, 1940.
  'Semiografia della danza e sue prospettive didattiche', *Nostra Tempa*, Rome, February-March 1955.

Saint-Léon, A., *La Sténochorégraphie*, pub. by author, Paris and St Petersburg, 1852, (L.N.; D.d.M., N.Y.P.L.).
  Par Arte de Danzar à la Francesa, (Spanish edition of La Sténochorégraphie), Madrid, 1858.

Saunders, R. D., *Danscore – The Easy Way to Write a Dance*, pub. by author, Hollywood, 1946.

Schwalb, Brame M., *Folk Dancing is for Everybody*, MS Method, Manhattan Beach, U.S.A., 1974.
  23 Israeli Dances Notated by MS Method, MS Method. Manhattan Beach, U.S.A., 1974.

Shade, A. E., 'An investigation into the possible uses of movement notation in the theatre', M.A. thesis, University of Colorado, 1972.

Shawn, T., *Every Little Movement*, Eagle Co. Pittsfield, Mass. (1963 edition describes Alfred Giraudet's "Nutographie", p.108), 1954, 1963.

Sheafe, A. J., 'Choreography, why is no effort made to record the dances of our period?', *The American Dancer*, July 1940.

Siris, P., *The Art of Dancing Demonstrated by Characters and Figures*, pub. by author, London, 1706.

Snell, Friedburg G., 'The beginnings of Kinetography Laban', *L.A.M.G. Magazine*, England, May 1979.

Stepanov, V. J., *L'Alphabet des Mouvements du Corps Humain*, M. Zouckermann, Paris, 1892.
  Alphabet of Movements of the Human Body (trans. by R. Lister), The Golden Head Press, Cambridge, 1958, (reprint: Dance Horizons, 1969).

Subrahmanyam, P., 'Dance notation of Adavus', chapter in *Bharata Natyam – Indian Classical Dance Art*, Marg Publications, Bombay, India, 1979.
  'The history, technique and a notation for Adavu System in dance', *South Indian Studies*, Vol. 1, Chap. 12, pp.109–125, 1979.

Suna, H., *Cinetography-Notation of Choreographic Movements*, Academy of Sciences of Latvian SSR, (English summary), 1965.
  Dejas Notacija (Dance Notation), Academy of Sciences of Latvian SSR, 1979.

Dejas Notacija II (in Latvian, Russian and English), Academy of Sciences of Latvian SSR, 1980.

Sutton, V., *Sutton Movement Shorthand Book I*, The Movement Shorthand Society, Irvine, California, 1973.

    Sutton Movement Shorthand Notation Supplement, The Movement Shorthand Society, Irvine, California, 1975.

    The Sign Writer (quarterly periodical), The Center for Sutton Movement Writing, Newport Beach, California, 1981.

Szentpal, M., *Lehrbuch der Kinetographie*, Zentralhaus für Volkskunst, Leipzig, 1958. (Laban system).

    Tanzjeliras (Laban-Kineografia), Vol. 1. Népmüvelesi Propaganda Troda, Budapest, 1964, 1976.

    Dance Notation Kinetography Laban (English translations, mss), Budapest, 1975–6 (L.O.D.C.).

Taubert, G., *Rechtschaffener Tanzmeister*, Friedrich Lanckischens Erben. Leipzig, 1717. (Feuillet system).

Tetley, G., 'Status of notation, "Choroscript"', *Dance Observer*, New York, November 1948. (Nikolais system).

Théleur, E. A., *Letters on Dancing*, pub. by author, London, 1831, 1832.

Tita, S., see Vasilescu.

Tomlinson, K., *The French Art of Dancing*, pub. by author, London, 1735, 1744, (later: *The Art of Dancing*) (D.d.M., B.L.), (Reprints: Dance Horizons 1970; Gregg 1971).

Toth, S., *Tanečné Písino*, Nakladatelstvo Slovensko Akademie, Bratyslava, 1952.

Totten, E., 'On the work of a choreologist', *The Guardian*, London, July 1973.

Turnbull, A., 'Teachers and teaching – the Institute of Choreology', *Dance and Dancers*, London, November 1969. (on Benesh notation).

Ullman, L., 'An international congress of dance and movement notation' *L.A.M.G. Magazine*, England, November 1977.

Vaillat, L., 'Orchésographie ou sténochorégraphie', *Arts et Métiers Graphiques*, Paris, 1935.

Vainio, R., *Ensimmainen Transsikirjani* (translation of *My First Dance Book* by N. Chilkovsky), Helsinki, c. 1963. (Laban system).

Van Aelbrouck, J.-Ph., *Notation du mouvement (Cinétographie Laban)*, pub. by author, Brussels, 1979.

Vasilescu, T., *Rumanian Choreographic Folklore*, State Committee of Culture and Art, Bucharest, 1969.

    Folclor Coregrafic Romànesc, Consiliul Culturii si Educatiei Socialiste, Bucharest, 1972.

Wailes, M., *Dancetype*, Milbank Press, London, 1928.

Weaver, J., *Orchesography*, pub. by author, London, 1706 (B.L., L.C., D.d.M.), (reprint: Gregg 1971). (Feuillet system).

    A Small Treatise of Time and Cadence in Dancing, London, 1706, (reprint: Gregg 1971). (Feuillet system).

White, J., 'An examination of systems of movement notation', M.A. Dissertation, Leeds University, England, 1977. (Appendix IV of this work contains a very useful bibliography of articles and news items on dance notation in *Dance and Dancers* and *The Dancing Times*, 1913 to 1976.)

Whitley, A., 'Writing down the Rambert repertoire', *Dancing Times*, London, 694,

July 1968. (on Benesh system).

Wiley, R. J., 'Dances from Russia: An Introduction to the Sergejev Collection' in *Harvard Library Bulletin*, Cambridge, Mass., January 1976, Vol. XXIV, No. 1. (see also Gorsky, *Two Essays on Stepanov Notation*, trans. by Wiley.)

Worth, F., 'My work as a choreologist with the Royal Ballet', *The Dancing Times*, London, June 1967. (on Benesh system).

Wynne, S., 'Feuillet's Choreographie and its implications in the society of France and England, 1700', M.A. thesis at Ohio State University, 1965.

Yanai, Z., 'Notation for liberation of movement', in *Mahshavot*, by IBM Company of Israel. (on Eshkol system).

Zadra, Rev. R., *Manual of Method Zadra*, Boston, (c. 1935).
'La rappresentazione grafica di atteggiamenti e movimenti ritunico-calisterie del corpo umano', *Il Diritti della Scuola*, N.11.15 Marzo 1957.

Zorn, F. A., *Grammatik der Tanzkunst*, J. J. Weber, Leipzig, 1887.
Grammar of the Art of Dancing, International Publishers, (edited by Sheafe, A. J.), Boston, 1905, (reprint: Dance Horizons, 1975).

Bibliography of computer articles

Abbie-Denton, M., 'Computers, choreography and choregraphy', 1982. Proceedings of the VII Commonwealth and International Conference on Sport, Physical Education, Recreation and Dance, Brisbane.

Allen, J., 'Recording movement in Labanotation on computer', *User's Manual*, University of Iowa, Cooperation of the Computer Assisted Instructional Laboratory of the Weeg Computing Centre, 1979.

Archer, L. B., 'A study of computer aided choreography', Royal College of Art, London, 1975.

Badler, N. I., 'Conceptual descriptions of physical activities', *American Journal of Computational Linguistics*, (Microfiche 35) pp.75–83, 1975.

Badler, N. I., 'Human body Models and animation', *IEEE Computer Graphics and Applications*, November 1982.

Badler, N. I., & Smoliar, S. W., 'Digital representations of human movement', *ACM Computing Surveys*, Vol. 11, pp.19–38, 1979.

Badler, N. I., Smoliar, S. W., & Weber, L., 'An architecture for the simulation of human movement', Proceedings 1978 Annual Conference: Association for Computing Machinery, Vol. 2, pp.737–745, 1978.

Badler, N. I., Smoliar, S. W., O'Rourke, J. & Weber, L., 'The simulation of human movement by computer', *Movement Project Report No. 14*. Dept. Computer & Information Science, University of Pennsylvania, July 1978.

Badler, N. I., O'Rourke, J. & Toltzis, H., 'A spherical human body model for visualizing movement', *IEEE Proceedings*, 67, 10, October 1979, pp.1397–1403.

Badler, N. I., O'Rourke, J. & Kaufman, B., 'Special problems in human movement simulation', *Computer Graphics*, 14 (3) July 1980.

Barenholz, J., Wolofsky, Z., Ganapathy, I., Calvert, T. W. & O'Hara, P., 'Computer interpretation of dance notation', Computing in the Humanities, Proc. Third Int'l Conf. on Computing in the Humanities, S. Lusignan and J. S. North, etc., University of Waterloo Press, 1977.

Beaman, J., 'Computer choreography', *Anthology of Impulse*, pp.62–4, Dance Horizons, New York, 1969.

Brown, M. D., & Smoliar, S. W., 'A graphic editor for Labanotation', *Computer Graphics*, 10.2 1976 pp.60–65.

Brown, M. D., Smoliar, S. W., & Weber, L., 'Preparing dance notation scores with a computer', *Computers and Graphics*, Vol. 3 pp.1–7, 1978.

Calvert, T. W., & Chapman, J., 'Notation of movement with computer assistance', Proc. 1978 ACM Conference, pp.731–734.

Calvert, T. W. & Chapman, J., 'The integration of subjective and objective data in the animation of human movement', *Computer Graphics*, Vol. 14, pp.170–6, 1980.

Collins, M. G. & Kane, G. R., 'An interactive computer graphics approach to the design of marching band routines', *Computers & Graphics*, Vol. 1, pp.319–24, 1975.

Copeland, L., 'Dance, a graphics program', University of Utah, *Computer Science Report*, 1968.

Cordiero, A., 'Computer dance TV', (Portuguese and English), Centro de Computacao da Universidade Estadual de Campinas, Brazil, 1974.

Crisp, C., 'No need to fear computer ballet', *Parade*, No. 153, London Press Service, 1975.

Eshkol, N., Melvin, P., Michl, J., Von Foerster, H. & Wachmann, A., 'Notation of movement', *Computer Laboratory Report* BCL 10.0, University of Illinois, 1970.

Fedak, J., 'An initial design specification of a syntactic analyzer for Labanotation', *Movement Project Report* No. 10, Dept. Computer & Information Science, University of Pennsylvania, January 1978.

Fetter, W., 'A human figure computer graphics development for multiple applications', Proc. Europcomp. Conf., London, 1974.

Goldberg, R., 'Performance: the art of notation', *Studio International*, July/August 1976, pp.54–68.

Herbison-Evans, D., 'Computer assistance to dance choreologist in residence', Basser Dept. of Computer Science, University of Sydney, 22 July 1980.
    'A human movement language for computer animation', Basser Dept. of Computer Science, University of Sydney, proceedings of a Symposium held at Sydney 10–11 September, 'Language Design and Programming Methodology', 1979.

Hirsch, V., 'The implementation of floor plans in the graphic editor for Labanotation', MSE thesis, Dept. Computer & Information Science, University of Pennsylvania, 1977.

Keen, J., 'Movement', Project, University of Sydney, 1973.

Lansdown, J., 'The computer in choreography', *Computer*, August, 1978, pp. 19–30.

Macourt, M., 'Ballet dancer advises on computer animation', *Sydney University Gazette*, Vol. 3, No. 11, September 1980.

McNair, B.G., 'Benesh movement language', M.Sc. Report, Basser Dept. of Computer Science, University of Sydney, 1979.

McNair, B. G., Herbison-Evans, D., & Neilands, N., 'Computer assisted choreograhy teaching', Proceedings of the 11th Australian Colleges of Advanced Education Computing Conference, Brisbane, Australia, May 12–14, 1980.

Menosky, J., 'Videographics & grand jetés' Choreography by Computer *Science '82*, May, 1982.

Noll, A. M., 'Choreography and computers', *Dance Magazine*, New York, January 1967.
    'Human or machine? Aesthetic preferences for pseudo-random computer generated patterns', *Creative Computing*, Vol. 3, No. 6, Nov.-Dec. 1977, pp.96–102. Shorter version of papers in *The Psychological Record*, Vol. 16, pp.1010, and

Vol. 22, pp.449–482.

O'Rourke, J. & Badler, N. I., 'Model based image analysis of human motion using constraint propagation', *IEEE PAMI* Vol. 2 No. 6, November 1980.

Reichardt, J., 'Computer programmed choreography', *Cybernetic Serendipity*, J. Reichardt (ed.), London and New York: Studio International, 1968.

Reiss, S. C., Winslow, A. B., & Yemini, S., 'Language involved in movement processing' (LIMP), U.C.L.A., unpublished, 1976.

Savage, G. J., & Officer, J. M., 'Choreo: an interactive computer model for choreography', *Proceedings of the Fifth Man-Machine Communication Conference*, Calgary, Alberta, 1977.

'Interactive computer graphic methods for choreography', presented at the Third Int. Conf. Computing in the Humanities, 1977, University of Waterloo.

Smoliar, S. W., 'Computers helping dance notation help the dance: a vision', National Computer Conference, 1980, pp.67–71.

Smoliar, S. W. & Tracton, W., 'A lexical analysis of Labanotation with an associated data structure', *Proceedings 1978 Annual Conference: Association for Computing Machinery*, Vol. 2, pp.727–730.

Smoliar, S. W. & Weber, L., 'Dance notation and the computer', submitted to *Computer*, 1977; available through IEEE Computer Society Repository.

'Using the computer for a semantic representation of Labanotation', Third Int. Conf., Computing in the Humanities, 1977, University of Waterloo.

Tracton, W. P., 'GEL: a graphic editor for Labanotation with an associated data structure', M.Sc thesis, University of Pennsylvania, 1979.

Tracton, W. & Yang, D., 'The representation of Labanotation symbols in the data structure of a page of a Labanotation score', Dept. of Computer & Information Science, University of Pennsylvania, 1977.

Ubell, E., 'Dance notation steps into a new era', *The New York Times*, Sec. 2, pp.12–19, 14 October, 1976.

Weber, L. & Smoliar, S. W., 'The computer as a tool for Labanotation', *Action! Recording!*, No. 7, September, 1977, The Language of Dance Centre.

Withrow, C., 'A dynamic model for computer aided choreography', report UTEC-CSc-70-103, University of Utah, 1970.

Wolofsky, Z., 'Computer interpretation of selected Labanotation commands', M.Sc. thesis, Simon Fraser University, 1974.

Articles on U.S. copyright laws

'Copyrighting choreography' by Lee Silvian, *Bravo Magazine*, Vol. 5, No. 2, 1965.

'The new copyright law and teachers', *The New York Teacher* (United Federation of Teachers publication), 1978 pp.29–31.

'A dancer's business – choreography and copyright, part one' by Nicholas Arcomano, *Dance Magazine*, April 1980, pp.58–9.

'A dancer's business – choreography and copyright, part two' by Nicholas Arcomano, *Dance Magazine*, May 1980, pp.70, 119.

'A dancer's business – choreography and copyright, part three' – conclusion' by Nicholas Arcomano, *Dance Magazine*, June 1980, pp.62–3.

'S.22: Copyrighted 1976 – Congress approves "Monumental" Bill', by Susan Wagner (first of two parts), *Publishers Weekly*.

'Copying and the Copyright Bill – Where the new revision stands on "Fair Use"' by Susan Wagner (second of two parts), *Publishers Weekly*.

Libraries contacted

Australia – University of Sydney.
Austria – Derra de Moroda Dance Archives, University of Salzburg.
Canada – Simon Fraser University.
          University of Waterloo
Denmark – Det Kongelige Bibliotek, Copenhagen.
England
   Leeds – University of Leeds.
   London – British Library,
         The British Computer Society.
         Language of Dance Centre.
         Library of the London School of Contemporary Dance.
         Royal Society of Arts.
         English Folk Dance and Song Society.
   Manchester – The John Rylands University Library.
   Salisbury – Cathedral Library.
   Worthing – South Eastern Divisional Library.
France
   Paris – Bibliothèque Nationale.
         Bibliothèque de l'Opéra.
Germany – Württembergische Landesbibliothek, Stuttgart.
         Bibliothek Deutsche Sporthochschule, Köln.
         Staatsbibliothek, Berlin.
         Stad – und Universitäts Bibliothek, Frankfurt-am-Main.
Ireland – National Library, Dublin.
Italy – La Scala, Milan.
Norway – Ringve Museum, Trondheim.
Scotland
   Dundee – Central Library.
   Edinburgh Museum and Library.
   Glasgow – University Library.
Spain – Biblioteca de Cataluna.
U.S.A. – Carnegie Library of Pittsburgh.
         Harvard University Theatre Collection.
         Honnold Library, California.
         Library of Congress, Washington D.C.
         Louisiana State University Library.
         New York Public Library Dance Collection.
         New York University.
         Ohio State University.
         University of Illinois.
         University of Iowa.
         University of Michigan, School of Music.
         University of Pennsylvania.
         University of Utah.
         Wellesley College Archives, Mass.

Appendix D

Names given to notation systems

Many names have been given to the writing down of dance. Most inventors have tried to find a significant, yet different name. In the eighteenth century notation was called 'Choreography' from the two Greek words for 'dance' and 'to write'. Today the word 'choreography' refers to the composition of dances, not to the writing of them down or to their written form. The term is therefore now quite inaccurate, but too widely used to be changed. Choreographers are, of course, the composers of ballets, not those who record them on paper. Since virtually all choreographers do not know or use any notation, it seems strange to read in the newspaper that 'Ashton has written a new ballet.' Below in alphabetical order are the names used over the centuries. Many, of course, were simply called 'dance notation' or 'movement notation' and identified by the inventor's name. Discounting the many ballroom methods and simple folk dance jottings, there are more than 85 dance or movement notation systems.

Anatomical system, *see* Fee, 1959.
Chirography, *see* Théleur, 1831.
Choregraphie, *see* Feuillet, 1700.
Choregraphy, term used by Noverre, 1760; and Rees, 1719.
Choreology,* *see* Benesh, 1956.
Chorography, *see* Essex, 1710.
Choroscript, *see* Nikolais, 1945/6.
Cinétographie Laban, *see* Laban (French publications), 1928.
Dancetype, *see* Wailes, 1928.
Grafico Della Danza, *see* Ruskaja, 1940.
J-Notation, *see* Jay, 1957.
Kahnotation, *see* Kahn, 1951.
Kinegraphs, *see* Birdwhistell, 1952.
Kinesiography, *see* Loring-Canna, 1955.
Kinetography Laban, *see* Laban, 1928.
Labanotation, *see* Laban, 1928.
Motation, *see* Halprin, 1965.
Motif Writing, *see* Laban, 1967.

---

*The term 'choreology', selected by the Beneshes for their system of notation, is a much older, generic term used by Serge Lifar among others to mean the science (branch of knowledge) relating to dance. The term itself has no reference to the writing of dance, i.e. to dance notation.

Motographia, *see* Chiesa, 1932.
Motography, *see* Valishev, 1972.
M S Method, *see* Schwalbe-Brame, 1973.
Nutographie, *see* A. Giraudet, 1892.
Orchésographie, *see* Arbeau, 1588.
Pictographs, *see* Jay, 1957.
Pitmanotation, *see* Harrison, 1956.
Rhythmographik, *see* Desmond, 1919.
Rithmografia, *see* Chiesa, 1932.
Romanotation, *see* Proca-Ciortea and Vasilescu, 1969.
Schrifttanz, *see* Laban, 1928.
Scoreography, *see* McCraw, 1964.
Semiografia Coreutica, *see* Ruskaja, 1940.
Sténochorégraphie, *see* Saint-Léon, 1852.
Stickmanotation, *see* Jay, 1957.
Tanzfigurenschrift, *see* Misslitz, 1954.
Tanznotenschrift, *see* Desmond, 1919.
Tanzschrift, *see* Korty, 1940.
Tanz und Bewegungs-Schrift, *see* Arndt, 1951.
Terprography, *see* Summero.
Terpsichorographie, *see* Despréaux, 1800(?).

Appendix E

Centres of dance and movement notation

Centres of training and publishing which incorporate a major library of notation materials.

Benesh System
The Institute of Choreology,
4 Margravine Gardens,
London W6 8RH, England.

Conté System
Association Ecriture du Mouvement,
7 rue de Dragon,
Paris 75006, France.

Eshkol-Wachmann System
The Movement Notation Society,
75 Arlozorov Street,
Holon, Israel.

Morris System
Margaret Morris Movement,
Suite 3/4, 39 Hope Street,
Glasgow G2 6AG, Scotland.

Sutton System
The Center for Sutton Movement Writing,
The Movement Shorthand Society, Inc.
P.O. Box 7344, Newport Beach,
California 92660. U.S.A.

Laban System
The Language of Dance Centre,
17 Holland Park,
London W11 3TD, England.

Laban Centre for Movement and Dance,
at University of London Goldsmiths' College,
New Cross, London SE14 6NW,
England.

The Dance Notation Bureau,
33 West 21st Street,
New York, N.Y. 10011, U.S.A.

The Dance Notation Bureau Extension,
Department of Dance,
College of the Arts,
Ohio State University,
1813 N. High Street,
Columbus, Ohio, 43210, U.S.A.

The Philadelphia Branch of the Dance Notation Bureau,
Philadelphia College for the Performing Arts,
Shubert Theatre Building,
250 Broad Street,
Philadelphia, PA. 19102, U.S.A.

Centre National d'Ecriture du Mouvement,
Place St. Arnoult,
60800 Crépy en Valois, France.

Kinetographisches Institut,
Folkwang Hochschule,
Essen-Werden, Germany.

Centre for Dance Studies,
Les Bois,
St Peter,
Jersey, Channel Islands.

Maria Szentpal, Director,
Budapest
Mártirok utja 7.
1024 Hungary.

Library,
Magyar Tudományos,
Akadémia Népzenei,
Intézete Néptánc Osztály,
1014 Budapest,
Országház u. 30, Hungary.

International Council of Kinetography
Laban,
Chairperson: Lucy Venable,
554 South 6th Street,
Columbus, Ohio. 43206, U.S.A.
(Biennial conferences for international
exchange on development and unifi-
cation.)